STRESS MANAGEMENT FOR LAWYERS

STRESS MANAGEMENT FOR LAWYERS

Third Edition

How To Increase Personal & Professional Satisfaction In The Law

Amiram Elwork, Ph.D.
Law-Psychology Graduate Program
Widener University

With Contributions By

Mark R. Siwik, J.D.
Risk International

Douglas B. Marlowe, Ph.D., J.D.
Treatment Research Institute
University of Pennsylvania

*V*orkell Group
North Wales, Pennsylvania

Vorkell Group
North Wales, PA 19454-3673
http://www.vorkell.com/
Discounts available on bulk orders. Call (215) 661-9330 or email
helpdesk@vorkell.com

Printed in the United States of America.
First edition published 1995.
Second edition published 1997.

This book is intended for educational and informational purposes
only. Nothing contained in this book is to be considered as the
rendering of medical, psychological or legal advice for specific cases.
If expert assistance in a specific case is required, the services of
licensed professional persons should be sought.

Cover design by 1106 Design, Phoenix, AZ.
Illustration by Todd Davidson – Illustration Works.

Publisher's Cataloging in Publication Data

Elwork, Amiram
    Stress management for lawyers: how to increase personal &
professional satisfaction in the law / Amiram Elwork ; with
contributions by Mark R. Siwik and Douglas B. Marlowe. – 3rd ed.
        p. cm.
    Includes bibliographic references.
    Library of Congress Catalog Card Number: 2006929970
    ISBN 978-0-9644727-3-0 (softcover: alk. paper)
    ISBN 978-0-9644727-5-4 (ebook)
    1. Stress management. 2. Practice of law -- United States --
Psychological aspects. 3. Lawyers -- Job stress -- United States.
    I. Siwik, Mark R. II. Marlowe, Douglas B.   III. Title.
    RA785 .E46 2007   155.9'042'088344— dc22

Dedicated to my daughters,

Rachael and Rebecca.

ABOUT THE AUTHOR
& CONTRIBUTORS

Amiram Elwork, Ph.D., is a psychologist who specializes in working with the legal profession. He is the Director of the Law-Psychology Graduate Training Program at Widener University near Philadelphia, PA, and the President of the Vorkell Group, a consulting firm serving the professions. He is a national speaker and consultant to lawyers, law firms, and bar associations on how to manage law practices and enhance the psychological and leadership skills of lawyers.

Dr. Elwork received a B.A. degree from Temple University, a Ph.D. in psychology from the University of Nebraska, and served his internship at the University of Pennsylvania's Center for Cognitive Therapy. He has written books and articles, and conducted research on a variety of "psycholegal" issues. For example, his first line of research was on the effectiveness of jury instructions and culminated in a book entitled *Making Jury Instructions Understandable.* Dr. Elwork's work with lawyers as a consultant throughout the years made him increasingly aware of the high level of stress they endure. As a result, he began to devote a significant portion of his time to this topic and wrote the first edition of this book in 1995. Along the same lines, he has also co-edited a book entitled, *Success Briefs for Lawyers.*

Douglas Marlowe, J.D., Ph.D., is Director of the Treatment Research Institute's Section on Law and Ethics and Adjunct Associate Professor of Psychiatry at the University of Pennsylvania School of Medicine, in Philadelphia, PA. A lawyer and psychologist who studies coercion in drug abuse treatment, Dr. Marlowe is a Fellow of the American Psychological Association and has published numerous articles and chapters on the topics of drug abuse and crime. He has played a leadership role in such organizations as the National Association of Drug Court Professionals, and has been instrumental in developing a national research agenda for drug courts and drug abuse public policy.

Mark Siwik, J.D., divides his time between the Vorkell Group, a consulting firm that focuses on the needs of lawyers and other professionals, and Risk International Services, Inc., near Cleveland, OH, where he helps policyholders negotiate and settle complex insurance claims. His legal career includes a federal clerkship, partnership in a leading Ohio law firm, and leadership roles in national, state, and local bar associations. He is the co-editor of a book entitled *Success Briefs for Lawyers* and a frequent lecturer on insurance coverage issues and professionalism.

ACKNOWLEDGMENTS

I greatly appreciate the help of many individuals whose aid and support made this 3rd edition of my book possible. First, I want to acknowledge the influence that my clients, graduate students, and seminar participants have had on shaping and improving my ideas. Thank you for the opportunity to work with you and for sharing your insights with me. I also want to thank the many book reviewers and letter writers who gave the earlier editions of this book constructive criticism. Hopefully, I have learned from you and incorporated your wisodm in this edition.

Thank you, Mark Siwik, a fine lawyer and friend, for writing the Foreword. Our joint seminars have greatly expanded my horizons. Many of the new ideas included in this edition reflect what I have learned from our inspirational discussions. I would also like to thank Douglas B. Marlowe, my friend and respected colleague, for contributing two chapters on impaired attorneys. Thank you, Susan Matour, for helping me better understand the concept of zealous representation from a typical lawyer's perspective.

Thank you, Steven Keeva, George Kaufman, Susan Daicoff, and Larry Richard, for reviewing the book and for endorsing it on the back cover. Coming from such established experts as you on this topic, your kind praise and willingness to help means a great deal to me. Finally, my wife, Andrea Elwork, and my daughters, Rachael Wells and Rebecca Elwork, deserve a special thanks for spending many hours editing and proofreading this book in its manuscript form. Their love gives me the courage to take risks and the energy to be creative.

CONTENTS

Things do not change, we do.

Henry David Thoreau

FOREWORD

I first learned about Amiram Elwork's work on lawyers and stress in 1993. At the time, I was a young lawyer finding my way in the profession. I remember the fairly constant drumbeat of my fears. Would I meet my ever-increasing quota of billable hours? Would I be able to satisfy the client? What if I made a mistake?

Guilt was another chronic emotion. It is hard to explain to your wife and your family why you are always working instead of spending time with them. The most recurring emotion for me, however, was anger. I felt trapped, powerless and frustrated by my inability to cope.

Oh, I tried to improve my time management skills by creating endless "to do" lists and prioritizing my tasks using the "A-B-C" technique. I gave an A to those items that were important and urgent, and a C to the less important or urgent items. After a while, however, I could not tell the difference between an A and a C item. Nearly every task seemed to warrant an A, and the tasks on my list just kept growing and growing.

I did not know where to turn for help. My loving wife, a lawyer too, was supportive. She was young and trying to figure things out as well. The older and more experienced lawyers around me gave me conflicting messages. They would tell me to ease up and relax, but their advice was often inconsistent with their own behaviors. In fact, they seemed just as stressed as I was, if not more.

This perception was reinforced by the fact that my state of Ohio required all attorneys to attend regular training sessions on preventing substance abuse. Don't get me wrong. I recognized the importance of this kind of intervention, but I thought it was comparable to fighting a saber-toothed tiger with a flyswatter. To me, the real issue was a gap in leadership and management training. I believed that we were good at teaching lawyers about the law (e.g., the elements of a contract or a tort) and practice skills (e.g., investigating, negotiating etc.). The problem was that lawyers received little or no training on managing themselves and other legal professionals. I theorized that if more of this training was provided, it might lessen the incidence of substance abuse. Perhaps more importantly, it would create a solid foundation for lawyers to achieve success and satisfaction in the law.

As you might guess, I found many of the answers I was looking for in an earlier edition of this book. Initially, Dr. Elwork helped me understand how certain environmental factors and personality traits commonly found in lawyers influenced my thoughts and emotions. From there, I learned that my emotions were a byproduct of my thoughts. That is, if I engaged in habitual dysfunctional thinking, I was bound to routinely feel fear, guilt and anger. With patience and practice, I learned to identify and replace my dysfunctional thinking with realistic alternatives and to align my goals and behaviors with my values. The end result is that, most of the time, I now feel happy and proud of my vocation.

Today, after ten years of collaborating with Dr. Elwork on seminars and various writings regarding the legal profession, I am privileged to call him my friend and colleague. Even so, it would be inaccurate to say that my growth was easy or effortless. I would characterize it as following the proverbial "two steps forward, one step back" method of personal growth. I am still a "Type A" personality in recovery.

A key component to this developmental process is mastering the body and mind so that they work together and produce optimal performance much of the time. As a long distance runner, I have learned to think of life as a marathon rather than a sprint, wherein pacing and balance are key. Similarly, I have learned that the goal of stress management is not to eliminate all stress. Instead, the goal is to adapt the mind and body to appropriate levels of stress which, in turn, yield consistent peak performance. With too little stress, we underachieve in life. With too much stress, we lapse into distress and the potential for breakdown of some kind. In short, managing your stress so that it is experienced at appropriate levels enables success.

Recently, I underwent open heart surgery for a previously undetected congenital heart condition. Talk about stress! I came through the operation just fine but stumbled during the recovery by attempting to do too much, too fast, thereby prolonging my recovery. That experience reminded me that stress management is a subject you master over the course of a lifetime in the same way that an apprentice becomes a master artisan.

Unfortunately, we still live at a time when we give stress management more attention and respect in the sports world than we do in the world of white collar professional services. Today, nearly every professional franchise has the services of a sports psychologist teaching athletes how to handle the mental and emotional sides of the game. Much of what athletes learn in order to achieve regular peak performance is in this book. The key to top performance and long-term success in sports is the same as it is for success in the world of white collar professionals: mastery of one's mind and emotions.

Based on my personal experience and the feedback from many lawyers over the years, I know this book will give you the tools to meet the century-old challenge posed by Oliver Wendell Holmes. Holmes often asked lawyers how they intended to make out a fulfilling life when at times it might seem that law was nothing more than "the laborious study of a dry and technical system, the greedy watch for clients, the practice of shopkeepers' arts, and the mannerless conflicts over often sordid interests." His answer was, "If the lawyer has the soul of Sancho Panza, the world to that lawyer will be Sancho Panza's world; but if the lawyer has the soul of an idealist, the lawyer will make – I do not say find – his or her world ideal."

What is missing in Holmes' challenge is specific advice for making one's life in the law ideal. For me, and I hope for you, that advice resides within this book. Good luck.

Mark Siwik, Esq.
Co-editor of
Success Briefs for Lawyers
Senior Counsel at
Risk International Services, Inc.

INTRODUCTION

The practice of law has become an increasingly difficult occupation. As I will document in the next chapter, the evidence for this claim is overwhelming. Recent national surveys of lawyers have consistently found high rates of job dissatisfaction. A significant number of attorneys are dropping out of law and switching to new careers. Even more alarming is the fact that lawyers have unusually high rates of depression, alcoholism and a variety of other mental and physical ailments. Researchers agree that these are not statistical anomalies but a reflection of how tough it is to be a lawyer today.

For example, take the case of one of my past clients - let's call him J.D. He had read an article I had written for a local legal magazine and decided to call. He was courteous but very direct. Right from the start, he wanted me to know that he did not have much faith in psychologists and doubted that anyone could help him. Out of desperation, however, he was willing to try anything.

His story was familiar. J.D. had started out as a solo practitioner many years earlier, when all one had to do was hang out a shingle and practice law. Things had become much more competitive and complicated since then. Even though he had other attorneys working for him, J.D. felt unable to slow down. In fact, although he was putting in more hours than ever, his profits were plummeting. After years of putting up with his hostile mood swings, his colleagues and family members were fed up with him. It seemed like he was failing in all areas of his life, and his self-esteem was at an all-time low.

Part of J.D.'s problems stemmed from psychological issues that had little to do with being a lawyer. Clearly, however, J.D.

also was experiencing a number of occupational stressors. Like most lawyers, he was under relentless time pressures and had more work to do than he could possibly finish. In addition, he was operating under the tension of fierce economic competition, in an adversarial environment that breeds hostility, conflict, and cynicism.

Unfortunately, J.D. did not know how to cope with the many stresses of a law practice in a healthy manner. Similarly, he knew very little about time management, marketing or billing, and he lacked the ability to manage other people. When confronted with these facts, his initial response was, "Why isn't it enough to just practice law?" He greatly resisted the idea that, although he was a good lawyer in the traditional sense, the solutions to many of the problems he was experiencing at work required certain skills that he had never learned.

J.D.'s story is very similar to the stories of other lawyers I have counseled. If you are a lawyer and chronic stress is damaging your health or diminishing your happiness, this book is written for you. It is designed to teach you how to stay calm during stressful times, reduce your negative thoughts and emotions, align your behaviors with your own core values, bring more balance to your professional and personal life, improve your physical and mental health, manage your time and your practice more effectively, improve your relationships with others, and get more satisfaction out of law and life.

I wrote this book with a keen awareness of the credibility problem that mental health professionals have with many lawyers. Whenever I think about that issue, I am reminded of a cartoon I saw once but cannot cite, depicting a street scene of a homeless ex-lawyer and his well dressed psychotherapist. Upon recognizing the therapist, the homeless ex-lawyer runs after him and calls out: "Doc, doc! Don't you recognize me? You're the one who advised me to take it easy and let my practice take care of itself!"

I want to assure you that, unlike the therapist in the cartoon, I will not be advising you to ignore the harsh realities of life. I am fully aware of how difficult it is to practice law. Unlike so-called realists, however, I do not believe that passive endurance of chronic stress is a sign of courage or character. Because chronic stress is so harmful to your physical and mental health, simply enduring it is generally a sign of bad judgment. Overcoming life's challenges, not just enduring them, is what takes real guts and ingenuity. That is what I would like to help you do.

MAKE IT SIMPLE

"Everything should be made as simple as possible,
but not simpler." *Albert Einstein*

I am going to help you understand complex concepts and self-help techniques at their most elemental level. Do not be fooled by the fact that some of the advice given will sound like common sense. The problem is that common sense is not so commonly practiced. In addition, do not confuse simplicity with lack of sophistication. Nobel prizes have been awarded to people who have explained complex phenomena in fundamental terms.

While my goals here are much less lofty, I think that it is extremely important to make very complex issues easy to understand. Simplification makes things more clear, more orderly, more memorable, less overwhelming, and easier to put into practice. In reading this book, do not just learn the basics, over-learn them. Make them a part of your natural thinking process. This way, when faced with the most complex of problems, you will know what to do automatically or at least know how to start.

Given how busy most lawyers are, each chapter is short and succinct, requiring only a few minutes of your attention. While the chapters are presented in a logical sequence, it is not necessary to read them in that order. Most chapters stand on their own. Therefore, you can turn to any section that happens to be of interest to you at a particular moment and get the needed information quickly.

My hope is that this is not the kind of book you read once and never open again. It is written as a reference guide that you can return to repeatedly, whenever you need a refresher or a solution to a specific and immediate problem. Hopefully, its brevity and simplicity will make it an inviting resource.

LIMITATIONS

Because this book speaks directly to lawyers, reading it is a good way to start your journey toward greater personal and professional satisfaction. To arrive at this destination, however, you will need to do much more than read this one book. Other books that are suggested throughout the succeeding pages will help expand your knowledge about a variety of issues. In addition, you will have to convert what you have learned into action.

Obviously, this book is not intended as a substitute for professional consultations. It is intended as an educational and informational resource; it is not to be considered as the rendering of medical, psychological or legal advice for specific cases. If your problems are serious or the advice in this book is not working for you, please consider engaging the services of a licensed professional.

WHY A THIRD EDITION?

This third edition is being published ten years after the publication of the second edition. In the last decade, a great deal of new information has become available about stress in general and stress among lawyers. In addition to what my readings have taught me, my consulting, counseling and speaking experiences over a ten year period have helped me grow and develop many new insights as well. If you are familiar with the earlier editions of this book, you will find that this one is considerably more comprehensive. It contains several new sections and a number of new chapters, as well as significant revisions of old chapters. I have done my best to make sure that the changes and additions represent substantive improvements, rather than superficialities.

SECTION I: A PROFESSION IN DISTRESS

Nothing in life is to be feared. It is only to be understood.

Marie Curie

It is easier to perceive error than to find the truth, for the former lies on the surface and is easily seen, while the latter lies in the depth, where few are willing to search for it.

Johann Wolfgang von Goethe

THE BASIS FOR CONCERN

In April of 1991, the American Bar Association (ABA) convened a conference entitled *At the Breaking Point*. Their report[1] concluded that "there is a growing trend in the legal profession which, left unchecked, threatens the well-being of all lawyers and firms in every part of the country." The trend was a clear deterioration of the legal work environment, accompanied by a decline in lawyers' career satisfaction, physical health and mental health. Although the report focused on the consequences of these developments for lawyers and law firms, it was obvious that litigants and the integrity of the entire legal process were also being affected.

Consequences of Distress On:

Lawyers & Law Firms - *e.g., job dissatisfaction, turnover, mental & physical illness, substance abuse, malpractice & health insurance costs.*

Litigants & Legal System - *e.g., incompetence, malpractice, ethical violations.*

Expressions of concern had begun more than a decade earlier as many legal magazines started to report a meaningful downturn in the quality of life among lawyers. Responding to such reports, in 1984 the ABA Young Lawyers Division[2] surveyed a randomly chosen national sample of close to 2,300 attorneys. The results suggested that while the earlier reports were somewhat exaggerated, it was still noteworthy that about 15 percent of the respondents were generally dissatisfied with their jobs. More noteworthy, however, was the fact that even lawyers who were generally satisfied with their careers, reported that their jobs required them to endure high levels of daily pressures and tensions.

In 1990, the ABA Young Lawyers Division[3] conducted a similar follow-up survey with a random national sample of approximately 2,200 attorneys. This time, 19 percent of all attorneys reported being generally dissatisfied with their jobs. This represented a 27 percent increase in the general level of dissatisfaction reported six years earlier. Over 70 percent of lawyers in all settings reported that pressure and tension on the job was considerable.

Another national survey of over 1,200 randomly selected attorneys, conducted as part of a doctoral dissertation at Temple University,[4] reported that 23 percent of the respondents were dissatisfied with their jobs in 1992. In 1999, over 600 of the most highly compensated partners at the nation's largest law firms were surveyed by The American Lawyer magazine.[5] Seventeen percent reported being less than content with their jobs, and 31 percent complained that their workload was too great.

In addition to these national surveys, local surveys have also been conducted. For example, in 1990 the North Carolina Bar Association[6] surveyed close to 2,600 attorneys. Like their national cohorts, over 18 percent of North Carolina attorneys reported being dissatisfied with their jobs. Even though close to 80 percent of them were generally satisfied with their lives and careers, they reported unusually high rates of negative psychological and physical symptoms. Close to 37 percent of them admitted to feeling depressed, and over 42 percent reported feeling lonely in the past few weeks. About 25 percent reported physical symptoms of depression (e.g., appetite loss, lethargy) and anxiety (e.g., trembling, heart racing). Over 11 percent reported suicidal ideation at least 1-2 times per month in the past year, and nearly 17 percent reported drinking 3-5 alcoholic beverages per day.

Similarly, in a 1999 survey conducted in Wisconsin, 91 percent of the lawyers who responded reported that the practice of law appeared to be increasingly more stressful each year.[7] In another survey of lawyers in Wisconsin a decade earlier, 32.5 percent of the respondents admitted to using alcohol on a regular basis as a way of reducing stress.[8] A survey of 1,809 lawyers in Minnesota, conducted between 1997-99, revealed that more than 25 percent were less than satisfied with the practice of law and that 21 percent were considering leaving the law.[9]

Other studies of lawyers have also been conducted using scientifically validated measures of mental illness. For example, it has been demonstrated that the mental health of lawyers begins to deteriorate in law school, as shown by significant increases in the prevalence of anxiety and depression.[10] A number of characteristics about law school appear to make it stressful: (1) Students are encouraged to compete for class rankings under time pressures; (2) The Socratic method evokes the fear of failure and embarrassment; (3) The lack of clarity in the law creates uncertainty; (4) Altruism, optimism and trust are considered naive, whereas cynicism, pessimism and paranoia are common.

One study demonstrated that although entering students at the School of Law at The University of Arizona were found to be similar to the general population, by the spring semester they were found to report significantly higher than average rates of psychopathological symptoms, including signs of depression, anxiety, hostility, and paranoia.[11] The symptoms continued to increase into the end of the law school program and did not return to pre-law school levels within the first two years of legal practice.

Another research study[12] surveyed 801 lawyers in the state of Washington and found alarming rates of reported depression and substance abuse. Again, using validated measures of mental health problems, this study found 19 percent of the respondents to be suffering from depression and 18 percent to be problem drinkers. Given a 5 percent overlap between the two groups, close to one third of the sample had a significant mental health problem. These figures represented rates that are at least twice the national average for the general population. With no reason to believe that lawyers in the state of Washington are unrepresentative, the researchers concluded that comparable rates of depression and problem drinking would be found in most jurisdictions in the United States.

Indeed, a Johns Hopkins University study[13] measured the prevalence of Major Depressive Disorder within a number of occupations across many locations (New Haven, CT, Baltimore, MD, Durham-Piedmont, NC, St. Louis, MO and Los Angeles, CA). Of the 28 occupations that could be compared in a statistically valid manner, lawyers were the most likely to suffer from depression and 3.6 times more likely than average for the group studied. The researchers hypothesized that the legal environment may be particularly conducive to depression due to the stress that results from such characteristics as high work loads and job complexity.

Another national study in 1987 measured depression in a sample of 8,486 employed people across 239 occupations.[14] These researchers found that, in general, professionals had among the lowest incidences of depression. However, a closer look at their data reveals that lawyers in particular were among the exceptions, in that they were more likely to experience depression than 70 percent of the other persons in the study. A 1992 study by the National Institute for Occupational Safety and Health also found that lawyers had higher suicide rates than average for professional groups.[15]

The statistics reviewed above explain why the ABA sponsored conference mentioned earlier was entitled *At The Breaking Point*. The title was not hyperbolic. It reflected a recognition by many[16] that an excessive number of lawyers are in distress.

The consequences of this fact go beyond causing lawyers to experience mental health problems. Chronic stress has been linked to a variety of physical ailments, including headaches, cardiovascular diseases and illnesses caused by immune system malfunctions.[17] In addition, it can trigger the deterioration of close personal relationships and contribute to unsuccessful child rearing and failed marriages.[18]

Chronic stress not only damages lawyers and their families but also affects their ability to serve clients effectively.[19] It has been estimated that 40-75 percent of the disciplinary actions taken against lawyers involve practitioners who are chemically dependent or mentally ill.[20] While most attorneys never experience serious impairment, even medium levels of chronic stress are likely to have a deleterious effect on their ability to work at peak effectiveness (e.g., meet deadlines, detect emerging problems). For example, in a survey of over 600 partners at large law firms, 40 percent reported making avoidable mistakes because of the pressure they are under to work fast.[21] Even though most of these mistakes may not get exposed, they still have a significant negative effect on litigants and the integrity of the entire legal system.

This problem also has ramifications at the firm level. The health consequences of stress raise health insurance costs and subject law firms to the risk of large lawsuit awards under various disability statutes. For example, one in-house counsel in San Francisco was awarded over one million dollars "because his company refused to 'accommodate' his depression by agreeing to shorter hours" or taking other supportive steps.[22]

In addition, stress has been linked to high rates of absenteeism and staff turnover. Statistics show that every year a significant number of lawyers either leave their firms or the practice of law altogether.[23] Finally, stress contributes to the various types of costs that law firms endure as a result of malpractice cases brought against them.[24]

WHY LAW IS STRESSFUL:
AN OVERVIEW

In a scholarly book[25] about the state of the legal profession in the late twentieth century, Harvard Law Professor, Mary Ann Glendon asked, "Why are so many lawyers so sad?" To understand the answer to Professor Glendon's question, we need to acknowledge its complexity. Clearly, lawyers' above-average rates of depression and substance abuse suggest that the occupational stressors they endure are at least partly responsible. While it is beyond my scope to describe them all, a variety of environmental stressors are implicated, in interaction with a number of predisposing individual characteristics.[26]

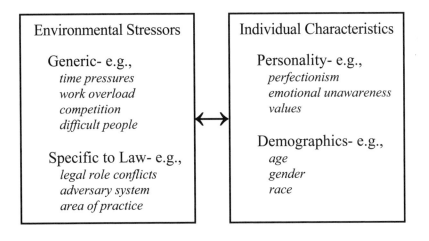

Some of the environmental stressors are generic and apply to a number of occupations besides law, whereas others are specifically indigenous to law. In addition, there are personality traits and demographic characteristics that make some lawyers more predisposed to experience stress. These factors do not act independently but are part of an intricate web. Depending on your analytical starting point, each factor is sometimes the cause and sometimes the effect.

As documented in the preceding chapter, among the primary complaints that lawyers cite as contributing to their stress are time pressures at work, work overload, and inadequate time for themselves and their families. Simple statistics as well as descriptive accounts suggest that many legal workplaces, such as some large law firms, are like blue collar sweat shops.[27] That is, they are overly focused on one thing, namely income. The typical lawyer is expected to log a minimum of 1,800-1,900 billable hours per year, and many lawyers are expected to far exceed this figure. Even an 1,800 hour minimum translates into almost 7 billable hours per day, 5 days per week, 52 weeks a year. Since this does not include eating, socializing, going to meetings, reading mail, seeking new clients, etc., it has been estimated that to bill 7 hours one must work 9-12 hours. Thus, it is common for lawyers to take work home or not go home for dinner, to work on weekends, and to not take their allotted vacation or holiday time.

As the number of lawyers climbs higher and higher, some blame their pressures on competition. Indeed, the growth in the number of attorneys in the U.S. has been enormous.[28] In 1950, there were 200,000 lawyers in the U.S., or one lawyer for every 750 people. The number of lawyers in this country grew to 280,000 by 1970, to over 400,000 by 1980, to over 700,000 by 1990, and to over 1 million by 2000 - one lawyer for every 300 people in the U.S.[29]

Other factors that have contributed to greater competition include periodic economic downturns in the general economy, corporate streamlining, and legal reforms. These and other developments have caused lower morale, job insecurity and less loyalty. To summarize, in recent years, lawyers as well as many other professional groups have found making a living to be increasingly difficult and time-consuming.

Some lawyers attribute their stress to a less than ideal work-site environment. They complain about political intrigue and backbiting, disrespect and incivility from superiors and adversaries, poor clerical and paralegal assistance, and unfair promotion procedures. Others point to the fact that the profit motive at many law firms is so strong that it often supersedes important humanistic values. These attorneys often feel like commodities that can be used, discarded, and easily replaced.

In addition, it is generally known that our adversarial legal system tends to promote a Machiavellian environment, in which aggression, selfishness, hostility, suspiciousness, and cynicism are widespread. This causes a number of distressful effects, including generalized irritability and anxiety.

Another set of concerns that lawyers experience involves conflict and ambiguity about their roles in society. Some lawyers report feeling conflicted between their roles as officers of the court and as advocates for their clients. Sometimes they feel the tremendous weight that comes with being responsible for solving other people's problems within a context where mistakes are very costly. At other times they report feeling guilty about the fact that they are often forced to advocate for unjust results or to hurt people who have already undergone tragic ordeals. As a consequence, too many lawyers also report that they lack a feeling of making a real contribution to society.

These issues also underlie the antipathy that the general public feels for lawyers, which is itself another source of stress. As Rodney Dangerfield, a comedian, might have said: Lawyers "get no respect." I don't know of any other profession that has been the subject of so many negative jokes. Today there are entire books and websites devoted to vicious jokes about lawyers. This is nothing new, however. Here is something Will Rogers once quipped back in 1926:

> Personally, I don't think you make a lawyer honest by an act of legislature. You've got to work on his conscience. And his lack of conscience is what makes him a lawyer.[30]

Indeed, if you examine the common themes of lawyer jokes, you will find that the great majority make one of two points: (1) Lawyers have no scruples (e.g., How can you tell when a lawyer is lying? His/her lips move.); (2) The world would be better off with fewer lawyers (e.g., What's a thousand dead lawyers at the bottom of the sea? A good start.). Some of these jokes are very funny, but they also evoke some sadness in me. Such an essential profession in our society should not be so negatively perceived.

Of course, not all areas of law or types of practice are equal. Although some would argue otherwise, the private practice environment generally tends to be somewhat more stressful than the corporate or government setting. One of the exceptions to this rule is the public defender's role, a government position that tends to be very stressful.[31] Litigators report more stress than other colleagues. Certain specific areas of practice, such as family and criminal law tend to be particularly stressful. Three underlying factors appear to make most of the difference: workload, time pressures, and amount of conflict.

In addition to the external stressors, there are individual traits that must be entered into the formula as well.[32] For example, perfectionism is a common personality trait among lawyers that makes them more susceptible to stress. Perfectionistic people live by the following rules: "I must do a perfect job, or I will fail. I need to be in total control. Details are extremely important." While some perfectionism is necessary in the practice of law, when taken too far, it creates an enormous amount of distress. Since the probability of everything going according to plan is close to zero, perfectionists tend to be perpetually disappointed.

Another common stress-inducing trait among lawyers is that they tend to be exceedingly analytical thinkers. In fact, a national study of over 1200 lawyers revealed that 77 percent of them prefer to make choices on the basis of emotionally detached logic.[33] These data suggest that a significant number of lawyers do not fully appreciate the positive role that emotions can play in human cognition. Thus, they tend to lack the ability to deal with their own emotions in the healthiest of ways and tend to be insensitive to the feelings of others.

To make matters worse, our adversarial legal system often stimulates feelings of hostility, cynicism, aggression, fear and low self-esteem. Thus, lawyers who are not adept at managing emotions in general or these negative emotions in particular, are more likely to feel stress. Similarly, because legal outcomes are not always "just," lawyers who are not skilled at handling their emotions may feel either too disappointed or too detached. Either extreme reduces job satisfaction and personal fulfillment.

Another factor that has been partly blamed for the stress lawyers experience is the ascendancy of materialistic values in the profession. Many lawyers and legal writers[34] nostalgically recall a time when law was more of a profession and less of a business. Their view is that by being less focused on economic self-interest, lawyers of an earlier era were more devoted to the rule of law, to helping others and society, and to such principles as integrity, commitment, and good will. They say that past generations of lawyers were more highly respected by others, felt more in control of their lives, and were less stressed.

Finally, certain demographic characteristics such as race, age and gender are also risk factors for stress among lawyers. Members of minority groups and women in the law complain about job discrimination.[35] Female attorneys also express higher rates of dissatisfaction due to sexual harassment. In addition, younger lawyers and female lawyers report more conflicts about balancing work with family obligations.

HOW STRESSED ARE YOU?

The following check list will give you a rough measure of your own stress levels and their underlying causes:

- ☐ My work requires me to do too much in too little time.
- ☐ I don't have enough time to spend with my family and friends or to pursue recreational and social activities.
- ☐ Competition is making it difficult to make a living.
- ☐ The people at my law firm or department lack collegiality – e.g., are cold, unfriendly or rude.
- ☐ My firm or department is mismanaged – e.g., we don't get good clerical help, compensation procedures are unfair.
- ☐ My firm or department is too focused on profit.
- ☐ The physical environment in which I work is unpleasant.
- ☐ My work bores me, or I don't feel that I'm good at it.
- ☐ I don't feel that I'm making a positive contribution to society or to other people's lives.
- ☐ I don't think that what I do deserves respect or gets the respect it deserves.
- ☐ I deal with too many difficult and unreasonable people.
- ☐ I feel overly responsible for everything and everyone.
- ☐ I overanalyze things and am too cautious.
- ☐ I often feel one or more of the following emotions: anger, irritation, rage, guilt, regret, shame, fear, anxiety.
- ☐ I often feel depressed, defeated, or hopeless.
- ☐ I often rely on alcohol or drugs to help me feel good.
- ☐ I think about quitting at least once a month.
- ☐ Occasionally, I think about committing suicide.

THE ANATOMY OF A WORKAHOLIC LAWYER

The single most frequent complaint about the practice of law is the "hours." [36] Indeed, the great majority of lawyers work more than the national standard of 40 hours per week. They commonly take work home after an exhausting day, come in to their offices on weekends, fail to take their full vacations, and operate in a crisis mode. For some (too many) lawyers, work pervades everything. Even what seems to be personal time (e.g., watching a movie) is often secretly spent thinking about work.

This image of a workaholic lawyer was keenly depicted in a cartoon I once saw somewhere, but unfortunately cannot cite. A lawyer is sitting in his underwear on a medical examining table, and a doctor is standing next to him, looking at the patient's records. The lawyer-patient says to the doctor: "Doc, give it to me straight. How many billable hours do I have left?" The cartoon was funny, but it also captured a certain underlying truth that made it disturbing.

The workaholic nature of too many law firms today was further captured for me by a true story that a young attorney once told me. One of the partners under whom he worked at his first law firm would periodically bring in his young associates for a chat. In essence, these were mentoring sessions in which the elder lawyer would try to impart some wisdom to a small group of young people, with a genuine desire to help them. Among the things he sometimes spoke about was the number of times he had dinner with his family that month. "I can count the number on one hand," he would say proudly, as if to show by example what "real" lawyers are supposed to do.

Workaholism does have the obvious benefit of helping lawyers get further ahead at work, but this comes at a price.[37] Workaholics tend to have a higher frequency of headaches, sleep disturbances, high blood pressure, and other more serious illnesses. They are prone to acquire various food, alcohol and drug addictions. In addition, they have difficulty establishing or maintaining close personal relationships, and they have higher divorce and failed parenting rates.

Furthermore, it is common for workaholics to eventually get "burned out" and to experience emotional exhaustion and a reduced sense of accomplishment.[38] A typical symptom of burnout is feeling drained and unable to give any more of yourself to others, wishing that "they would all just go away." This can result in callous, rude, and inappropriate responses toward clients, colleagues and staff. The person may also feel inadequate and lacking in personal achievement and purpose.

It should be noted that although mental health professionals use the term "burnout" regularly, it is not an official mental health diagnosis. However, people who are seriously burned out usually exhibit the symptoms of at least a mild form of depression (e.g., pessimism, sadness), which *is* a mental health disorder. And so, it may be more accurate to think of burnout as a form of depression. Lawyers who suffer from burnout can also experience clinical anxiety as well as other more serious emotional illnesses.

The stressors usually associated with the practice of law makes workaholic lifestyles even more risky. Lawyers constantly take on the weight of other people's problems. They commonly deal with clients who are emotionally strained and at their worst. And, of course, attorneys are often embroiled in conflict with hostile adversaries. Law professors also may work long hours but, because they do not experience these other stressors, are much less likely to feel the same deleterious effects.

From a health perspective, all of this suggests that many lawyers need to work less than the average number of hours, not more. So, why are so many of them workaholics? Who or what is to blame?

Accusing senior partners of being too demanding is easy, but this explanation is probably simplistic. Although many senior partners do indeed pay little attention to the personal human needs of their associates and staff, they are usually even worse at taking care of their own needs and work at least as hard as their associates.[39] It is true that large law firms tend to have more workaholic cultures than small ones, but there are plenty of workaholic lawyers in small and solo practices as well.[40] Similarly, workaholism cannot be totally blamed on a recession or on increased competition; working long hours is a way of life for many lawyers even during prosperous times.

The truth is, workaholism among lawyers has a number of intertwined root causes.[41] Although the following causes are neither exhaustive nor universally applicable, they have an effect on a considerable number of attorneys.

JUSTIFIABLE PARANOIA

One root cause of workaholism is in the very nature of our adversarial legal system, which requires many lawyers to adopt a dog-eat-dog, pessimistic world view. Within this environment, it is realistic for lawyers at times to suspect that people have ulterior motives, that it is safer to be secretive, that others will seize every opportunity to take advantage, and that manipulation and selfishness is widespread. It is also reasonable for lawyers to be skeptical sometimes, and to anticipate all possible hazards, as well as set low expectations. In an adversarial context, thinking this way is often necessary for victorious survival and reflects nothing more than defensive competence.

This point is illustrated in a study of students at the University of Virginia Law School.[42] Building on previous studies that confirmed the positive effects of optimism, the researchers expected optimistic law students to outperform their pessimistic classmates academically. Instead, the researchers were surprised to find that, in this instance, pessimism was correlated with higher grades in law school. It seems that law school rewards a pessimistic-fearful attitude as a way of preparing the student for the "real world."

When mentally ill patients have unwarranted suspicions about the actions of other people, clinicians call that "paranoid ideation." The most common effects of paranoid thinking include generalized irritability, anxiety, and fear, along with physical symptoms like "butterflies in the stomach" and insomnia. These emotions drive paranoid people to invest enormous amounts of energy into thinking of ways to avoid anticipated harm.

Although the suspiciousness and pessimism that lawyers experience is often justified and cannot itself be clinically classified as paranoia, it does have similar ill effects. At the very least, performance anxieties are likely to force many lawyers into workaholic behavior and thought patterns. In addition, since suspicious ideation is difficult to turn off and on at will, it is likely to spill into and damage relationships with associates, friends, and family members. In turn, this causes feelings of isolation and loneliness.

The best advice for people who are forced to work in a psychologically antagonistic environment is to limit their exposure to it. Workaholic schedules should be minimized and more time should be spent in activities with family and friends, so that humanistic feelings can be rekindled. Given all of the other forces that drive workaholic attorneys, however, this advice is easier given than followed.

PERFECTIONISTIC THINKING

Another cause of workaholism among lawyers is the fact that "law" is driven by rules, order and organization, and thus, requires logical thought, objective analysis, and close attention to details. Lawyers are regularly judged on their ability to apply these skills within a context where errors are not well tolerated. This raises performance anxiety and induces perfectionistic thinking, which in turn leads to an obsessive dedication to work.

On the one hand, perfectionism drives people to achieve professional success and is reinforced through praise and recognition. On the other hand, the urge to be perfect can lead to indecision, procrastination, and excessive thoroughness. Thus, when taken to extremes, it actually inhibits productivity. In addition, since perfection cannot be fully achieved, striving for perfection can cause chronic discontent and low job satisfaction. In other words, it takes the fun out of work.

Those who enter the law with perfectionistic tendencies are particularly susceptible to having work take over their lives. Since there is always room for improvement, perfectionists have difficulty knowing when to let go of their work and stop researching, rewriting and preparing. At times, deadlines are their only salvation. Perfectionistic lawyers also tend to spread themselves too thin. That is, they anticipate (imagine) that events in the future will go more smoothly (perfectly) than they have in the past and, as a result, tend to take on more work than they can handle.

This type of thinking also spills into lawyers' personal lives in a number of ways. Being excessively in control at work tends to choke off spontaneity everywhere else. Perfectionists are often viewed by family members and friends as people who are critical and demanding, and who do not know how to relax or have fun. In addition, they are susceptible to making too many promises they cannot keep; just as in the workplace, perfectionists tend to spread themselves too thin in their personal lives as well. These qualities have a negative effect on their relationships with spouses, children, and friends. Unfortunately, workaholic perfectionists sometimes compensate for their failures at home by devoting even more time to work.

INSATIABLE DESIRE FOR SUCCESS

Many lawyers become workaholics because they are driven by an insatiable desire to achieve an ever increasing level of professional success. They make the mistake of believing that professional success has a satiation point and that one can get there more quickly by "temporarily" sacrificing one's personal life. For example, some may say, "As soon as I make partner, I'll pay attention to my other needs." Since past professional goals are constantly replaced by new ones, other needs are in fact permanently deferred for many lawyers. These lawyers seldom enjoy their success. They live in the future, not in the present. No level of achievement is savored for very long before it is interrupted by the pressures of newly set ambitions. Success is elusive in that it is eternally anticipated rather than experienced. Happiness is always foreseen, but seldom felt.

Some lawyers also make the mistake of assuming that the word "success" is synonymous with professional achievement and material wealth.[43] Thus, they become preoccupied with work. Contrary to their expectations, however, the idea that professional and financial achievement is all that is necessary for happiness has been disproved in a number of studies.[44] For example, in a survey of University of Michigan Law School alumni several years ago, it was found that attorneys with the highest annual hours worked did report the largest incomes, but they also had the lowest job satisfaction ratings.[45] In other surveys, attorneys have admitted that the high pressure to bill more hours has become so strong in some law firms that it sometimes results in fraudulent billing practices.[46] In my mind, if you are dissatisfied with your career and engage in fraudulent billing, you cannot call yourself "successful."

From a casual outsider's perspective, many workaholic attorneys have it all. Privately, however, too many of them "lead lives of quiet desperation."[47] Professional achievement and wealth in part represent ways of getting love, self-esteem, and security. In reality, they can attain these psychological goals more effectively by leading balanced lives. Sadly, most workaholics don't understand or accept this fact, and are out of touch with the underlying psychological needs they are trying to satisfy.

My bottom line on this topic is that the best synonym for "success" is "happiness." No matter what you have achieved professionally or financially, you cannot call yourself successful unless you are happy. It's not that professional and financial achievements don't contribute to happiness. It's that, for most people, such achievements are only part of the formula.

I am not asserting that workaholism is wrong for everyone, just for most of us. There are people who simply love what they do professionally so much that they immerse themselves in it completely. For them, work is play, and they are very happy to play most of the time. Some of them still manage to do more than work and some do not. The key to their success is whether they are happy. And so, to those readers who are genuinely happy being workaholics, I encourage you to keep doing what you are doing.

THE PLIGHT OF YOUNG AND FEMALE ATTORNEYS

"At the end of your life, you will never regret not having passed one more test, not winning one more verdict or not closing one more deal. You will regret time not spent with a husband, a friend, a child or a parent." *Barbara Bush*

Several surveys have suggested that an excessive number of young attorneys and female attorneys are dissatisfied with their jobs.[48] For example, a national ABA survey[49] conducted in 1984 found that although 15 percent of all respondents expressed significant job dissatisfaction, women did so at almost twice that rate (29 percent). A follow-up national survey[50] in 1990 found that whereas 19 percent of all attorneys reported being generally dissatisfied with their jobs, a much more dramatic picture emerged when the sample was broken down by age and gender. Among male attorneys who had graduated from law school after 1967 and were currently in private practice, 28 percent reported being generally dissatisfied with their jobs. As many as 41 percent of their female cohorts reported general dissatisfaction with their jobs.

Given their higher levels of job dissatisfaction, it is not surprising to find that young lawyers (associates) have high attrition rates.[51] A vivid illustration of this point is provided by two studies[52] published in 1998 and 2000 by the National Association for Law Placement (NALP), in which it tracked 10,300 associates within 154 law firms (of all sizes) and 5,500 lawyers in 175 firms, respectively. NALP's findings show that approximately 8-9 percent of new associates leave their firms in the first year of employment, 38-43 percent leave by the third year, and 60-65 percent leave by the fifth year. Annual average attrition rates are at 15 percent. Turnover rates for women and minority lawyers tend to be significantly higher than those of their counterparts.

WHAT TROUBLES ASSOCIATES

Many associates start their careers by valuing high income and prestige above other factors and are wooed into accepting jobs that provide such benefits in return for very hard work. The law firms at which they get their start are often highly focused on work accomplishments and employ lawyers who are excellent at their craft. Commonly, the new recruits reason that working in such an environment will be a good learning experience and that the affiliation can open doors in the future. Soon, however, a significant number of them become unhappy and begin to question their choices.[53]

Ultimately, many associates discover that what they really want is personal and professional satisfaction, and a balanced quality of life. They find it difficult and sometimes impossible to achieve these goals in a workaholic environment, where success is measured primarily by the income that one produces. Even though the war stories of their predecessors are well known, many associates are still surprised by their first hand experience of just how oppressive the workload is at some law firms and also how hostile the lawyers they work for can be when associates don't perform as expected.[54]

A 1995 survey[55] conducted by the ABA Young Lawyers Division, found that 30 percent of ABA members who were under the age of 36 or admitted into practice for less than 3 years were dissatisfied with the allocation of time between their work and personal lives. This complaint was significantly more prevalent among lawyers working for large firms, however. Compared to 23 percent of young lawyers in 1-2 person firms, over 62 percent of young lawyers in 150+ person firms expressed unhappiness about their inability to live a balanced life. It was often the case that the associates at these firms were expected to work exceedingly long hours at the expense of most other activities.

What do these data really mean in experiential terms? Here is an excerpt from one lawyer's description of what it was like to be an associate:

> In the six years that I was an associate working in that large general-practice firm, a knot of Gordian proportions grew in the pit of my stomach. Every waking moment and even some sleeping ones were accompanied by a specific conscious awareness that time was divided into billable minutes and non-billable minutes, minutes that counted toward my annual bogey, and minutes that were wasted. Time spent eating and socializing felt like wasted minutes. Sure I ate, sure I socialized, but the knot was there, keeping me from really relaxing and enjoying myself.[56]

In a survey[57] published in 1999, another associate summed it up this way: "I Bill, Therefore I Am." A more in depth personal account of what it is like to be an associate can be found in a book entitled "Anonymous Lawyer," authored by Harvard Law School graduate, Jeremy Blachman.[58] Based on the author's Internet blog (anonymouslawyer.blogspot.com) and written as a novel, the book is eerily true to life.

Samuel B. Fortenbaugh III, former managing partner at Morgan, Lewis & Bockius, New York, and Harvard Law School graduate of the Class of 1960, compared his generation's experience to that of current associates in the following terms:

> Young Harvard lawyers are less content today than we were. They work harder, longer hours. They don't

have the time to indulge themselves, to become Renaissance people. My classmates still believed that it was possible to go to plays – every night if we wished- to learn music, to have intellectual discourses. We led pretty decent lives in law firms. Today, a Harvard Law graduate comes in conditioned to give up large parts of his life for a number of years. I don't know if it's a pretty decent life.[59]

Even though associates are concerned about a variety of problems with the practice of law, it is not surprising that "work overdose" is their most frequent complaint. Typically, young attorneys are in the stages of life where they need more personal time to find a mate and get married or to spend with their newly formed families. Too often, they find that they cannot do that and get ahead in law at the same time.[60]

In a study conducted by the North Carolina Bar Association,[61] 43 percent of the close to 2600 attorneys surveyed in that state, reported that "the demands of their work do not allow them to have a satisfying non-work life (i.e., personal, family, social, civic)." Of those who were divorced or separated, 36 percent blamed the failure of their marriages partly on the pressures of their jobs. Among lawyers who had never been married, 46 percent said that the pressures of their jobs were partly to blame for that as well. A consistent finding in this study was that younger lawyers and female lawyers were significantly more dissatisfied with the quality and quantity of their leisure time than older attorneys and male attorneys.

In summary, law firms are highly successful at attracting many talented associates to work for them by offering very high incomes. Their most frequent strategy for retaining associates is to offer them even higher salaries, bonuses and benefits.[62] Yet, surveys indicate that while many associates are highly satisfied with their salaries, after a time money stops being their biggest draw and working conditions become even more important.[63]

Among the things they want are: shorter work weeks, flex-time, the ability to work from home and leave early on occasion without being stigmatized, interesting and fun work, mentors who truly care about them, collegiality and open communication. In short, the colloquial term for what they want is a "life." In one national survey, 45 percent of the associates polled indicated their willingness to take a significant salary cut in return for a lower billable hour requirement.[64]

There are data to suggest that when associates don't get what they truly want, turnover increases. That causes much organizational disruption and damage, and significantly increases recruitment and training costs.[65] Firms that respond to the needs of associates for a more balanced life tend to have lower attrition rates.[66]

WHAT TROUBLES FEMALE ATTORNEYS

Although our society has come a long way in terms of civil rights, some observers believe that women's liberation has also turned into a partial trap.[67] That is, even though it is a positive outcome that there are many more female lawyers today, their duties at home have not been reduced to that of their male counterparts; working women in our society are still also expected to be homemakers and primary caretakers of their children and elderly parents, whereas it is still more socially acceptable (though not healthy) for men to focus primarily on their careers. This, plus the fact that female attorneys tend to be more in touch with their emotions[68] than their male cohorts, and more predisposed to please others before themselves,[69] creates more internal turmoil regarding their time allocations.[70]

Another challenge faced by many female attorneys is the ethical orientation that they bring to the practice of law. As a group, women tend to be more predisposed than men to give weight to humanistic values, to care about the general well being of all parties involved, and to strive for cooperation, harmony and civility in the practice of law.[71] Even though these are admirable values, they are not in line with the established traditions of a profession that was once dominated by men. As a result, some women attorneys have a difficult time fitting into the profession.

The end result is that female attorneys report a significantly higher rate of dissatisfaction with their jobs than their male cohorts.[72] In addition, when compared to males, female attorneys tend to be less likely to enter the practice of law upon graduation from law school,[73] more likely to switch jobs,[74] and more likely to leave the profession.[75] One survey of 1009 lawyers in Ontario, Canada, showed that women left the profession 60 percent more quickly than their male counterparts.[76] In another survey[77] of 1809 lawyers in Minnesota, female attorneys consistently reported more symptoms of stress than their male colleagues (e.g., depression, anxiety, concentration problems, sleeplessness, eating disorders, irritability, and fatigue).

It has been known for a number of years that women with graduate level degrees have lower marriage and higher divorce rates than their male counterparts.[78] In recent years, however, it has been discovered that law is a particularly unfriendly profession toward women who want to have a family.[79] In 1983, the ABA Journal conducted a survey of 1736 attorneys, and found that female lawyers were more than twice as likely to be single as their male colleagues.[80] A few years later, in a study comparing female attorneys with female physicians and college professors, it was shown that female lawyers were least likely to marry or have children, significantly more likely to get divorced, and least likely to re-marry after a divorce.[81]

In a more recent survey of female lawyers,[82] it was found that job stress was correlated with the number of hours worked each week and that over 50 percent of the respondents reported difficulties raising children because of their employment. The most disturbing finding in this study was that the number of hours female attorneys reported working each week was a significant predictor of their probability for experiencing a spontaneous abortion during the first trimester of pregnancy. Working over 45 hours per week was found to be particularly predictive in this regard.

THE TYPE OF PRACTICE ALSO MATTERS

To some extent, the stressors that affect lawyers are a product of the type of organization in which they work, the types of law they practice and the kinds of clients they represent. Approximately 75 percent of lawyers who have legal positions are in a private practice setting, whereas most of the rest are employed in corporate legal departments or in government agencies.[83] These settings range in size from one lawyer to several hundred. Since law regulates almost every type of human behavior, there are a variety of substantive areas in which lawyers develop special expertise, including: commercial, torts, tax, real estate, criminal, labor, matrimonial, patent, public interest, etc. All of these differences affect the types of stress they experience.

For example, when compared to their peers in private practice, lawyers in corporate legal departments tend to complain more often about such problems as lack of opportunity for advancement and professional development, political intrigue and backbiting.[84] In addition, one of the most stressful issues corporate counsel have to deal with is cost control and budget restrictions.[85] On the other hand, lawyers in private practice are more likely to suffer the effects of not having enough time for themselves and their families, and of being under pressure to produce income.

Large private practice firms are more likely to place their attorneys under the pressure of greater billable hour requirements, more staff meetings and other administrative duties. The larger the firm, the more likely its lawyers are to have to contend with office politics, power plays, and competition for advancement or the firm's resources. Unless their work climates are carefully and explicitly managed, larger law firms tend to have more authoritarian, overly demanding and personally insensitive environments. Lawyers in the middle and lower levels of the hierarchy don't feel in control of their lives or careers.

In contrast, solo practitioners do have the advantage of being their own bosses. No one tells them what cases to take or how many hours to work, and they don't have to share their income with others. On the other hand, in addition to providing legal services, "solos" have to find time to create bills, pay bills, make purchasing decisions, market their practice, file and type. "Solos" take the risk of being totally responsible for their own decisions and are exclusively in charge of the "complaint department." In addition, they have to deal with feelings of isolation and the fears that accompany slow business months.

Litigators of all stripes probably endure more stress than non-litigators, especially when they go to trial.[86] One study[87] found that male and female trial lawyers had higher testosterone levels than non-trial lawyers of the same gender. Testosterone is a hormone associated with aggression and competitiveness. Starting with the pretrial phase, litigators report various physical symptoms, including headaches, skin rashes, gastrointestinal ailments, and insomnia. Out of a fear of forgetting something, they spend endless hours preparing, only to be disappointed by inevitable postponements. Once the trial phase begins, the anticipatory anxiety diminishes, but is replaced by aggressive negative emotions and physical exhaustion. Handling their clients' emotionality and preparing for each day of trial can take up every available waking minute. Family and other obligations are often simply not attended to and create their own pressures. After the trial, there is the inescapable letdown and obsessive replaying of all questions that should have been asked and closing statements that should have been made. In addition, they also have to catch up with other clients and cases that have been ignored during a trial.

Finally, substantive areas of specialization also contribute to stress. For example, family law is a particularly stressful type of practice,[88] in part because divorcing clients are often highly emotional and on their worst behavior. Since the couple's relationship often continues to unravel throughout the divorce action, family lawyers and their staff commonly operate in crisis mode. Feelings of hostility, guilt, fear and frustration are rampant. Clients who want to do rotten things to their spouses look for willing lawyers. Thus, part of the job often involves contending with S.O.B. lawyers. With half of the population having experienced a divorce, announcing that you are a divorce lawyer at a cocktail party has its hazards as well.

While it is beyond my scope to describe them all, each substantive area of practice has its stressors. Lawyers who deal with commercial paper all day sometimes complain about the tedium and the lack of a sense of contributing to the social good. Like family lawyers, bankruptcy attorneys also have to interact with clients who are highly emotional and at the worst time of their lives. Criminal lawyers frequently have to endure the stress of witnessing the most evil aspects of human nature. Those who specialize in the emerging area of elder law often have to witness family tragedies that come at the end of life. In summary, as advocates, lawyers cannot help but be touched by the problems of their clients.

SECTION II: OVERVIEW OF STRESS MANAGEMENT

The best way out is always through.
                                    Robert Frost

The worst cynicism: a belief in luck.
                                    Joyce Carol Oates

WHAT IS STRESS?

From prehistoric times, human beings have experienced stress that is either physical or psychological in nature, or both. People who do strenuous manual labor are likely to experience more physical stress (e.g., tired muscles) than others, whereas people in occupations that primarily require complex mental activity and human interaction are more likely than others to experience psychological stress. Thus, when lawyers report having a stressful day, more often than not they are referring to the mental and emotional strains of their jobs. For this reason, we will focus primarily on psychological stress.

ELEMENTS OF PSYCHOLOGICAL STRESS

The human experience we call psychological stress can be viewed as being composed of the following sequence of elements:[89]

$$\text{Stimulus} \rightarrow \text{Thought} \rightarrow \text{Emotion} \rightarrow \text{Behavior}$$

For example, consider what happens when you see a car coming toward you in your lane of traffic. Your central nervous system first perceives the situation, and then it begins to appraise it. The initial appraisals are swift and unconscious. As soon as you become conscious of your thoughts, you may say to yourself, "That passing car may not have enough time to get back into its lane. I'm in danger, and I have to avoid it." Similar judgments may occur in one or more sensory forms (e.g., visual, auditory). Thus, for example, you may experience visual images that depict a car accident.

As soon as your central nervous system recognizes an imminent danger, it begins to trigger several "sympathetic" bodily responses. Breathing gets faster. Digestion slows down. Heart rate and blood pressure go up. Perspiration increases. Your total being becomes focused on the car that is coming toward you. Your central nervous system appraisals along with your internal bodily reactions combine to create the experience we call an emotion, which in this case is most likely fear. The emotion pushes your body to react (behave) externally and you move your car in ways that avoid a collision. It is not a coincidence that the word emotion has the word "motion" in it.

Note that only the stimulus and behavior occur in external objective reality.[90] Thoughts and emotions occur internally and are subjective; they are partly a function of our unique personalities (habitual ways of responding to things) and are changeable. If this were not true, then all of us would react to this car scene exactly the same way. We don't, of course.

For some people, the fear created by a car coming towards them is so great that they either panic or get off the road much earlier than necessary. At the other extreme, there are people who say to themselves, "I have the right of way and should not have to be the one to move." The righteous anger that such thoughts produce, may cause them to play "chicken" with the other driver and wait a long time before getting off the road. Hopefully, most people have a reaction that is somewhere in between these two extremes.

Understanding how the elements of a stress response are interconnected gives us the ability to control our reactions by simply interrupting or changing their automatic flow. For example, it is obvious that if the stimulus is interrupted or changed, the rest of the stress experience will be different. When we cannot control the stress-producing stimulus, then another way to control our stress reaction is to interrupt or change our appraisal of it. Indeed, many of the upcoming chapters in this book focus on how to do this.

STRESS IS HEALTHY
DISTRESS IS NOT

Certain forms of stress are inevitable and necessary to a healthy, productive, and happy life. Some of the stressors in our lives energize our positive emotions and motivate us to get up in the morning, solve problems, and be creative. Thus, getting rid of all stress is both a naive and harmful goal; it is often associated with running away from it all, which is not a formula for success.

Instead, your focus should be on reducing a destructive form of stress called *distress*. This type of stress is characterized by negative emotions such as fear, guilt, and anger. When such emotions are chronic and strong, they tend to destroy our ability to enjoy life, stay healthy, and work productively.

Some people assume that an ability to endure distress is a sign of strong character or courage. Because chronic distress is so harmful both physically and psychologically, I believe that passive endurance of it is more often a sign of bad judgment and fear of change. My objective is to help you overcome life's harmful challenges, not just endure them. That does require strong character and courage.

MYTH: MIND AND BODY ARE SEPARATE

For every thought and emotion we experience, there is a corresponding biochemical correlate. Thus, thoughts and emotions are both physiological and psychological. They are reflections of the same phenomenon, measured from different levels of analysis.[91] When we experience psychological distress several things happen concurrently: We appraise something as being negative, biochemical changes occur in our brains and the rest of our nervous system, and we undergo several internal bodily changes (e.g., heart rate rises).

It should not be surprising that when harm is done in the psychological realm, it can concurrently occur in the physical realm as well. For example, recent studies have shown that diseases associated with the blood circulatory system as well as the immune system can be influenced by our thoughts and emotions.[92] These findings suggest that stress management is much more than just a way to achieve psychological health. It is something you do to maintain both your psychological and physical health, for they are interrelated.

THE BASIC PRINCIPLES OF STRESS MANAGEMENT

Turning to what you can do about stress, let me begin by bringing the principles of stress management down to the simplest of terms. From time immemorial, threats of all kinds have left both animals and humans with only three options: *surrender, flee, or fight.* Although we may use different descriptors today, the choices we face in reacting to the stressful events of our modern society are still remarkably similar.

THE SURRENDER OPTION

A current form of surrender is when you passively accept your stressful circumstances as inevitable and simply suffer the consequences. Of course some acts of endurance over stress are courageous, but many are not. I am referring to people who accept their stressors when they can do something about them. Usually, the emotions that drive such behaviors are fear and helplessness.[93] In turn, these emotions often result in anxiety disorders and clinical depression.

Interestingly, when you cope with psychological stress in a passive-depressive manner, a type of surrender also occurs at the biochemical level. Your central nervous system adapts to prolonged distress by accepting it as normal and begins to suppress the activity of your immune system, which in turn makes you more susceptible to various types of physical illnesses.[94] For these reasons, surrender is not a good option.

THE FLIGHT OPTION

The underlying strategy of the flight option is to reduce stress by removing yourself from its sources. You can remove yourself from or avoid the causes of your stress either *externally* or *internally*. Quitting your job, being assigned to a new department, working fewer hours, and taking a vacation or a sabbatical are examples of how we remove ourselves from stressful activities externally. Some of these tactics rejuvenate our ability to endure stress in the future (e.g., sabbatical).

Daydreaming is one way that we remove ourselves from stressful situations internally, without ever physically leaving our offices. The most effective way to do this is through formal *relaxation techniques* that involve breathing exercises, muscle relaxation, and mental imagery (e.g., meditation, Yoga). These techniques work because they allow you to focus your mind on something peaceful and different. In addition, they have positive biochemical effects, such as reducing your blood pressure.[95]

I have categorized relaxation techniques under the flight option because their immediate effect is only temporary. It should be mentioned, however, that people who do these exercises on a regular basis also experience long-term attitudinal transformations. For this reason, an argument could be made for categorizing relaxation techniques under the fight option below, as a way of making enduring changes in how you interact with your world.

THE FIGHT OPTION

Another way to reduce stress is to confront its sources and alter them. In the short run, it is generally easier to avoid rather than confront a problem. However, avoidance is seldom effective in the long run. Its results are short-term, as in the case of a vacation, or costly, as in the case of a career change. Obviously, I encourage all lawyers to take their vacations and some lawyers to switch careers, but usually these are not the ultimate solutions to most of their problems. Thus, while confronting problems head-on is the most difficult option, it does lead to long-term solutions.

You can tackle your sources of distress in two ways: either *externally*, by making your work environment less stressful, or *internally*, by making your body and mind more resilient to the work environment. Workplaces with environments that are least stressful are characterized by reasonable and flexible workloads, supportive mentors, collegiality, civility and professionalism. Lawyers who are resilient to workplace stress tend to get proper nutrition, exercise and sleep, to manage their negative thoughts and emotions effectively, and to act in harmony with their core values. In the chapters that follow, I will explain how you can do the same.

In keeping with the aim of this book, I will devote more pages to what you can do to become more resilient to stress than to how you can make your workplace less stressful. Please don't infer from this that the latter is less important. In fact, I maintain that it is unrealistic for lawyers to expect all of the changes to come from within. The stressors in today's legal system and workplaces are so strong that, unless more is done to lessen them, law will remain a very stressful profession. Workplace improvements, however, require organizational and systemic interventions that are beyond the ability of individual lawyers to make.

Of course, one of the things that you can do as an individual is get involved in group efforts to improve the legal workplace, through law firm committees and bar organizations. Historically, lawyers have been in the forefront of helping others achieve humane labor environments. There is no reason why lawyers cannot apply those same talents toward improving their own working conditions. I urge you to do that.

SECTION III: IMPROVE YOUR WORK ENVIRONMENT

A person comes under the control of a stimulating environment..............(it) selects behavior and, on the analogy of natural selection, takes over the role of creative thought, purpose, and plans.

B.F. Skinner

REDUCE WORKLOADS

As discussed earlier, the most frequent complaint among lawyers is "the hours." The cultural pressure to work long hours can be so strong that many lawyers blame themselves for their distress rather than their work environments. These unhappy lawyers spend years struggling to satisfy external expectations that do not fit them, hoping that in time they will adjust and find happiness. Even in the face of indisputable evidence that their colleagues are also miserable and sometimes feel forced to pad their hours, many unhappy lawyers still assume that there must be something wrong with *them*. Such thoughts lead to chronic feelings of guilt, which in turn can result in burnout and even clinical depression. In reality, most lawyers are not at fault for feeling distressed in workaholic environments. Usually, either there is a simple mismatch, for which no one is to blame, or the culture in which they work is toxic.

CREATE CULTURAL CHANGE

If your workaholic environment (not you) causes you significant stress, you must recognize and confront that fact, or nothing will change. There are only two things you can do to reduce your stress: either transform your current work environment or leave it for a healthier one.

How do you make an office less workaholic and hence less stressful? Partly, it depends on the size of your firm or department. In a medium to large organization, you will probably need to develop a new written policy on workloads and then convince management and colleagues to adopt it. Don't reinvent the wheel in developing a new policy, however; read the recommendations published by various bar organizations in recent years on how law firms and legal departments can adopt alternative work schedules and flexible hours.[96] If you work in a small firm or department, the new policy on reduced workloads may not need to be in writing, but the challenge of convincing management and colleagues to accept it is the same.

Adopting a new work-schedule policy is an important step, but it is not sufficient to cause real change. A survey published in 2000 by the National Association for Law Placement (NALP) showed that although 95 percent of large law firms claimed that they made part-time schedules available, very few lawyers (about 3 percent) actually worked part-time.[97] Since other professions have more part-time workers, the NALP suggests that the problem among lawyers is a cultural one.

Indeed, when lawyers ask for reduced workloads, most law firms and legal departments, large and small, are hesitant to grant them permission. Partners and associates report in surveys that their law firms are most likely to approve requests for part-time work from lawyers who are good performers and difficult to replace, who have strong connections, and who threaten to leave if their requests are denied.[98] They also think that women are more likely to get their requests approved than men, and that requesting time for child care is more likely to get a favorable response than a desire to pursue other interests.

The strong resistance by law firms to reduce workloads is vividly illustrated by a case in which an associate had to go to court to seek relief.[99] This litigator claimed that because the 16-hour days she was expected to work increased her blood pressure, she was disabled and required accommodations. Her law firm countered by saying that she was not disabled because she could work a 40-hour week. The judge ruled against the law firm.

Lawyers who are given permission to work fewer hours or to work from home some of the time, often report feeling stigmatized and marginalized.[100] This is true even for lawyers who work what most people consider to be full time (40 hours per week) in law firms that expect much more (50-70 hours). For example, lawyers who work part-time report that important meetings are often scheduled when they are out of the office, and that sometimes they are not given their own business cards.

In summary, lawyers who work fewer hours than is the norm at their firms report that they would be happy if the consequence to them was just lower salaries and bonuses. That would be fair and expected. What hurts and makes them want to leave their jobs or the profession is the fact that they are also made to feel inferior. Thus, before you can even begin to create real change at your workplace, you need to understand the psychological dynamics of your current culture.

One of the obstacles you may encounter is that some law firms are run like white-collar sweat shops. In describing today's profit driven law firms, Scott Turow, a lawyer and novelist put it this way: "The only sure ingredients of growth are new clients, bigger bills, and especially more people at the bottom, each a little profit center, toiling into the wee hours and earning more for the partnership than they take home."[101] If the workaholic culture of your firm or legal department is driven at least in part by a strong financial motive, base your arguments for a change at least in part on economic factors.

The leaders in your workaholic workplace may believe that they are following modern business principles. They must be persuaded that their business model is actually outdated. That is, some of our most competitive world class corporations and successful law firms have found that helping employees balance work with personal and family life helps - not hurts - their organizations' survival in the long run. It increases loyalty, productivity, and client service, while reducing the costs associated with burnout and turnover.[102]

You must present this type of evidence, along with financial projections for your firm or department, or management will not even give alternative work schedules serious consideration. You must demonstrate in concrete terms that your suggested policy and cultural changes will not threaten the financial stability of the firm or department, or reduce its ability to serve clients – that it may, in fact, ensure the organization's long-term health.[103]

You should be clear about the type of culture you are trying to achieve. The idea is not to turn your office into a place where people are now prohibited from working long hours. Propose a vision for a workplace where lawyers with diverse values, in differing stages of their lives and with various obligations are allowed and encouraged to contribute and flourish. You want to help create a culture of mutual respect, so that neither lawyers who work long hours nor lawyers who allocate more time to their personal lives are made to feel inferior.

Expect some resistance no matter what your data show or how reasonable your proposal is. One-size-fits-all attitudes are difficult to break. Some leaders who focus solely on the short-term bottom line will not be willing to take any financial risks. Others will be afraid that changing the status quo in any way will upset the cultural stability of the office. Still others will not care about morale and job satisfaction.

You must also understand that for some workplace leaders, work defines their worthiness and that of their organization. For those who believe in the virtues of hard work and long hours, it's not just about the money. They will not want to foster a culture that they think will diminish the reputation of their firm or department.

To illustrate my point, allow me to describe a conversation my wife and I once had with a lawyer-acquaintance who was coming out of his building on a Saturday. Having confirmed that he had come in to his office to do some work, somehow our conversation shifted to a comment he made about the law firm next to his. "They can't be a very good firm or at least they can't be doing well financially," he said. "How do you know?" I asked. "I'm here on weekends all of the time and I never see anyone over there," he replied. The possibility would not occur to him that perhaps the lawyers next door were the real success stories – that they might have been doing so well that they did not need to work on weekends. Attempts to convince this lawyer that his firm should reduce its emphasis on long hours might be futile.

Although some leaders will resist change, others will be persuaded. They will genuinely share your vision of a workplace where the quality of an attorney's work is not negotiable, but where his or her work schedule is. Still, leaders who are open to your ideas may not know how to implement them. Thus, you have to be prepared to do the work that will produce a concrete plan of action. Execute your plan effectively the first time. You may not get another chance.

If you decide that you are powerless to change your organization's workaholic culture, consider leaving it. If your values and those of your colleagues are simply too different, you may belong somewhere else. Similarly, if you always feel like a fish out of water, switch to a workplace where you can breathe easily again.

Don't make the same mistake again and again, however. Don't be lured by pitches from prospective colleagues who assure you that theirs is a workplace where a lawyer's right to a personal life is valued. Verify the concrete numerical criteria by which you will be judged (e.g., billable hours). Calculate precisely how and when you will need to arrive and leave from the office on most days, how early you will need to get up in the mornings, whether you will have ample time to eat dinners with your family, take vacations and holidays, and, in general, have a life outside of the office.

BECOME YOUR OWN BOSS

Another option to consider is starting your own firm either as a sole practitioner or with colleagues who share your values. As your own boss you can determine your own work schedule. One lawyer who formed his own firm described the experience this way:

> I am happy to announce that I eventually found the ideal law job. I am referring to the law firm I started ...... (where) lawyers work when and where they want. I work at home at least one day a week. There is no specified limit for vacation time......Since almost all of the work we do is for fixed fees, for the most part, I don't even keep track of the time I spend. There are no timesheets and no knots in my stomach.[104]

Running your own law firm does require you to avoid some traps that can turn you into a workaholic very easily. That is, some sole practitioners find it difficult to limit their hours because besides practicing law, they sometimes have to file, type, create bills, pay bills, make purchasing decisions, and market their practices. They also need to deal with increased risks and the negative emotions that accompany them. Sole practitioners are responsible for all decisions, in charge of the "complaint department," and liable for all mistakes. In addition, they must be prepared for collection problems and slow months.

Sole practitioners who do control their workload effectively have specific psychological skills. They tend to be solution-oriented thinkers. That is, they focus on problems long enough to recognize them, then begin to think about solutions. They also tend to be emotionally self-aware. For example, with regard to answering the phone at all hours, the self-aware lawyer will ask: "Is it really true that my clients will leave me if I don't answer the phone after business hours?" In response, they will consider alternative views: "Isn't it possible that if I live a balanced life and show how much I value my family, clients will respect me more and remain loyal? How can I set limits to my working hours and still be responsive to my clients' needs? How can I limit my practice to clients who will respect my right to a balanced life?"

IN RE LITIGATORS

At least two masters control the work schedules of litigators: their law firms and the courts. In addition to the burden of their office workloads, many litigators find that some judges care little about the mental health of lawyers, as evidenced by the unpredictable and disruptive ways in which they schedule hearings, trials, and other matters.[105]

A few bar associations have begun to push for reforms designed to help litigators. For example, in 1999 the Supreme Court of North Carolina approved a rule that guarantees attorneys the right to take a planned vacation of up to three weeks - without having to appear in court or be called upon to be involved in any other litigation activities during that period.[106] These types of advances show that it is possible to improve the lives of litigators, but more lawyers need to become actively involved in pushing for them.

Even under the best conditions, however, when litigators go to trial they work long hours and experience high stress.[107] They spend endless hours preparing before a trial. Once a trial begins, handling their clients' emotional responses and daily preparations can take up every waking minute. During such times, they tend to neglect family and other obligations, which creates further stress. After a trial, they must find time to catch up with other clients that they have ignored.

Even though workaholism may be inevitable before, during, and after many trials, most litigators make the mistake of failing to bring their lives back into balance by taking extra time off. In the same way that soldiers in battle are given leaves to revitalize themselves, the best way to combat the negative effects of litigation is to take short vacations after every difficult or lengthy trial whenever possible. This will not only normalize your physical and psychological functions, but also renew your relationships with family members and friends.

CONCLUSION

Each of us is unique and defines a balanced life differently. Ask yourself whether your current work schedule interferes with other important needs. If you are happy working as hard and as much as you do currently, there is little reason to change. On the other hand, if your usual workload causes you chronic stress, don't waste time imagining that things will change on their own. Do something about it.

It is true that my suggestions for reducing lawyers' workloads are easier said than done. However, as documented in a number of testimonials, some lawyers have taken bold steps to bring more balance into their lives and have succeeded.[108] I suggest that you at least consider the possibility of doing the same. Making a real change will admittedly require courage and even some sacrifices. It may not be easy, but it is definitely worth a try.

CREATE COMARADERIE

Isolation is a major source of stress for many lawyers. Law firms and legal departments of all sizes can be lonely places, where lawyers toil behind closed doors and seldom interact with colleagues unless there is a business matter or a crisis to handle. Part of the reason for this is that the legal community places a high value on productivity, financial success, ambition, personal advancement, and social status. Friendships, group affiliations, relationships and social interactions are thought to interfere with these values. Consequently, colleagues are discouraged from sharing and discussing their daily stressors and problems.

Unfortunately, this uneven view of what is important has its costs. For example, several surveys have shown that a lack of camaraderie, communication and mentorship are among the top reasons many young lawyers give for leaving their law firms and sometimes the profession.[109] One study found that having several mentoring relationships (not just one) is important to a young lawyer's job satisfaction and success.[110] Another study found that access to same gender mentors is also important.[111] Interestingly, female attorneys who had male mentors earned higher incomes, but those who had female mentors reported higher career satisfaction, greater intent to continue practicing law, and fewer conflicts between their work and personal lives.

George W. Kaufman, author of "The Lawyers Guide To Balancing Life And Work,"[112] has summarized the problem of isolation this way:

> In contrast to my early days in law, our profession is currently in trouble. The roots of our problem can be found in the dissatisfaction that so many lawyers

experience while practicing their craft. Part of the problem is that today's young lawyers have few models to draw upon and receive little comfort from their seniors. Intimate conversations that lead to changes in jobs or careers are usually reserved for families and therapists, rather than other attorneys who actually have the experience that young lawyers need to hear.[113]

Kaufman believes that good mentoring supplies young lawyers with the values and connectivity that are necessary for a satisfying career. I totally agree, but I would add the obvious point that all lawyers, not just young ones, gain from collegial relationships with others at work. The benefits include lower stress levels, higher job satisfaction, and greater loyalty to an organization and its mission. This improves client service and secures organizational stability and long-term financial health.

For these reasons, I encourage workplace leaders to create organizational climates that reward (or at least don't punish) mentoring, group cohesion, and friendships. They need not create an environment where lawyers socialize so much that little work gets done, but simply tilt the balance just enough to reap the benefits of higher loyalty, job satisfaction, and client service, as well as lower stress and burnout.

Lawyers in organizations where friendships are subtly or actively discouraged should consider helping to create a new culture. Adding a few more social events to the obligatory annual holiday party is not the solution, however. You must strive for a genuine reordering of your organization's daily priorities to include interpersonal relationships. It requires integrating a new set of values that emphasize the importance of the people with whom you work. Once that is understood and accepted, the appropriate daily behaviors become the natural things to do. Words like "thank you" and "please" get used more often. Taking a few minutes to ask others about their children and to listen to their answers becomes normal.

If you feel dissatisfied by an unfriendly workplace and know that it is highly resistant to change, consider looking for one with a different culture. Don't spend years feeling guilty about not fitting in or trying to revise your own values.

If you are a solo practitioner and suffer from feelings of isolation, there are several obvious steps to consider: Think about bringing in a partner or an associate, expanding your affiliations with other colleagues by participating in more bar association functions, or simply finding a few friends with whom you can have lunch on a regular basis. To paraphrase what an unusually healthy sole practitioner told me once, it's all a matter of perception. Don't think of yourself as a sole practitioner, but as a member of a mammoth law firm that just happens to be composed of all of the solos and small firms in your community. Make a point of keeping in touch with all of your "partners" just as if their offices were right next door. This way, you will never be lonely.

PROMOTE CIVILITY

Our system of justice is adversarial in nature and requires lawyers to represent their clients with zeal. This characteristic guarantees that many of the tasks lawyers take on will have some stress associated with them. It just comes with the territory. Even so, many legal scholars have concluded that the practice of law has become too adversarial and uncivil in recent years.[114]

Overzealousness and incivility are evident when lawyers participate in shouting matches, send hostile letters, employ unreasonable delay tactics, and flood the opposition with interrogatories, depositions, motions, and pleadings.[115] This has become a major concern among lawyers, as evidenced by the fact that a majority of them complain about it in surveys.[116] Furthermore, it has decreased public respect for the profession and for our system of justice.

The legal community has responded to the overzealousness problem in multiple ways. For example, some courts[117] and bar associations[118] have developed "civility" guidelines as a way to rekindle what is commonly called "professionalism" in the practice of law. Thus far, these guidelines have been intended to be inspirational; lawyers are not required to adhere to them as in the case of ethical codes of professional responsibility. Some jurisdictions have taken the additional step of requiring lawyers to get continuing education credits in "professionalism."

Regrettably, the majority of surveyed lawyers have reported that the current "professionalism" guidelines are ineffective - that there is a need to make them mandatory and to attach penalties for noncompliance.[119] These same surveyed lawyers have suggested that there is also a need for more concrete limitations on the number and scope of interrogatories, depositions, pleadings, and motions permitted in a single case.[120] The idea is that streamlining these procedures may decrease the worst types of antagonistic games that the system encourages.

Another step that many jurisdictions have taken is to expand the availability of alternative dispute resolution (ADR) options such as mediation and arbitration. Since part of the stress that lawyers experience results from the adversarial nature of our legal process, it follows that ADR methods should lead to less stress for all parties - clients and lawyers alike. So far, however, ADR methods have not gained great popularity.

Finally, another response to the overzealousness problem has been the emergence of several new practice models that emphasize humanistic, altruistic, and interpersonally oriented values. These models include: Collaborative Law, Comprehensive Law, Holistic Law, Therapeutic Jurisprudence, and Preventive Law.[121] They all advocate a need for lawyers to consider the law's effect on the general well being of all persons (clients and lawyers) in the legal context, and to do more counseling with clients so that future problems and disputes can be avoided. Proponents argue that these practice models will result in better outcomes for litigants, improve the lives of lawyers, and lead to greater public respect for lawyers and our legal system.

All of the preceding ways of making the practice of law more civil are based on a common central assumption. Namely, the ethical duty to represent clients zealously has been taken to extremes and needs to be tamed. This position is somewhat controversial in the legal community, and that may be one reason why the professionalism movement has had limited success. The mainstream position on zealous representation is exemplified by the advice that Harvard law professor, Alan Dershowitz, typically gives young lawyers:

Zealous representation requires subordinating *all* other interests – ideological, career, personal – to the legitimate interest of the client. You are the surgeon in the operating room whose *only* goal is to save the patient, whether the patient is a good person or a bad person, a saint or a criminal.[122] (italics added)

Many and perhaps the majority of American lawyers and judges, consider this definition of zealous representation to be a well-established ethical duty. That is, most American lawyers learn a similar definition of zealous representation early in their careers, along with a number of due process arguments to defend it.[123] The problem is that the duty to represent clients this way may be incompatible with a definition of professionalism that requires civility. If, as Dershowitz asserts, zealous representation requires lawyers to subordinate *all* other interests to those of the client, then incivility is appropriate at times because it works. Under our current adversarial system, nice guys who are unwilling to engage in uncivil behavior do finish last sometimes.

Is there a solution to this problem? If you will permit a psychologist to engage in a little legal philosophizing, I do think there is a solution, but I believe that it requires a reassessment of several basic tenets of our adversarial system. We are all so accustomed to repeating the legal and behavioral assumptions on which our current system is based that we accept them as fact.

I am suggesting that the currently popular interpretation of the "zealousness" concept is just that – current interpretation. In fact, there is a developmental history to this concept, and it has evolved over the years. The currently accepted interpretation is not written in stone, and it would behoove us to study and revisit its various past interpretations, as well as consider new ones. Additionally, I am suggesting that we have a romanticized faith in our entire adversarial system of justice. We are fond of thinking of it as imperfect but still the best in the world. This is a belief, not an empirically demonstrated fact. There are various points of view on how our adversary system can be improved, and the only way to truly know who is right is to test them in a scientifically prescribed manner.

I don't claim to know exactly how our current system can be improved, but it seems obvious to me and most Americans that we can do better. Unfortunately, I don't detect an outcry for reform among lawyers. A very articulate business acquaintance of mine once summarized the layman's point of view on this topic as follows: "Here is what I think is the crux of the problem with the legal profession today: It really upsets me when criminal defense lawyers brag about the number of cases they've won. Instead, I wish they would cite the number of innocent people they have successfully defended. There is a difference. I'm not saying that we should do away with lawyers, the right to a fair trial, or any of that. I'm just saying that something is wrong when the distinction I'm making isn't considered relevant, or when a lawyer's achievements are measured by the same criteria as that of a professional athlete. Law shouldn't be likened to a professional sport. A lawyer's accomplishments should not be measured by how many cases he's won or how much money she's made."

HOW LAW SCHOOLS CAN HELP

Many observers believe that environmental stress reduction for lawyers needs to begin in law school. A number of studies have shown that attending law school is stressful and has mental health consequences for some students, such as chronic depression and anxiety disorders.[124] While students consider law schools to be intellectually stimulating, they also often describe them as cold and hostile environments in which adversarial skills and workaholism are highly valued, while relationships and balanced lives are implicitly devalued. The Socratic method is intended to prepare students for the real world, but is often experienced as abusive and demeaning. Some researchers have concluded that instead of inoculating students to stress and its health consequences, law school training does the opposite.[125]

Logical reasoning, moral neutrality, respect for facts and details, skepticism, and pragmatism are among the skills and attitudes that are emphasized in law schools.[126] It is part of what law professors mean when they say proudly to their new crop of students each year, "We are going to teach you how to think like a lawyer." Those who cannot "think" this way are encouraged to leave the law. In fact, one study showed that law students who find it difficult to abandon their personal feelings about what is right and wrong, have a dropout rate that is four times higher than the rest of their colleagues.[127]

I think that law school curriculums overemphasize logical reasoning to the exclusion of other characteristics that are also important to being a lawyer, such as interpersonal and counseling skills, empathy, emotional intelligence, and moral integrity.[128] Training in these areas would reduce stress among lawyers by raising the level of professionalism and civility in law. Indeed, several educators have called on law schools to reform their training models so that more emphasis is placed on these areas, but law schools have been slow to change.[129] More urgent pressure for such changes is needed from the profession.

I would suggest that law schools also need to become more selective in their admissions processes, by making "character" a more important selection criterion. The typical law school admissions process relies primarily on an applicant's academic achievements and intellectual abilities. Character is considered, but it is often defined merely as the absence of police arrests, criminal convictions, academic violations, and other officially recorded legal or ethical stains. In contrast, graduate training programs in health care not only require applicants to submit a variety of character oriented written materials, such as letters of recommendation and goal statements, but they also commonly ask for face-to-face interviews. During such interviews, the applicant's character is implicitly assessed.

Since lawyers are no different than health professionals in taking on the weight of other people's important problems, law schools should be equally diligent in selecting future lawyers of high character. This is the most effective way to raise the level of professionalism and civility in the law. Basic character traits are so deeply ingrained in a person that they are difficult to change in or after law school with just a few hours of formal training in ethics. In the words of the comic actor Robin Williams, "You can't churn butter with a toothpick."

SECTION IV: MAINTAIN A HEALTHY BODY

The preservation of health is a duty. Few seem conscious that there is such a thing as physical morality.

Herbert Spencer

A sound mind in a sound body, is a short, but full description of a happy state in this World: he that has these two, has little more to wish for; and he that wants either of them, will be little the better for anything else.

John Locke

GOOD NUTRITION

The benefits of good nutrition are well known. It helps prevent illness, increases physical energy, extends life expectancy, and improves physical appearance. Good nutrition also improves the biochemistry of your brain so that you experience more positive moods, higher mental energy and sharper concentration levels. Thus, if you want to manage stress more effectively, then proper nutrition needs to be part of your strategy.

The first thing you should do is arm yourself with reliable information. Most educated people already know that they are supposed to be selective in the foods they eat. When pressed for specifics, we can all recite some of the hazards of foods that contain too much sugar, fat, cholesterol, and salt, as well as too many calories. We know that there are several food groupings (breads and cereals, vegetables and fruits, meats and dairy products, etc.), but most of us probably don't know exactly how much of each food group we should eat. Thus, we tend to rely on the old adage that everything should be eaten in moderation.

Well, recent research indicates that some of what we have been taught for a number of decades has been wrong, and that our understanding of nutrition needs to be updated and made more precise. At this writing, one of the best summaries of the scientific nutrition literature can be found in a book entitled "Eat, Drink, And Be Healthy," written by Walter Willett, M.D., the chairman of the Department of Nutrition at Harvard's School of Public Health.[130] In summary, Dr. Willett recommends the following:

- Eat whole grain foods, vegetables, fruits, nuts, beans, fish, poultry, eggs, and plant oils.

- Avoid or eat less red meats, butter and margarine, white rice, white bread, potatoes, pasta, sweets and anything that is considered to be "junk" food (e.g., potato chips).

- Take a daily multi-vitamin supplement and possibly a calcium supplement, just for insurance.

- If you drink alcohol, do so in moderation.

Although some of this advice should be familiar to most readers, there are aspects of it that are very different than what we have been taught traditionally. For example, it has been known for a long time that simple carbohydrates (sugars) should be eaten sparingly, but until recently it was thought that all complex carbohydrates were the same and could be eaten in large quantities, as long as they were within a person's daily caloric needs. This is not true, however. There are "good" and "bad" complex carbohydrates.

Recent scientific findings indicate that several sources of complex carbohydrates, such as processed foods or baked goods made from white flour (e.g., bread, pretzels, chips), pasta, white rice, and potatoes should be avoided almost as much as sugars.[131] The problem with these "bad" carbohydrates is that they contain few nutrients, and our digestive systems quickly turn them into glucose (sugar), which then gets distributed into our bloodstreams almost as fast as when we eat desserts. Given the large quantities of breads, potatoes, pasta, and rice that are commonly served with many meals, it is critical that we make an effort to limit our intake of these foods or at least insist on brown rice, whole-wheat bread, and whole-wheat pasta. In contrast, "good" carbohydrates (most whole grains, beans, fruits and vegetables) contain vitamins, minerals, and fiber that are important to our nutritional health and help protect us against colon cancer, heart disease, and diabetes.[132]

The current research indicates that fats need to be better understood as well. Saturated fats found in red meat and whole milk and the trans fats found in margarine tend to clog our arteries, as we have been taught. In contrast, however, it has been found that the "unsaturated" fats found in vegetable oils, nuts, whole grains and fish actually contribute to our health. For example, they help your body raise its so called "good" (HDL) cholesterol and decrease its "bad" (LDL) cholesterol.

Finally, it is clear that protein sources are important parts of our diets, but our knowledge about how they relate to health and disease is somewhat more limited than it is with fats and carbohydrates. We do know that of the animal sources of protein, red meat is the worst for your health because of the amount of saturated fat it contains;[133] poultry (without the skin) and eggs are better than red meats, but fish is our best option. In fact, fish contains the unsaturated oils (omega-3s) that are actually good for your health. Beans, nuts, grains and other vegetable sources of protein are also healthier than red meats because they are low in saturated fats and contain healthy unsaturated oils (omega-3s and omega-6s) and fiber. However, individual sources of vegetarian proteins contain a less varied and incomplete mix of the amino acids we need for good nutrition than do animal sources. Thus, if you are going to take a vegetarian route, make sure to eat a variety of vegetarian protein sources to insure the intake of a complete variety of amino acids.

WEIGHT CONTROL

Next to not smoking, keeping your weight in the healthy zone is the single best step you can take to maintain long-term health.[134] Being overweight has been linked to all forms of cardiovascular disease, diabetes, cancer, arthritis, infertility, gallstones, asthma, sleep apnea, mental health problems related to low self-esteem, etc. Even though our knowledge about the ills of being overweight has been getting increasingly more clear in recent years, obesity has been on the rise – just the opposite of what logic would dictate. The majority of Americans are at least somewhat overweight, and about 25 percent are obese. Studies have shown that although most overweight people try to lose weight multiple times in their lives, 95 percent of them fail to maintain a healthy weight for very long.

What should you do? First, determine whether you are overweight. Second, if you have a weight problem, figure out what that 5 percent of the population has done to conquer it, and do the same.

What is a healthy weight? The currently recommended way to determine your ideal weight range is to calculate your body mass index (BMI), as follows:[135] (1) Multiply your weight in pounds by 703; (2) Calculate the square (x^2) of your height in inches; (3) Divide the number derived in step # 1 by the number derived in step # 2; the resulting number is your BMI.

If your BMI is under 25, you are in the healthy zone. That is, there is a consensus in the scientific community that people with BMIs of 25 and above (except for body builders) have a higher risk of dying prematurely. Most people in the healthy zone have a BMI of 19-25. Figuring out exactly where your optimum BMI is within that range is best done by looking at yourself in the mirror or by comparing yourself to photos of when you were at your peak in appearance.

If your BMI is between 25-29, consider yourself overweight. You are obese if your BMI is 30 and above. If you want to calculate what you would need to weigh in order to have a BMI of 24, do the following: (1) Calculate the square (x^2) of your height in inches and multiply it by 24; (2) Divide the number derived in step #1 by 703. The resulting number is what you would need to weigh for your BMI to be on the outer edge of the healthy zone.

Once you have determined that you need to lower your BMI, your next step should be to take the time to develop and follow through on a plan of action that works. Why bother doing what 95 percent of dieters do, which is to fail in the long-term? Keep in mind that weight loss has become a multi-billion dollar industry that is highly dependent on repeat business. It feeds on our hopes that if we simply invest in one more diet book, one more piece of exercise equipment, or health club membership, we will finally get control of our weight.

The "truth" about how to best achieve a healthy weight has been researched in a number of studies recently.[136] While it is a fact that most dieters eventually fail, a certain percentage of people with a weight problem do get control over it for life. These "losers" teach us that gaining control of your weight is possible. Research on how they achieve their success reveals that what most of them *don't do* is follow the advice of the latest diet guru, enroll in weight-loss programs, buy special foods, take pills or get suckered in by advertisements that promise fast results. What do they do to achieve long-term success? In a nutshell, they do three things:

- Successful dieters develop a lifetime habit of eating the right foods. Their diets are similar to what is presently recommended by nutritionists. This is not a coincidence because the nutrition recommendations summarized in the preceding chapter are based partly on studies of successful dieters.

- Successful dieters control their intake of calories without feeling hungry. They understand that we are hard-wired to be intolerant of hunger, and that any diet that creates hunger is guaranteed to fail. Thus, most of them eat whenever it is necessary to reduce their hunger, but control their portions - some become nibblers.

- Most successful dieters learn that they simply cannot maintain a healthy weight without doing fairly rigorous exercise on a regular basis, as described in the next chapter.

At this writing, a number of researchers on obesity believe that recent findings about the functions of a hormone called "leptin" represent a significant advance in our knowledge about weight control.[137] Leptin is one of several hormones released by our fat cells that regulate our appetites and metabolism rates. Researchers have discovered that even though people who are overweight produce plenty of leptin, somehow it is blocked from doing its job. Exactly why this occurs is still being researched, but the condition is called "leptin resistance."

One theory is that leptin resistance is caused partly by the ingestion of the wrong foods, as defined in the preceding chapter (e.g., sweets, bad carbohydrates, red meats). The idea is that these foods are so toxic to our bodies that they block such hormones as leptin from performing their natural functions. Several of the latest bestselling diet books assert that if we would just stick to the right foods, most of us would maintain a healthy weight without much effort or the need to count calories.[138] These claims have not been adequately tested at this point for us to know whether they are just part of the newest fad in dieting or represent a true turning point in our understanding of weight control. It should be noted, however, that people who have gained long-term control over their weight do appear to have eating habits that are similar to those recommended by the leptin theorists. Thus, maybe their claims have validity. Time will tell.

EXERCISE

Exercise is recommended by virtually all health experts.[139] It prolongs life and reduces the risks of developing and dying from heart disease, high blood pressure, diabetes, and colon cancer. Exercise helps persons of all ages maintain healthy bones, muscles, and joints. It also promotes psychological well being, and reduces feelings of stress, depression, and anxiety. Given the universal agreement that exists about its benefits, the only real questions regarding exercise that are still being researched and discussed concern the kinds of exercise we should do and how much.

All experts agree that those of us who are engaged in sedentary, deskbound professional lives (e.g., most lawyers) need to first focus on becoming more physically active in our daily routines. The idea is to not be so focused on taking the easy way all of the time and instead to welcome physical exertion as an opportunity to improve or maintain our health. For example, whenever possible we should choose to walk rather than ride (e.g., skip elevators, escalators, and taxis), carry things rather than have someone else do it, and do some of our own house and office chores. To follow this prescription, we need to accept the fact that becoming more physically active is not the most efficient way to do get our daily tasks done, but that it is the preferred way to do things if we value our health.

To be physically fit, it is also necessary for all of us to get into the habit of doing more formal forms of regular exercise. Two types of exercise are recommended: aerobic and anaerobic. Aerobic exercise improves your body's ability to deliver oxygen to your muscles and other tissues. Examples include sustained (more than just a few minutes) fast walking, jogging, cycling, swimming, rowing, and aerobic dancing. These exercises tone your muscles, burn up calories, and exert your heart and lungs, thereby improving their efficiency and endurance. Anaerobic exercise, on the other hand, which includes weight lifting, push-ups, pull-ups and any other type of resistance training, increases muscle strength and mass and helps your body burn more calories throughout the day. In fact, the most recent findings indicate that muscle tissue, even at rest, uses up more than twenty times as many calories as fat tissue does. Stretching is another form of anaerobic exercise that improves muscle flexibility and helps prevent injuries.

How much exercise should a person with a desk job do, in terms of intensity and length? You are not going to like the answer. Even though any activity is better than none, the latest scientific findings indicate that to achieve cardiovascular fitness and maintain a healthy weight, you need to do moderately intense aerobic exercise for one hour per day, 6-7 days per week.[140] That is the equivalent of walking at a speed of 4 miles per hour for one hour, most days of the week. Fortunately, the effects of exercise are cumulative. Thus, two thirty minute walks per day accomplish the same goal. Similarly, if you engage in an intense form of physical activity such as running, you can spend less time exercising (e.g., 30 minutes per day or 4 days per week.)

Because walking and jogging are so easy to do and don't require special equipment other than good sport shoes, they are probably the most popular forms of aerobic exercise and are used as "referents" by most experts. Nevertheless, the same benefits can be achieved with many other forms of aerobic exercise (e.g., golf without a cart, tennis), which can be mixed to add variety and fun. It is also suggested that some time be devoted to building and maintaining muscle through resistance training. A few minutes a day in addition to the aerobic routine, or one-two sessions per week instead of the aerobic exercises is the recommended dose.

PLEASURE-PAIN PRINCIPLE
IS KEY TO SUCCESS

"The only way to keep your health is to eat what you
don't want, drink what you don't like, and do
what you'd rather not." *Mark Twain*

One might predict that once people are informed about the
benefits that good nutrition, exercise and weight control bring,
they generally develop a desire to do the right things and then
just do them. Dream on! As I have already discussed, most
people (95 percent) who go on diets to lose weight generally
fail in the long run.[141] Similarly, most people who try to become
more physically active through exercise eventually quit.[142] The
truth is that when it comes to nutrition, exercise, and weight
control, as well as many other things in life, most of us have a
difficult time getting ourselves to do the right things.

At this point, you might be wondering what my purpose is
in repeating these depressing facts. I want you to succeed, of
course, but I also know that it will not happen unless you learn
to overcome the strong pull of negative habits. The worst
mistake you can make is underestimate their power. And so,
before you start improving your nutrition and exercise habits,
prepare yourself to fully understand and do battle with the
strong forces that will tempt you to fail. This is exactly what the
few people who are successful at changing their habits over the
long haul learn to do. Because it is going to require a lot of
customized ingenuity on your part, my purpose here is to
simply introduce you to some core principles and strategies that
will help you succeed.

The basic problem most of us have with developing and
sustaining good nutrition and exercise habits is that the pain

comes before the gain. To overcome this problem you must first understand and fully accept the fact that we humans are all biologically wired to avoid pain and seek pleasure. We do this automatically. It is called the "pleasure-pain principle" of human nature. This is one reason why bad habits are so difficult to break. For example, when we eat that extra dessert or skip our exercise, pleasure precedes pain.

The bottom line on how to develop healthy nutrition and exercise habits is this: You have to come up with strategies for change predicated on the fact that human beings are hedonistic (pleasure-seeking & pain-avoiding) animals and that you are no exception. Don't feel guilty about it. Accept this fact and use it to your advantage.

Thus, your first order of business should be to devise an individualized plan that will make the healthy eating and exercise behaviors you need to turn into long-term habits as pleasurable and painless as possible. Furthermore, in order to fully succeed, you need to apply the pleasure-pain principle at three different levels of experience: physiological, psychological and environmental.

At the physiological level, for example, your application of the pleasure-pain principle would mean the following: Don't go on a diet that makes you feel hungry and deprived much of the time. Fight mother nature on this, and you will fail. Remember that you are an individual with unique genetic predispositions, habits, and lifestyles. Through trial and error, you will need to figure out which of the healthy food categories are more likely to be tasty and satisfy your hunger, how often you need to eat (1-6 times a day) to avoid hunger and its side effects (e.g., headaches), what your total caloric needs are, etc.

A similar approach should be taken when you develop an exercise habit. Figure out what types of exercises are most pleasurable physically and start with them. Start small, branch out and work your way up to the desired activity levels slowly. Again, to the extent that it is possible, try to maximize physical pleasure and minimize physical pain. It is the most effective way of turning your new eating and exercise behaviors into long-term lifestyle habits.

Also be prepared to do battle at the psychological level. Your negative old habits took a long time to develop, and they will not loosen their grip on you easily. No matter how good your plan is at minimizing physical pain and maximizing physical pleasure, it still takes psychological determination to turn down some of your old favorite foods (e.g., sugars to which you have probably become somewhat addicted) or to turn down an opportunity to be sedentary. These options will still represent short-term pleasure of the highest order. Sooner or later, your well tested excuses for practicing bad habits will tempt you to fail: "I'm too busy and don't have time. It's too difficult, and I can't do this."

One thing you can do to overcome a strong psychological desire to eat poorly, or to refrain from exercise, is to get into the habit of mentally accentuating the costs of such behaviors. For example, whenever you find yourself automatically thinking that you don't have the time to eat well or exercise, interrupt yourself and rephrase your sentences. Say something ridiculous like the following to yourself: "Let's get this straight! I don't have the time to prolong my life, reduce my chances of getting seriously ill, or make myself look more attractive. These are just not my priorities. Billing my clients for a few extra hours this month is much more important than my health." Since your brain is programmed to avoid psychological pain, cynically emphasizing this illogical self-talk and its costs will hopefully trigger fear and guilt in you, which in turn will motivate you to do the right things.

At the same time, get into the habit of repeating to yourself, on a daily basis, the positive gains that come with good nutrition and proper exercise. Everyday, take a few seconds here and there to literally picture yourself as a healthy, energetic and attractive person. Keep telling yourself why you are trying to develop healthier habits in the first place, and that in fact they are somewhat pleasurable and minimally painful. In addition, repeatedly visualize yourself as someone who is ultimately in control of your life. Tell yourself that regardless of life's daily ups and downs or your occasional failings, you are an effective problem solver in the long run. Frequently remind yourself that the game is not over until the clock stops ticking, and that does not happen until you die. The idea is to reprogram your brain through repetition to automatically associate pleasure with thinking about healthy behaviors and pain with thinking about unhealthy behaviors.

Finally, if you truly want to get control of your nutrition and exercise program, create environmental stimuli that elicit positive behaviors from you. Don't spend hours philosophizing about your inability to exercise free will, or feeling guilty about it. If you really want to get control of yourself, accept the fact that subtle external cues play a powerful role in directing human behaviors. For example, there is only one way to stop me from eventually eating that dark semi-sweet chocolate that I love so much: leave it at the store.

With regard to exercise, make a list of the environmental factors that are likely to make it more pleasurable and less painful. For example, if you find exercise boring, then devise ways to make the time go by quickly and productively (e.g., watch the news or listen to a book while exercising). If you find it lonely, find one or more people to share the experience (e.g., walk with your spouse – it is also great for the relationship). If your calendar makes it impossible to do moderate amounts of daily exercise, then schedule yourself for less frequent but longer and more vigorous sessions. When choosing between placing your exercise equipment in your cold basement or in your bedroom, choose the latter. You will be much more likely to use it in the comfort of your bedroom, especially when it stares at you each morning and cries out: "Use me!" Again, my examples are intended only as illustrations of the core principle you should follow, which is to maximize pleasure and minimize pain. The specifics have to be customized to your unique needs and likes.

Another step you need to take at the environmental level is to create several feedback loops that reinforce your goals. Some people join weight-loss support groups while others get a friend or family member to provide encouragement and keep them accountable. These are good short-term strategies, but I suggest also developing long-term feedback loops that do not depend on other people. For example, making a habit of confronting your naked body in front of a mirror is always a good reality check. (It has certainly frightened me into shaping up a few times.) Another similar strategy is to become more willing to be in photographs or videos in the first place and then to confront yourself in them.

The natural tendency to avoid pain leads most people who are out of shape to avoid looking at themselves in the mirror, in photographs or in videos. However, if you can conquer the fear of confronting yourself, you can make the pleasure-pain principle work in your favor. Each time you look at yourself, you will either feel the pleasure of pride or the pain of guilt that comes with either taking good care or not taking good care of your body. Either way, this strategy will motivate you to do the right things.

While looking at yourself, remember that feeling shameful about aging or about not being endowed with the physical beauty of a fashion model is neither healthy nor smart. I will be discussing self-esteem issues elsewhere in this book, but for now I want to emphasize the fact that I am proposing only that you allow the pain of guilt to operate on your unhealthy eating behaviors or lack of exercise. The things you cannot reverse, such as aging, need to be met with pride. The way to do that is to tell yourself what you would tell your dearest friend.

One of the best feedback loops you can create is a chart of your progress. All it really requires is a pencil and a paper to keep track of what you eat, how much exercise you do and what you weigh on a daily basis. However, an easier and more effective way to track your success is to use a computer program designed for this purpose, which runs either on your desktop or on a handheld computer.[143] By tracking your actual behaviors, you are less likely than normal to underestimate the number of calories you eat, more likely to eat the right things and amounts, and more likely to adhere to an exercise program. Tracking your behaviors makes you more aware of your own automatic habits and allows you to slowly work through various challenges that keep you from developing new habits. This type of feedback is powerful in that it uses pride and guilt to make you accountable and keep you on track.

All of the advice I have given you regarding the power of the pleasure-pain principle is effective, but it does depend on whether you follow through on it. As someone once asked: "How many psychologists does it take to change a light bulb?" Answer: "Only one, but the light has to want to change."

In conclusion, I want to make one other point. Without question, proper nutrition, exercise, and weight control will have a positive biochemical effect on your brain and help you manage stress more effectively. However, it is also true that people who experience a great deal of psychological stress have a more difficult time getting proper nutrition and exercise. For example, people who experience stomach butterflies that are symptomatic of anxiety often try to quell them through mindless eating. Thus, in reality, your strategy for stress reduction must be a multifaceted one. The rest of this book is devoted to the other strategies you will need to invoke.

IF YOU SMOKE

STOP!*

*Any questions? Should you need more information, see the websites of the U.S. Department of Health and Human Services, the American Heart Association, the American Cancer Society and every other health organization in the United States.

RELAXATION TECHNIQUES

Imagine that it is two o'clock in the afternoon. The phone has been interrupting you all day. You have been insulted numerous times, and you just cannot seem to concentrate on the brief that is due tomorrow morning. You don't have the time to ponder the meaning of it all, and just saying "relax" to yourself is not going to work. What you need is a fast way to calm down. This is a good time to use relaxation exercises. They provide effective temporary relief of stress symptoms, such as negative thoughts and emotions, muscle tension, upset stomach, and high blood pressure.

People who practice relaxation techniques on a regular basis also experience long-term mental and physical benefits.[144] To understand why, it is instructive to know that in order to get good at relaxation, you must learn to focus on the task of relaxing and not allow distractions, such as noises or your own thoughts, to interrupt you. The ability to "let go of things" is an important element of stress reduction in general. People who get good at it during their relaxation exercises tend to be better at maintaining that attitude throughout the day. This helps them develop a greater sense of calm and control over a variety of annoyances. In addition, it stimulates them to reexamine what is truly worth getting upset about in their lives, and it can lead to long-term physical health benefits, such as less cardiovascular disease and a stronger immune system.

In general, there are three types of relaxation exercises you can learn and use in various combinations:[145]

- Muscle Relaxation
- Breathing Exercises
- Mental Imagery

To understand how these techniques work, remember that the mind and body are not separate entities. Thus, whenever we experience stressful thoughts, there are concurrent physiological correlates such as muscle tension, faster breathing, higher blood pressure, etc. Conversely, whenever we feel physical symptoms of distress, we are also more likely to have stressful thoughts.

Relaxation techniques are based on the idea that since mind and body are part of one unified whole, it is possible to affect the body through the mind and the mind through the body. With muscle relaxation and breathing exercises, you focus primarily on the body, whereas with mental imagery your focus is on the mind. In each instance, however, the purpose is to interrupt the stress pattern at any level and thereby reduce stress in the whole organism.

A typical muscle relaxation exercise is one in which you find a comfortable place to sit and begin by concentrating on your muscular tensions. The idea is to focus your total attention on your body. Start either at the top or the bottom and progressively move to the other end. Then begin tensing and relaxing each muscle group. For example, wiggle and tighten the muscles in your feet and toes for a few seconds and then release them, noticing how it feels to relax. Then, doing the same thing, progressively move up your body to the other muscle areas, such as those in your legs, hips, stomach, back, arms, shoulders, neck and, finally, your head.

Another type of exercise, which you can use alone or in combination with the others, is breathing. Again, find a comfortable and quiet place to sit, close your eyes, and begin breathing more deeply than usual. As you do this, chase all intruding thoughts away, and concentrate on just your breathing. Listen to the sounds as if they were waves in the ocean. Feel the air bathing your lungs, and imagine the extra cleansing your blood stream is getting.

Finally, you can try a variety of imagery exercises. Here the idea is to create relaxing images in your mind and experience the pleasure they bring. You might picture yourself on a sail boat, lying under a tree, or playing with your children. Use all of your senses in your images. For example, listen to the sounds of a summer wind and feel its warmth. Also, create interpretative verbal messages; silently comment on how peaceful it is or how much you love watching your children smile.

If you are reluctant to try relaxation techniques, you are not alone. Many lawyers feel awkward trying them because of the mysticism that is often attached to discussions about meditation. Do not be put off by such connections. You really don't need to adopt a new religion or burn incense to benefit from relaxation exercises. Some lawyers are reluctant to try relaxation exercises out of a puritanical belief that there is something wrong with relaxation. Others have a mistaken fear that relaxation will cause them to have less energy and make them lose their desire to work. In fact, relaxation exercises take just 10-20 minutes, and make you more alert, more able to withstand long hours, and more able to be productive.

Obviously, my description of relaxation techniques has been introductory at best. If you want to try these techniques, I would suggest that you read one of the many available books that explain the theory behind them,[146] followed by one or more books that provide you with specific scripts and drills.[147] I also suggest trying a commercially produced relaxation audiotape, as it should make the practice of these exercises much easier; such tapes walk you through each step and provide you with soothing background music.[148]

SLEEP

One of my favorite Frank Sinatra songs is called "In the Wee Small Hours of the Morning." It is a bitter-sweet ballad that evokes memories of lying awake in the middle of the night, when the rest of the world is fast asleep, thinking about a lost love. It is not just Sinatra's voice and articulation, the poetic words, musical arrangement, and orchestration that make the song stand out. It is also the fact that most of us can readily identify with the experience of being agitated about something and losing sleep over it.

An occasional sleepless night is both unavoidable and not particularly damaging. The next day we simply pay the price by feeling stressed out and fatigued and by not being able to think clearly. Chronic sleeplessness is much more serious, however. In addition to always feeling tired, foggy, and moody, people who are constantly sleep deprived are less resilient to physical and mental stress and more susceptible to physical and mental illness (e.g., hypertension, anxiety).[149] Sleeplessness can have a significant negative effect on your relationships and on your ability to work productively.

Gauging by the number of confidential questions I get from lawyers about insomnia, I suspect that it is a significant problem within the legal community. If you are an insomniac, I urge you to not ignore the problem, as that will only interfere with your ability to succeed in life and may result in an illness. This chapter contains some basic information about sleep disorders, but since the topic is very complex, I suggest that you also read one of several excellent books that deal with it exclusively.[150]

WHAT IS INSOMNIA?

There are several kinds of insomnia, and they are generally categorized either by their symptoms or their causes.[151] In terms of symptoms, there are people who experience difficulty falling asleep, who get awakened repeatedly throughout the night, who wake up too early, or who have a mixture of these symptoms. All of these symptoms result in an inadequate amount or quality of sleep.

The causes of insomnia are either medical, environmental, psychological, or a combination of these factors. The medical causes of sleeplessness range from chronic indigestion and heartburn to kidney diseases and brain tumors. In addition, a sleep disorder can be a side effect of medications, foods that contain caffeine, alcohol, and nicotine. Another medical sleep disorder that affects millions of people is "sleep apnea."[152] Unbeknownst to most people who are afflicted with sleep apnea, they have a problem breathing throughout the night and are frequently awakened by their need to catch their breaths. Thus, their sleep tends to be very fragmented and unhealthy.

At the environmental level, sleep disturbances can be caused by living with a baby who does not share your sleep schedule, a fidgety dog who sleeps in your bed, a local airport or railroad that shares your airspace, etc. In addition to the physiological causes of sleep disorders, about half are psychological in nature. Sometimes, insomnia is caused by the psychological excitement that follows positive experiences such as the birth of a child or a major job promotion. Oftentimes, it is caused by the negative emotions we experience in reaction to anticipated or actual negative events, such as the death of a loved one or some personal failure. Perfectionistic people who are obsessive about unfinished tasks tend to lose sleep over them, even when they are unimportant. Note that sleep deprivation can itself be the cause of new psychological problems, or it can exacerbate old ones.

WHAT IS AN INSOMNIAC TO DO?

Obviously, one of the first things an insomniac should do is determine the causes of his or her sleeplessness. First, eliminate the possibility that a purely physical ailment is at the root of the problem by consulting a physician. In addition to getting a full examination, ask your physician to review the side effects of all your medications and remove them from the list of possible causes. Then, consider the possibility that an environmental irritant is a contributing cause (e.g., barking dog, bright neon alarm clock). Having eliminated these causes from your list, you should proceed to several other possible physical causes: lack of exercise, poor nutrition, caffeine, nicotine, alcohol and sleeping pills.

As explained in the preceding chapters, people who eat the right foods and exercise regularly report experiencing more positive moods, having more energy and higher concentration levels, and being more able to withstand the daily stresses that surround them. They also report getting more sleep.

One of the most effective things you can do nutritionally is reduce or eliminate your intake of caffeine. Reducing caffeine intake not only improves your brain's sleep patterns, but it also improves the functioning of your urinary tract and reduces the number of nighttime visits you make to the bathroom. A great many insomniacs grossly underestimate the amount of caffeine they ingest daily. For example, they are often unaware of the actual number of cups of coffee they drink and don't recognize all of the other foods that contain caffeine (e.g., cola, chocolate). Keeping a daily written log of all foods ingested is the only way to accurately measure your intake of caffeine.

Reducing or eliminating your cigarette smoking, ingestion of alcohol, and intake of sleeping pills is another step you can take to improve your sleep patterns. Since nicotine is a stimulant like caffeine, insomnia is highly common among smokers. Alcohol and sleeping pills help you fall asleep, but their effectiveness is limited in that they produce fragmented types of sleep patterns that will not give you the rest you need. In addition, sleeping pills and alcohol have various side effects, addictive properties, and physical dangers.

Another step you can take to improve your sleep patterns is to get good at managing your psychological stress. Since the rest of this book is devoted to teaching you psychological stress management techniques, I will only point out here that the trick is to become happier. People who are prone to think positive thoughts followed by positive emotions simply sleep better than people who constantly think negative thoughts and feel negative emotions.

Finally, if none of the self-help techniques greatly improve your sleep patterns and you continue to feel chronically sleepy, you should seek the help of a health professional. Start with your physician to determine whether the cause is physical. If you think that the cause is psychological, then consult a mental health professional. If neither of these steps lead to significant improvement or you suspect a complicated sleep disorder such as sleep apnea, then you should go to a sleep disorders clinic that is accredited by the American Academy of Sleep Medicine.[153]

SECTION V: IMPROVE YOUR THINKING

*There is nothing either good or bad, but thinking
makes it so.*

William Shakespeare

*The greatest discovery of my generation is that
human beings can alter their lives by altering their
attitudes of mind.*

William James

Ninety percent of the game is half mental.

Yogi Berra

IT'S THE THOUGHT THAT COUNTS

Consider a situation in which two lawyers have a number of meetings with a broker to close a deal for their clients. Each time, the broker is late in arriving. Both lawyers have a reaction to the broker's chronic lateness, but their judgments about him differ. As a result, they exhibit different feelings and behaviors at their meetings. That, in turn, makes a difference in the type and amount of stress each lawyer experiences.

One lawyer concludes that the latecomer must not have much respect for the lawyers' time. This thought leads him to feel angry and to be somewhat cool and hostile at the meetings. In contrast, his colleague concludes that the broker is just one of those people who constantly tries to squeeze more out of a day than is realistic. Her thoughts also lead to mild annoyance, but not anger. More importantly, she feels some apprehension about the possibility that the rushed broker may do careless work. Thus, she decides to be friendly at the meetings, but to proofread all materials with extra caution.

How can the same situation create such different reactions? We humans are simply not automatons who respond in purely mechanical ways. Our various physiological constitutions and learning experiences result in a unique blend of personality traits - ways of thinking, feeling, and behaving. In turn, our personalities have a great deal to do with how we interpret situations and respond to them, and that makes a significant difference in how much stress we experience.

As you may recall from an earlier chapter, psychological stress can be viewed as being composed of the following sequence of elements:[154]

Stimulus → Thought → Emotion → Behavior

In the scenario above, the broker's chronic lateness is the stimulus. The judgments (thoughts) that the two lawyers make in response to the stimulus trigger their individual emotions and behaviors. The reason that their emotions and behaviors differ is that their judgments are composed of two additional elements: objective-external reality and subjective-internal interpretation. The fact that the subjective portions of all judgments are open to reinterpretation logically leads to a very important psychological principle: *You can control your emotional response to a stressful stimulus by controlling your mental interpretations of it.*

Here is a simple demonstration of how our perceptions are a function of both objective reality and subjective interpretation. Just look at the cube below:

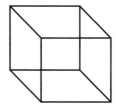

There are two ways to perceive this cube. One way is to view its front panel facing down and to the right. The other way is to see the front panel facing up and to the left:

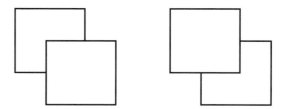

Now look at the full cube above and try to shift views at will. Your ability to do this demonstrates the fact that although the external stimuli that represent the cube remain the same, we have the ability to look at it from several points of view and to create different perceptions of it at will. This also illustrates the idea that we give meaning to things through an active process in which we construct our individual realities. Most lawyers already know this to be true and can point to many instances of it in their work. An example is how jurors interpret the so called "facts" of a case.

In the next few chapters, I am going to teach you how to willingly shift your points of view in matters that cause you distress. The strategy involves evaluating your own thoughts and considering how alternative interpretations of the same situations and events can have a profound and constructive effect on your emotions and behaviors.

Note that the strategies I will cover are easy to explain, but difficult to put into effect. In fact, some people seek the help of professionals to implement these techniques and you may want to do that also. Before turning to that option, however, note that there are many people who learn these strategies on their own and achieve happiness without professional help.[155] No matter what you decide to do, the stress management techniques that follow require a great deal of practice and patience.

IMPROVED THINKING 101

Even though I have spoken in front of graduate students and professionals for most of my adult life, I still get a bit anxious whenever I am about to give a speech to a new audience. The "what ifs" take over. "What if my ideas aren't well received? What if I forget some important points? What if I go on for too long and am unable to finish on time? What if my jokes don't work? What if....? What if....? What if....?"

I have been doing this long enough to know that if I don't interrupt my negative thoughts, eventually they trigger a strong sense of fear and hinder my effectiveness. And so, as a way of taking control, I bring to life my paraphrased memories of what I heard a comedian (Jackie Mason) once say upon walking out on a Broadway stage. "Ladies and gentlemen," he said, "I want you to know that it is a pleasure - a pleasure - for *you* to see me! Why? Because people are standing in line to get tickets to see my show, and you were lucky enough to get one." He then paused and said, "I only mention this in case you think I stink - then you'll know that it is your problem and not mine."

His opening lines, delivered in a New York Jewish accent, were more than funny. There was a great deal of wisdom in them about stress management. Like most performers, I imagine that this comedian got nervous prior to walking out on stage. Being a veteran, however, he must have learned to confront his emotions by: (1) becoming conscious of and *understanding* his stress - producing thoughts; (2) *evaluating* some of his habitual negative thoughts as harmful; and (3) *improving* matters by replacing his maladaptive thoughts with beneficial ones. In this way, he turned his original fear-producing logic literally upside down and got big laughs at the same time.

FIRST, UNDERSTAND YOUR
STRESSFUL THOUGHTS

Your typical stress-producing thoughts are likely to be so automatic that you may not even be aware of them. The road to improvement starts with slowing your thoughts down to the point where you do become fully aware of them. Only then will you be able to turn off the automatic pilot and steer yourself in new directions.

The best way to become aware of the specific thoughts that contribute to your distress is to keep a daily log of them for about two weeks. Simply divide a blank sheet of paper into four columns: stimuli, thoughts, emotions, and behaviors. If you prefer, make copies of and use the top portion of the sample form provided at the end of this chapter. Then, choose one or two stress-producing events per day, and record them as you would in a diary. The only difference is that this log requires you to dissect each experience down to its elements and become aware of their cause-and-effect connections.

For example, suppose an associate upsets you by turning in a legal brief that does not meet your expectations. To fully understand your reactions, you would record the fact that you received such a brief in the first column. In the second column you would record thoughts such as: "This is unacceptable. You are incompetent. I need to do this myself." The resulting emotions like anger and fear of failure, would get entered in the third column. Finally, in the last column you would write the fact that you expressed your hostility toward your associate and began rewriting the brief yourself.

The first and last columns may be easier to complete than the two in the middle. Generally, it is easy to identify the external events that triggered your distress and your outward reactions to them. (An exception to this is that sometimes your own thoughts are the triggering events, and not anything in the environment.) Identifying the thoughts and emotions that occur in-between will probably be more difficult. However, once you work through the initial difficulties and are able to record your thoughts and emotions a few dozen times, you will discover that the same limited number of themes will occur over and over again. At this point they will become easier to recognize, less automatic, and more conscious.

Recording your stress reactions a number of times should make you increasingly mindful of several facts. First, what underlies most distress are one or more negative emotions such as anger, guilt or fear. In other words, when we say that we have had a stressful day, we often mean that we have had a day in which we experienced strong negative emotions. Second, you will come to realize that negative emotions are triggered by negative thoughts. For example, there is no way that you can feel angry without first thinking, either consciously or unconsciously, that someone has done or is doing something objectionable.

The next thing you will realize is that many of your negative thinking patterns are the products of years of repetition. They get activated without much conscious effort on your part. What makes them particularly destructive is that they do occur automatically, regardless of whether they are inappropriate and dysfunctional. To improve the way you typically react to things, you will need to break through your own conditioning by repeatedly *interrupting* its automatic flow. One way to do that is to persistently flesh out your automatic thoughts, thus bringing them into full consciousness. Becoming fully aware of how your negative thoughts cause your distressful emotions is not all you have to do to bring your stress under control, but it will be a very significant step.

THEN, EVALUATE AND IMPROVE YOUR
DYSFUNCTIONAL THINKING HABITS

In addition to becoming fully aware of your thoughts and interrupting their automatic flow, *challenge* them. Since people differ in how they perceive similar events, ask yourself how others might perceive your predicament. Consider all alternative interpretations and *evaluate* their validity. When it is reasonable, consider *replacing* your initial automatic thoughts with more adaptive ones. Sometimes, your problem will dissipate as soon as you change your view of it. It will be a case of "mind over matter" – meaning that if you don't mind, it will not matter.

Of course, some problems will remain real regardless of how you perceive them. In such instances, you need to take the additional mental step of asking future and solution oriented questions such as, "What can/will I do about this?" In other words, shift your focus away from simply repeating your problem or perceiving it differently, and try to *generate solutions* to it. Then, imagine the emotions and behaviors that a solution-oriented line of reasoning will stimulate. Choose the solution that will result in the most positive outcomes.

Allow me to illustrate this technique by way of a simple example. Suppose you get stuck with an unexpected amount of additional work and observe yourself thinking: "How will I ever find the time to handle all of these cases? I can't readjust my calendar. I will have to work this weekend and disappoint the kids again. What can I do?" Chances are that as soon as you begin thinking this way, certain emotions will get evoked, such as fear of failure, guilt, and anger. You may find yourself unable to concentrate or work as efficiently as usual, and you may become more irritable with others.

What *can* you do? First, break your full reaction down to its elements as described above. Then, begin to question your automatic thought patterns. You might say to yourself: "Wait a minute! These are my automatic thoughts. That does not make them automatically right. When I say, 'How will I find the time?,' I am making an automatic judgment that there is no better solution to my problem than to work through the weekend. In addition, I am automatically predicting that terrible things will happen if I make adjustments to my calendar."

In continuing your internal dialogue, consider such thoughts as: "Suppose I reverse my current thinking. Let me assume the possibility that there is a solution to my problem and that others might not think less of me if I adjust my calendar appropriately. Instead of asking the question in a rhetorical way, let me ask it again as a real question: 'How can I find the time to do all of this without sacrificing my personal life?' One thing I can do is call one of these clients and ask if a delay would be acceptable." As you begin to explore various solutions to your problem in a creative and open ended way, you will notice your emotions and behaviors begin to change for the better.

At the end of this chapter there is a daily log that you can use to practice the technique just described. The top row asks you to simply become aware of the stimuli, the thoughts, the emotions and the behaviors that together define your stressful experience. The bottom row asks you to evaluate your thoughts and to consider how alternative thoughts might improve your emotions and behaviors.

It is best to do this exercise on paper at least a few times, just to fully grasp the steps that are involved. As unnatural as it may seem, recording your internal dialogue on paper will have a strong positive effect on you. If you find yourself too reluctant to try the exercise on paper, don't give up on the entire approach. Just do as much of the exercise as you can in your mind. Particularly good times to practice the exercise in your mind are while you are taking a shower or driving a car. If you do it often enough, the exercise will become easier and easier. Eventually, it will become a natural part of the way you think.

Although the process I have described is effective, because it involves changing a part of your personality, it could be one of the most difficult tasks you will ever undertake. Changing your habitual ways of thinking will take strength and courage, and it will require you to break through much emotional resistance. Do not expect quick results. I wish I could offer an easier solution, but if dysfunctional thinking is your problem, then there is no better way. Although the technique I am proposing is difficult, I offer it as something that is both doable and worthwhile.

The next several chapters are designed to help you carry out the details of this technique. If you find it too difficult to put into practice or continue to experience high levels of distress, you may want to consider the help of a mental health professional. Should you decide to seek professional help, note that my approach is based on a technique known as cognitive-behavioral or rational-emotive psychotherapy. Because the vast majority of lawyers place great value on their rational and analytical skills, I have found that this approach is a natural match.

DAILY LOG OF STRESS REACTIONS & SOLUTIONS

	WHAT HAPPENED? IDENTIFY EVENTS, SITUATIONS, OR THOUGHTS THAT STIMULATED STRESS.	IDENTIFY NEGATIVE THOUGHTS: SPECIFIC PERCEPTIONS & GENERAL RULES (e.g., "I am a failure.").	LABEL THE EMOTIONS YOUR THOUGHTS CREATED (e.g., Angry, Afraid, Guilty, Sad, Hurt, Suspicious, Jealous).	RESULTING BEHAVIORS: (e.g., Yelled, Withdrew, Could not Work, Complained).
1ST UNDERSTAND				
2ND EVALUATE	ARE YOUR THOUGHTS & EMOTIONS JUSTIFIED? IF NO, IDENTIFY DISTORTED PERCEPTIONS & DYSFUNCTIONAL RULES & CONSIDER ALTERNATIVES. IF YES, ASK SOLUTION/FUTURE ORIENTED QUESTIONS (e.g., "What can I do about this?").		PREDICT/DESCRIBE YOUR EMOTIONS UNDER A REVISED LINE OF REASONING.	PREDICT/DESCRIBE YOUR BEHAVIORS UNDER A REVISED LINE OF REASONING.
3RD IMPROVE				

IMPROVED THINKING 102

As discussed earlier, an effective way to reduce emotional stress is to change some of your thinking habits. To achieve this, you should *understand* that your stress reactions are composed of four elements: stimuli, thoughts, emotions, and behaviors. In addition, you need to realize that stressful emotions are usually preceded by negative thoughts. Thus, once you identify the specific negative thoughts that underlie your emotional distress, you then need to *evaluate* their validity and *improve* them. Since this technique is complicated and difficult to implement, allow me to explain it in more detail.

ADOPT AN INVESTIGATIVE ATTITUDE

To successfully improve your thinking habits, you have to first adopt an investigative attitude in which you assume nothing about the validity of your stress-producing thoughts. This is hard to do because your thoughts are likely to be so automatic that they seem indisputable. Like most people, you probably act as if the mere fact that they come to mind makes them true. Can you imagine acting this way when you develop legal arguments? Yet, with regard to personal matters, this is the kind of illogic that makes some people accept a great deal of their own internal negative dialogue at face value.

Even though your conscious mind will readily admit that not all of your automatic thoughts can possibly be true, expect your habitual unconscious self to fight that notion strenuously. Thus, until your full being is thoroughly convinced, repeatedly tell yourself this irrefutable fact:

"Just because I think or feel something automatically, does not make it automatically valid."

Note that there is no need to assume that you are always wrong about everything. Just stop assuming that your automatic negative thoughts are always right. If you can do this, you will have figuratively tipped over the first of a series of dominoes. Your remaining victories will be won much more readily.

IDENTIFY YOUR DISTORTED PERCEPTIONS AND DYSFUNCTIONAL RULES

Before you can replace your negative thinking habits with more constructive ones, you need to get good at recognizing your negative thoughts in the first place. This task becomes easier once you realize that there are only a limited number of them. General themes such as failure, rejection, guilt, financial security, and self-fulfillment are likely to recur many times.

Furthermore, regardless of their specific content, there are only two universal categories of negative statements that people make to themselves. The first type is negative perceptions or observations about *specific* individuals or events in the present, past or future. The second category of negative statements includes universal beliefs, rules, and assumptions about people and life in *general*. To make the distinctions between these types of negative thoughts more understandable, consider the following list of examples:

<u>*Specific Perceptions*</u>

Future
"If I don't get this right, we are not going to prevail."
"How will I ever get this work done on time?"
"What if I embarrass myself?"

Present
"I don't spend any time with my family."
"The senior partners think I don't bill enough hours."
"I am not competent to take on this project."

Past

"What happened here was totally unfair."
"They never treated me with respect in that firm."
"She was always negative and insulting."

General Beliefs, Rules And Assumptions

"People are not trustworthy. They are all selfish."
"The only way to get it done is to do it yourself."
"Mistakes can't be tolerated because they lead to failure."
"There is nothing worse than being humiliated in public."
"Life is a jungle. Only the strong survive."
"Unpleasant situations need to be avoided at all costs."
"If you ignore problems they usually go away."
"Do things your way. Don't be controlled by others."
"You have to look out for yourself. No one else will."

Note that thoughts do not occur just in linguistic forms. They are also experienced as visual, auditory and other types of sensory images. For example, instead of saying "I really failed in this case," you may see yourself in a courtroom looking embarrassed. Whenever you experience such images but are not sure of their meaning, try to translate them into their linguistic forms for greater clarity.

You will find that sometimes your specific observations are objectively inaccurate. Let's call these *distorted perceptions*. Similarly, there are times when your generalized beliefs and assumptions do not lead you to desired results. Let's call these *dysfunctional rules*. Given the enormous effect that distorted perceptions and dysfunctional rules can have on your emotions and behaviors, it behooves you to identify and revise them on a regular basis.

In the case of *specific perceptions*, ask yourself to produce the evidence for them to make sure that they are not *distorted*. Some distortions are not based on any evidence at all. Most distortions, however, are based on kernels of truth that are overstated. Such errors are often reflected in negative statements that include words like "always, never, absolutely, terrible, awful, can't stand, must." Whenever I hear such words in my clients' negative sentences, I generally find them easy to refute. "Is it really true that *none* of the things you do turn out successfully?" I'll ask. Once you start looking for similar exaggerations in your own automatic thoughts, you will find them easy to disprove as well. Disprove them you should, for they are responsible for much of the psychological stress you experience.

To illustrate how you might uncover a *distorted perception*, imagine that one day you find yourself repeating the following prediction: "I am going to totally blow this case." The anxious emotions and behaviors that such a thought is likely to create requires you to at least evaluate its validity. Cross-examine yourself the same way that you would a witness. Say to yourself: "How do you know that you are going to blow this case even before it has begun? How many times has that happened to you in the past, even though you have said the same thing? Maybe, what you really mean is that you need more time to prepare. Your original statement is not based on fact; it is your own insecurity jumping to negative conclusions. You are paying an emotional price for it, so get yourself together, and revise your original statement. The truth is that you just need more time to prepare."

Generalized beliefs and rules that are negative and cause you stress are much more difficult to prove or disprove than specific perceptions. For example, take a common general rule such as: "If you want something done right, you have to do it yourself." All of us can point to instances in which someone to whom we delegated a task failed us. However, we also can point to instances in which we were more than satisfied with the work of another person.

To determine how often a general belief or rule is true, we would have to do an empirical study of some sort. Thus, proving or disproving its accuracy is not the practical thing to do. What is more useful to ascertain is whether your negative beliefs or rules help you achieve positive results. Those that do not are *dysfunctional*.

For example, let us examine the functionality of believing that "if you want things done right, you do them yourself." One of the most important ramifications of living by this rule is that it encourages you not to delegate work. In turn, this means that you will not be an effective manager of other people. Ask yourself what kinds of lawyers tend to be more productive – lawyers who delegate effectively or those who do everything themselves? Similarly, consider what types of lawyers achieve senior partnerships or are successful at this role. Soon you might decide that even though your original belief contains a kernel of truth, it limits your ability to succeed and should be revised.

CONSIDER ALTERNATIVE THOUGHTS

One of our most powerful cognitive abilities is to think dialectically. As you probably know, dialectics is a method of argument in which one purposefully weighs contradictory ideas. This ability is responsible for a great deal of human creativity and is much relied upon in the practice of law. It also happens to be an effective way to break through a number of personal problems. Whenever you feel as though you are stuck in the mud mentally or emotionally, apply those same dialectical skills you use in thinking about legal matters to personal ones.

The easiest way to generate alternative points of view is to simply consider the opposite of whatever your perceptions and rules might be. Another easy way is to take on the role of other people you know. Literally ask yourself, "What would my significant other say about this or how would he/she view it?" A variant of this is for you to take on the role of a different you. For example, if you tend to be a perfectionist, imagine yourself as someone who is competent but not bothered by mistakes. Then ask yourself the same question, "If I were this other person, how would I view this same situation?" You will be pleasantly surprised by how powerfully role playing will loosen up your thinking.

ASK AND ANSWER SOLUTION/FUTURE ORIENTED QUESTIONS

Once you recognize your negative thoughts and evaluate their validity, only two possibilities exist. Either your negative thoughts are distorted and dysfunctional or they are accurate and adaptive. Each possibility requires a different response. The healthy and most effective thing to do with your distorted and dysfunctional thoughts is to correct and improve them. When your negative thoughts are valid, however, the thing to do is to solve the problem(s) they reveal.

For example, let us assume that you have been disturbed by the thought that your secretary does not like working for you. The best way to proceed is to first check out the validity of your thought, and then do one of two things: If you are mistaken, simply change your opinion. If you are accurate, either get another secretary or look for ways to improve your relationship. The idea is to learn from the past, and move on to a better future.

Many of the people who suffer from anxiety and depression do so in part because they fail to take this last step. When asked to confront their problems, some will report that they are doing so when that is not true. What they do, in fact, is mentally rehearse their problems over and over again, without moving on to solve them. "Yes, I confront my problems. I think about them all of the time," some will say. When asked for details, they will explain that they chronically ask themselves questions such as: "Why am I a failure?" What they do not realize is that when the human brain is on automatic pilot, it often assumes the validity of the questions that are asked of it. Thus, when you ask your brain to tell you why you are an idiot, it is likely to go into its database and print out all of the reasons you are an idiot. If you ask it for a second opinion, it will also tell you that you are ugly.

My point is that beating yourself up or perseverating on the past is not the way to confront your problems. That will only increase your stress. Once you have uncovered and validated a real problem, the best way to confront it is to ask yourself a series of solution/future oriented questions like:

How can I fix this?
What can I do about this now?
What can I do to improve matters?
How can I solve this problem in the future?

Your next task is to answer these questions. When your brain shifts into "solution" mode, it goes into its database and starts to create ideas. As soon as that occurs, something magical happens: your emotions change from negative to positive, as fear, anger, guilt, pessimism, etc., begin to be swept away by courage, forgiveness, pride and hope. Of course, some of your ideas will be good and some will be bad. Your final task will be to make a distinction between the two and to act on the good ideas.

I have found that knowing the solution-oriented questions to ask is often not enough to generate answers. The reason for this is that many of us tend to ask questions in a rhetorical way. That is, the question mark is not real. We shrug our shoulders and say, "What can I do?" Our actual intent is to say, "I can't do anything about this." Thus, if you catch yourself asking such rhetorical questions, first try to place a real question mark at the end of your sentence, and then generate genuine answers. If you get no answers, then consider the possibility that your question is really a negative thought, and evaluate its validity.

For example, here is a list of several negative rhetorical questions that I have heard lawyers ask:

Where will our next client come from?
How do I ensure that the quality of our work is high?
How do we insure the future of this firm, given the competitive and changing nature of law practice?
How do I deal with partners who give me complex tasks, but no instruction, no training, no guidance, and no sympathy?
How do I deal with too many masters, when each of them doesn't know or care what I am doing for the others?
How can I make partner, when I don't really know the rules?
What if I don't make partner?

These are all legitimate questions, but not when they are asked in a rhetorical form. If you want to get rid of the stress they cause, convert them into real questions, and begin to answer them in solution-oriented ways. For example, let us take the first question on the list, "Where will our next client come from?" When you try to truly confront this question, you will be forced to think of ways that your firm can bring in new clients or get new business from current clients. Once you shift into solution-mode, you should feel much less apprehensive about this question. And, if you follow through on your marketing ideas, you will feel very good indeed.

BREAK OLD HABITS

Imagine that a judge criticizes you in open court, in front of your colleagues, your client and the jury. Such an event might stimulate you to think, "This is making me look bad! I should have been better prepared! I'm going to lose this case! The judge really didn't have to treat me this way!" Thoughts like these tend to evoke negative emotions such as embarrassment, fear, guilt, and anger. The bodily reactions that are part of these emotions jolt you into behaving differently.

Although the initial negative reactions to a critical judge may be universal, how long they persist depends on you. You may continue to say to yourself, "I am going to lose this case and the respect of everyone in the courtroom!" On the other hand, you may switch gears and say to yourself, "What is it that the judge wants me to do, and how can I move on?"

The choice you make has significant consequences. If your thoughts continue to focus on the problem and its repercussions, what you fear may indeed occur, and your level of distress will increase. In contrast, if you begin thinking about solutions to the problem, positive results are more likely to follow, and your level of stress will diminish.

What causes some people to concentrate on problems and others on solutions? In one word, the answer is habits. Some people would say that personality is the determining factor, but the word "personality" is nothing more than a label we attach to habitual ways of thinking, feeling, and acting. For example, someone with a perfectionistic personality is a person with a habit of thinking that everything he or she does must be perfect.

From an evolutionary perspective, your ability to develop habits has adaptive value. Habits allow you to respond to events automatically and alleviate the need to reanalyze each situation as if it is a new experience. Imagine what life would be like if you could not rely on your automatic pilot to do such things as walk up a staircase or stop a car at a red light. As we all know, however, the downside is that some of the habits we develop are not so adaptive. In fact, some of our maladaptive mental habits make stressful situations worse rather than better. For example, when perfectionists make mistakes, they are often so distressed that it interferes with their ability to make corrections.

Obviously, the thing to do is to unlearn your maladaptive mental habits and replace them with adaptive ones. After years of repetition, however, habitual thoughts become so deeply ingrained that they feel permanent. Since no learned response is etched in stone, however, this is only an illusion. No matter how unchangeable your habitual thoughts may appear, remember that they are learned patterns of behavior.

To my knowledge, few theorists argue that humans are born with specific ideas in their brains such as, "I'm a loser." Such thoughts are learned, not inborn. No matter how well-learned they are, they can be unlearned. It is just a matter of time, practice, and the right techniques. Thus, don't ever allow yourself to conclude that you are incapable of changing. You do have the power to break old habits. Furthermore, once you get a few successes under your belt, old habits become increasingly easier to break.

CONQUER THOSE INNER VOICES

Be prepared for several inner voices that will urge you to resist change. One of them will say: "This is too frustrating. I can't change." As discussed in the preceding chapter, this will occur because your old thought patterns are exceedingly well-learned habits that have taken many years to develop. They have become as automatic as walking up a staircase. In fact, the core of the problem is that they are too automatic and need to be switched into manual. Don't expect a transition to occur without effort. Be patient with yourself and confident that you do have the power to change.

Another likely inner voice tempting you to quit will say, "I don't have time to do this now. I'll face up to my problems tomorrow." In response, you should ask yourself, "What are the chances of that happening?" You know what the answer is. Thus, whenever you catch yourself thinking this way, switch your focus to the lifelong pain you will feel if you fail to do anything about your stressful existence. Literally make a list in your mind: constant time pressures, low job satisfaction, anger, fear, misgivings about your personal life, heart disease, etc. Contrast that against what you will gain if you bite the bullet now: less psychological pressure, better physical health, higher self-esteem, greater job satisfaction, positive relationships with associates, spouse and children, etc. This will help you conclude that change is not only possible but also well worth the price - now, not later.

Finally, the most insidious of your inner voices may call out and say to you, "If I admit that my thinking style in the past has been erroneous, then I will have to live with the idea that I have failed in some way. Also, what if I try to change and don't succeed?" Notice that these types of negative predictions and conclusions will evoke guilt and fear of failure in you, which in turn will tempt you to quit. No thoughts are more harmful than those that prevent you from growing. Let them be your primary targets. Argue against such ideas as you would in a legal brief or a case. Here are two sample responses: "First, it is more functional to think of the past as learning experiences, not failures. Second, if you don't change, then you will wind up failing in the future as well as in the past. Is that what you want?"

What if you try and don't succeed? You try again! And after that, you keep trying as many times as it takes to succeed. The only reason not to try is if you honestly think that you are so defective in some way as to be incapable of change. If you really think that, however, then you owe it to yourself to evaluate the validity of this conclusion by seeing a mental health professional.

MORE THAN JUST HAPPY TALK

When you share your apprehensions with a well-meaning friend or family member, the advice that you are most likely to receive is: "Think positive. Everything will turn out for the better. You'll see." Essentially, this is a form of cheerleading in which the underlying message is: "Don't worry! Be happy!" I call this "happy talk."

Sometimes this is the right advice. Many of us waste too much emotional energy anticipating negative events that never occur. If we would just lighten up, life would be less stressful. Much of the time, however, this type of advice is inappropriate and ineffective. In case you are confusing it with the advice I am giving you, allow me to distinguish myself.

Happy talk encourages you to ignore problems in the hope that they will disappear on their own. I am advising you to confront problems and fix them. Happy talk assumes that all negative thoughts are dysfunctional and should be dismissed. I am advising you to heed your negative thoughts because they have a strong adaptive value. They get your attention and motivate you to examine and improve whatever is wrong.

Undoubtedly, sometimes you will find that your negative thoughts have no foundation and should be revised. My advice calls on you to come to this conclusion only after you have fully examined them. I am also of the opinion that sometimes your negative thoughts will be valid and you will have good reason to feel angry, guilty or fearful. In such cases, I advise you to make improvements, either in the environment or within yourself.

SECTION VI: HEED YOUR EMOTIONS

Hear reason, or she'll make you feel her.
Benjamin Franklin

The quality of strength lined with tenderness is an unbeatable combination.
Maya Angelou

By starving emotions we become humorless, rigid and stereotyped; by repressing them we become literal, reformatory and holier-than-thou; encouraged they perfume life; discouraged they poison it.
Joseph Collins

EMOTIONAL INTELLIGENCE IS KEY

Why is it that some people do so well in life, while others who are equally smart do so poorly? Oftentimes, the answer lies in an ability called "emotional intelligence."[156] It improves decision making, social skills, motivation, willpower, and impulse control. It also increases your ability to manage stress and leads to better health. Emotional intelligence is as powerful a determinant of success as intellectual ability. People who excel in both the intellectual and emotional realms are the truly gifted among us.

What is emotional intelligence (EI)? Unless you have studied the concept, the definitions that first come to mind tend to be wrong. For example, some people think of it as the ability to be polite and respectful on a consistent basis. Others think of it as the ability to express one's emotions without restraint and "let it all hang out." Neither of these definitions are correct, however.

As I define it, EI is the practical ability to *understand, evaluate, and improve* the role that emotions play in our lives.[157] Specifically, emotionally intelligent people have the ability to effectively: (1) recognize their own and others' emotions; (2) identify the causes and consequences (stimuli, cognitions, and behaviors) of their own and others' emotions; and (3) respond to their own and others' emotions in ways that advance personal and professional success, as well as physical and mental health.

As suggested by a number of observers, these skills should be taught in law school, but they seldom are.[158] In fact, EI training should start in kindergarten, yet it is rarely offered in any of our educational curricula. Given how important EI is in managing stress, this book would not be complete if I did not cover it here.

HEED OUR EMOTIONS?

My task here is formidable. I am going to advise you to heed your emotions, knowing that lawyers prefer to suppress them instead. That is, current national statistics show that the vast majority of lawyers view themselves as thinkers; they prefer to make decisions purely on the basis of logical analysis rather than feelings and tend to have a low regard for "touchy-feely" people.[159] Yet, I want to dissuade you from this point of view.

A prevalent belief among lawyers is that while cognition is a high level human ability, emotions are mere vestiges of our biological ties to lower forms of life. Some lawyers I have met believe that the human race would be better off if we were to eliminate our emotions altogether. Like the "Spock" character on the *Star Trek* television and film series, they think that the healthy way to deal with emotions is to contain them. In fact, many legal workplaces consider the repression of feelings to be a hallmark of professionalism.[160]

The rationale for suppressing emotions is based on the idea that passion and reason are separate entities, and that the former interferes with the latter. This idea is deeply-rooted in American law and society, and it dates back to Plato, Descartes, and Locke.[161] It is based on the following assumption: to be in control, it is best to be rational; and to be rational, it is best to restrain the more inferior, emotional elements of our nature. Take, for example, why it is that crimes of passion are punished less severely than cold ones. The core assumption is that people have less cognitive control (mental intent) of their behaviors when they are under the spell of their emotions.

Traditionally, because feelings have been assumed to interfere with clear thinking, they have been presumed to reside in the heart or somewhere else in the body, away from the head.

Some Greek philosophers even associated human emotions with disease.[162] That is why the Greek word for passion, *"pathe,"* is the root of several English words that imply illness or weakness (e.g., *patient, pathology, pathetic,* etc.).

Although these beliefs about emotions have a long history and are ingrained in the minds of many people, there is one problem with them. They are wrong! They don't reflect the latest scientific knowledge about human cognitions and emotions[163] and underestimate the adaptive power of millions of years of evolution. Recent studies have established that heeding your emotions is one of life's key skills, and that repressing them is *not* the thing to do most of the time.

Emotions are like indicator gauges. The only difference is that instead of seeing these gauges, you feel them. From an evolutionary standpoint, this type of wiring has great survival value. Emotions get your attention by creating either pain or pleasure, and that helps you judge your circumstances. The more emotional pain you feel, the more seriously you consider your distress. By feeling your distress, you become more likely to pay attention to it, reflect on it, and do something about it.

Continually repressing your negative emotions makes about as much sense as choosing to ignore a fire alarm. Unless you listen to the alarm and acknowledge the fact that there is a fire, you are likely to get burned. Furthermore, the appropriate response to a fire alarm is not to turn it off, but to put out the fire that turned it on. Similarly, to reduce your stress you need to become more aware of your internal signals of distress in the first place. Only then can you be in a position to do something about their root causes. This gives you the ability to have greater control, not less.

HOW EMOTIONS REALLY WORK

The leading modern theories on how emotions really function are based on what is called an information processing model of our central nervous system.[164] The idea is that after millions of years of evolution, one of the primary roles of our nervous system is to monitor our internal and external environments, in order to detect positive and negative stimuli and make judgments about them. These judgments create the physical arousals we call emotions, which in turn serve the purpose of energizing us to either avoid or reduce some harm or pain, or to approach or increase some benefit or pleasure. Emotions literally "move" us to action; ergo, the word "motion" is embedded in "emotion."

Researchers now agree that emotions and cognitions are interdependent elements of the same integrated central nervous system, and that they usually operate in harmony rather than in conflict with each other.[165] That is, emotions and cognitions usually influence each other in a continuous and cooperative interplay. It is true that sometimes our emotions malfunction and lead us down the wrong path, but so do our thoughts at times. Therefore, it makes no more sense to repress all of our emotions than to repress all of our thoughts. Obviously, the thing to do is to make them both function effectively as often as possible.

EMOTIONS INCREASE AWARENESS

As discussed in previous chapters, the stream of human experience is composed of the following interrelated elements:

Stimulus → Thought → Emotion → Behavior

For example, assume that you are taking a leisurely hike and see a snake (stimulus). Your central nervous system appraises (thought) this to be a dangerous animal and creates an arousal (emotion) we call fear. This energizes you to focus on the danger and take actions (behavior) that are consistent with the goals of preventing harm and surviving.

Note that not all appraisals occur in the form of a conscious or linguistically phrased thought like, "That looks like a snake and it could be dangerous." In this example, the initial central nervous system appraisals that stimulate an emotion are probably instantaneous and unconscious. In fact, researchers have concluded that our emotions often result from unconscious appraisals, and that they themselves can be unconscious.[166] There is even evidence that some of our nervous system judgments and emotions originate outside of the brain. For example, researchers have found a brain-like set of cells within our digestive tracts. This "second brain" interacts with the rest of our nervous system but also acts independently and gives the phrase "gut feeling" a new meaning.[167]

Frequently, however, both our thoughts and emotions are very conscious. For example, assume that a colleague intentionally criticizes you in front of other people (stimulus). You say to yourself (thought): "That was nasty. You shouldn't have done that." Your thoughts trigger an arousal called anger (emotion). Then you say something to defend yourself (behavior).

Regardless of whether they start out being conscious, one of the adaptive functions of our emotions is to cause physical reactions in our bodies that make us and others more aware of them. This increases our focus on the stimuli and cognitions that trigger our emotions and thus improves our ability to control our behaviors. In addition, emotions tend to improve our memory of the significant events that surround them and that makes us more likely to recognize similar situations in the future.

It is believed that humans and other animals are wired to emote more strongly and quickly in reaction to negative stimuli than to positive ones.[168] This disposition has survival value in that negative emotions must be powerful enough to propel us to make swift changes either in the environment or in ourselves, whereas positive emotions only have to induce us to stay the course.

EMOTIONS PROMOTE WISDOM

Contrary to the traditional view, a number of research studies have shown that emotional awareness promotes better judgment. Such studies prove that emotions and cognitions function best interactively, and that both are critical to the achievement of wisdom. For example, it has been discovered that people whose emotions are suppressed due to brain damage, but whose intellectual abilities are fully intact, exhibit very unwise decisions and behaviors.[169]

How can this be? Remember that emotions usually emanate from and are only as logical as the thoughts that precede them. When you are truly mindful of your emotions, you become more conscious of your underlying mental appraisals as well. Once that happens, you are more likely to evaluate the logic of your reasoning. This helps you become more logical, make wiser decisions, and behave more effectively.

Similarly, when you are attentive to the emotions of others, you are more likely to interact with them effectively. Again, the reason is that emotions often reveal a person's true underlying cognitions. Once you understand a person's thoughts, you are in a better position to appraise their logic and react accordingly.

EMOTIONS REVEAL OUR GOALS

Among our most important motives for doing things is our anticipation of how they will make us feel. Most of us agree on the ultimate goal of achieving happiness, and we are happiest when we minimize the pain of negative emotions and maximize the pleasure of positive ones. What distinguishes us from each other is that we differ in what triggers our various emotions. For some, arguing in front of a jury is exhilarating, whereas for others, it is frightening.

Emotions are not only the driving forces behind some of our most basic goals in life, but they are also very self-revealing and instructive. So, if you want to know what goals you are trying to achieve or avoid, pay attention to your emotions. Imagine that you have been saying to yourself and others: "I'm going to try to bring in new clients." Months pass, nothing happens, and you do not really understand why you have not followed through. Becoming aware of your emotions whenever you think about or attempt to market your services can be revealingly helpful. If you feel fearful, it may be that the goal of your inaction is to protect you from experiencing rejection or failure. If you feel guilty, it may be that your inaction is intended to help you pay more attention to your current clients, family members and others. If you feel angry, your true goal may be to protect yourself from allowing your firm to get more work out of you than it already does.

FIRST LEARN TO IDENTIFY SPECIFIC EMOTIONS

Because the great majority of lawyers are thinkers rather than feelers, [170] many of them are not as emotionally aware as they should be. One of the errors lawyers often make is to equate emotions with thoughts. For example, if asked, "How did this event make you *feel?*," many lawyers reply with: "I *thought* it was unfair," instead of, "It made me *feel* angry." For some, this type of response reflects the fact that they need to direct more of their attention to feeling their emotions. For others, it may mean that they just need to become more adept at naming their emotions. My purpose here is to help you improve your skills in either case.

To begin with, you need to understand how to categorize your emotions. The specific classification system that follows is my own creation, born of a need to become skilled at this myself. Although it is still a work in progress, my classification system is based on the wisdom of numerous researchers, [171] and I urge you to try it.

Like hues on a color wheel, the number of emotions we are capable of feeling is very extensive. Identifying them is not as complicated as it seems, however, because most are associated with just six categories or clusters of emotions: *guilt, pride, anger, affection, fear, or hope*. Once you understand the underlying themes of these clusters, identifying your own and others' emotions will become easy and yield great rewards.

As shown in the table that follows, each of the primary emotions reflects an expression of a specific type of appraisal across three bipolar dimensions: negative vs. positive, self vs. other, and past vs. future.

TABLE OF HUMAN EMOTIONS

Primary Emotions		
Appraisals Of:	*Negative*	*Positive*
Self In The Past (Self-Evaluative Emotions)	**Guilt Cluster** *(Guilt, Embarrassment, Low Self-Esteem, Regret, Remorse, Shame, etc.)*	**Pride Cluster** *(Self-Acceptance, Self-Esteem, Pride, Self-Regard, Self-Respect, etc.)*
Other Living Beings, Things Or Events In The Past (Relational Emotions)	**Anger Cluster** *(Anger, Annoyance, Contempt, Dislike, Disgust, Hate, Irritation, Rage, etc.)*	**Affection Cluster** *(Affection, Approval, Attraction, Fondness, Friendliness, Lust, Love, etc.)*
The Effects Of Future Events On Self Or Others (Anticipatory Emotions)	**Fear Cluster** *(Anxiety, Apprehension, Despai,r Fear, Hopelessness, Panic, Pessimism, Worry, Terror, etc.)*	**Hope Cluster** *(Assuredness, Courage, Confidence, Hope, Optimism, Trust, etc.)*
Compound Emotions		
Combination Of Two Or More Primary Emotions	**Unhappy Cluster** *(Depression, Despair, Envy, Gloom, Grief, Jealousy, Sadness, Unhappiness, etc.)*	**Happy Cluster** *(Cheerful, Delight, Happiness, Joy, Euphoria, Satisfaction, etc.)*

For example, the guilt cluster represents emotions that express a negative judgment about the self in reference to past failures. In contrast, the pride cluster represents emotions that convey a positive evaluation of the self in reference to previous successes. Similarly, the anger and affection clusters represent negative and positive judgments about other living beings, environments or events in the past, and how one should relate to them. The emotions in the fear and hope clusters express negative and positive anticipations about the effects of future events on the self or others.

Although the differences between clusters are qualitative, within each cluster the differences are typically quantitative. That is, each cluster contains stronger and weaker versions of the same or similar emotion (e.g., annoyance → anger → rage). In addition to the six basic clusters, there are compound emotions that combine two or more of the primary ones. For example, when we say that we are unhappy, we are usually referring to a combination of negative emotions from the guilt, anger, and fear clusters. Similarly, happiness is normally a blend of positive emotions from the pride, affection and hope clusters. The term "mixed feelings" often refers to a conflicting combination of positive and negative emotions.

If you memorize the six primary clusters of emotions, you will find the task of becoming emotionally aware to be greatly simplified. For example, let's assume that a colleague's criticisms are beginning to stir up feelings in you. Almost immediately, you can assume that your emotions are probably negative. Now you are left with just three options: the guilt, anger, or fear clusters. To determine the specific emotions you are feeling, simply trace them back to their antecedent thoughts.

If you think that your colleague has a valid criticism, then you are likely to feel an emotion within the guilt cluster. If you believe that your colleague's criticism is unjust, then you are likely to feel one of the emotions in the anger cluster. Finally, if you think that the criticism has negative implications for your future, then you will probably experience some type of fear. Of course, there is always the possibility that you will experience a combination of two or more of these thoughts and emotions.

Grasping your colleague's emotions may be more difficult because that requires greater interpretation. You can start by considering the possibility that your colleague is expressing an emotion in the anger cluster, but also consider the possibility that he or she is just trying to be helpful and is actually expressing affection instead. In addition, consider the possibility that your colleague may be criticizing you as a way to diminish his or her own guilt or fear, and that these feelings may be unconscious.

Once you identify the emotions that you and your colleague are feeling, you then need to evaluate them and respond to them effectively. Since it all starts with awareness and understanding, however, it behooves you to know as much as possible about a range of specific emotions. The next several chapters should help in this regard.

SELF-EVALUATIVE EMOTIONS: GUILT VS. PRIDE

The guilt and pride clusters represent the negative and positive sides of the self-evaluative emotions. These are the emotions that express either a negative or a positive appraisal of the self in reference to past failures or achievements. Pay close attention to these emotions because one's evaluation of the self is an essential element of happiness. I am continually amazed at the high percentage of people for whom chronic guilt (low self-esteem) is a core issue.

The guilt cluster subsumes such feelings as shame, regret, remorse, repentance, embarrassment, disgrace, humiliation, self-disappointment, self-rejection, and self-disapproval. In contrast, the pride cluster includes such emotions as positive self-regard, self-respect, honor, self-acceptance, self-approval, and self-worth. For our purposes, it is not important for you to distinguish and label every specific emotion under each cluster. Just use the examples I have listed to understand the core themes of each cluster, and you will be ahead of most people.

When you are ready to explore the nuanced differences between the more specific emotions, you will find that the labels we attach to them are personalized and that getting consensus on their meanings can be difficult. For example, some people define shame as a public emotion in which one feels external disapproval and guilt as a private emotion in which one feels internal disapproval. Other people reverse these definitions. If you ever experience such definitional confusions, remember that meanings are more important than labels.

GUILT IS ANGER
DIRECTED AT YOURSELF

Many years ago, one of my clients taught me that guilt and anger are related. After listening to her complaints about her spouse for several sessions, I gently suggested that the chronic anger she felt towards him was both unhealthy and ineffective. She swiftly replied that by holding on to her anger she was able to prevent herself from becoming depressed. When asked what would cause her to be depressed, she listed a number of regrets about herself. "You mean that you would feel guilty about who you are?" I asked. "Yes," she said partly in jest, "if I didn't blame him for my problems, who else could I blame?"

That was when I realized that the core themes within the anger and guilt clusters differ only in that they are directed at different people. We feel one of the emotions in the anger cluster when we criticize others and one of the emotions in the guilt cluster when we criticize ourselves. In other words, we experience a variant of anger when we point to another person and say, "You! It's your fault!" On the other hand, we experience a type of guilt when we point to ourselves and say, "Me! It's my fault! Guilt is anger directed at yourself.

The emotions in the guilt cluster get triggered when your image of an ideal self does not match up with your perception of a real self. They get evoked when you violate your own moral or ethical values or when you think that you do not measure up in any other way. For example, people who do not think that they are as successful financially as they "should" be tend to feel guilty. People who do not think that they are as good at parenting as they "should" be also feel guilty. In fact, whenever you use the words "I should," you are bound to arouse one of the emotions in the guilt cluster.

There is a major difference between short-term or situation-specific guilt and chronic or global guilt. In the former instance, you make a specific behavioral mistake, and your guilt motivates you to ask yourself what you can do to correct the situation. In the latter case, your mistakes reinforce the feeling that you lack worth as a person and that there is no reason to try harder.

Short-term or situation-specific guilt is healthy because it helps you adapt and grow. Chronic or global guilt is the equivalent of eternal low self-esteem; the sense of hopelessness it creates retards your growth, leads to lower productivity, causes sleep disorders, and can lower the effectiveness of your immune system.[172]

Perfectionists are especially susceptible to chronic guilt. That is, since perfection cannot be achieved, striving for perfection causes constant self-discontent. Perfectionists also find it difficult to let go of their work and tend to become workaholics. This leads to chronic guilt about their family lives as well as their work. Women are more likely than men to feel guilty about family issues because their social expectations lead to stronger role conflicts.

I will never forget the following illustrative incident: After several sessions of prodding and digging with a perfectionistic lawyer-client, I said to him, "You sound like you feel guilty about something other than what we have been discussing." He became very pensive and then revealed to me and to himself for the first time: "I think I feel guilty about not having had a heart attack yet." He then went on to explain that he recently had a vivid dream in which he felt relieved about having suffered a heart attack. In his office, a heart attack was like a badge of honor. It meant that you had given your all to the firm and no longer had to prove yourself. As I listened to this explanation, my mouth must have dropped because he looked at me and said:

"That's crazy, isn't it?" I thought for a few seconds and finally decided that it was safe to be unequivocal in this instance. "Yes," I said, "that certainly is crazy."

SELF-ESTEEM IS AFFECTION
DIRECTED AT YOURSELF

Since the middle of the 20th century, American mental health professionals, educators, and leaders have promoted the benefits of positive self-regard. We've been taught that feeling good about ourselves is a most important goal and that low self-esteem is a sign of a mental health problem. As a mental health professional myself, I too have noticed how often low self-regard stymies one's progress in the world. At the same time, however, I have found that there is a great deal of confusion about the ways to create a sense of self-worth.

In the minds of most people, there is a bidirectional cause-effect relationship between self-esteem and success in life. The idea is that people who feel good about themselves are more motivated to achieve, and people who achieve are more likely to feel good about themselves. Under this theory, parents are advised to do two things for their children: create an environment in which children feel loved, and expose them to as many successful experiences as possible.

While feeling loved and experiencing success are important to the development of self-esteem, the data suggest that there must be more to it than that. We all know people who have been surrounded by love and encouragement all of their lives but who suffer from low self-worth anyway. Likewise, we all know people who have achieved a great deal in their lives and still feel that they are not good enough. At the same time, there are people who were neglected as children, and who have achieved a great deal less than the American dream, but somehow manage to like and accept themselves.

I have thought and read about this paradox for many years and think that I have come closer to unraveling what is wrong with the typical "feel loved and experience success" strategy. One of the mistakes we make is to assume that feeling loved and admired by others translates directly into self-worth. By definition, self-esteem is an internal form of approval, whereas being loved is an external form of approval.[173] Getting approval from others is a good thing, but it does not automatically turn into positive self-regard. Ultimately, it's what you think and tell yourself about your own self-worth that really counts.[174]

Another mistake we make is to inflate the power of successful outcomes and downplay the importance of effort and struggle to the development of pride.[175] This error motivates some parents to shield their children from frustrating challenges and educators to inflate their grades. Ultimately, that only leads to lower standards, more failure, and lower self-esteem. I urge you to not make the same mistake. Confronting frustrating challenges helps you grow, gain confidence, and conclude that you truly deserve to feel good about yourself.

A final mistake we make is to misinterpret the implications that follow from life's inevitable failures. That is, we don't adequately distinguish between short-term (situation-specific) and long-term (global) self-esteem. As discussed in the preceding section, short-term or situation-specific guilt is a healthy reaction to failure. The emotional pain you feel in such instances motivates you to get better at adapting to your environment's daily challenges. It's an unhealthy mistake, however, to allow your short-term guilt to reduce your global self-worth.[176]

When your overall self-esteem fluctuates with your daily ups and downs and depends on what you have done lately, you tend to become perfectionistic. Inevitable mistakes remind you of your flaws and cause you to be perpetually dissatisfied with your general self-worth. What I and many other mental health professionals advise you to do is to shift strategies: Don't wait to become perfect before you feel good about yourself in a general sense. Why? Because it will never happen, and life is too short. Instead, develop a feeling that mental health professionals call *unconditional positive self-regard*.[177] I am referring to a global sense of self-worth that is constant and unaffected by short-term successes or failures.

The goal is to get to the point where you can look in the mirror and honestly say to yourself, "Even though I am not perfect and make my share of mistakes, I feel good about myself on the whole as a person." In order to get there, you will need to answer one of life's most important questions: How good do I have to be to deserve my own overall affection and acceptance?

One way to answer this question is to think about your standards for other people. Take the people you love the most - for instance, your children. Are the standards that you apply to them more forgiving than the ones you apply to yourself? Do you not love them a great deal even though they are imperfect? Assuming that you are more forgiving of your loved ones than of yourself, also ask yourself these rhetorical questions: Why shouldn't I give myself the same "break" I give others? What's wrong with applying the golden rule to myself?

Once you develop a stable feeling of general self-worth, your chronic sense of guilt will dissipate and so will some of your anger and fear. That is, when you learn to accept yourself, you become more tolerant of others. Why? Because accepting yourself requires you to shed your perfectionism and replace it with a genuine belief in continuous growth – for yourself and for others. When you reduce your perfectionism you diminish your fear of rejection and failure. That encourages you to engage in more trial and error, which in turn allows you to learn and grow more easily. This is when processes tend to become just as enjoyable as outcomes. No longer do you view success as a way to achieve happiness. Instead, you try to happily succeed.

I have discovered that as good as I make the benefits of self-esteem sound, some people still don't want to work toward it. The reason is that they have been taught to think of self-esteem as an evil ambition. This is a belief that is strongly prevalent in a number of cultural and religious traditions. For example, several Christian communities consider the sin of pride as one of the seven deadly sins, the sin from which all other sins arise.[178] As a result, many well meaning people who counsel others to feel good about themselves fail to have an effect. They fail to understand that people generally do not follow another's lead unless they perceive the goal to be a positive one.

So, with my clients I first explain what I mean by pride. The type of pride I am advocating is not arrogant, narcissistic or grandiose; it's quiet, unassuming, modest, and accepting of the fact that humans have flaws. It does not lead you to think that you are better than anyone else, only that you and others have intrinsic value and an inalienable right to pursue happiness. It's a type of self-regard that makes you feel a deeper level of reverence for life and the rights of others.

With religious clients, I try to explain that the type of pride I am advocating is not at all sinful in that it allows you to feel an even greater reverence for God. I explain that this alternative point of view is equally prevalent in a number of cultural and religious traditions, and is well-expressed in the following words by Marianne Williamson:

> Our deepest fear is not that we are inadequate. Our deepest fear is that we are powerful beyond measure. It is our light, not our darkness, that most frightens us.

We ask ourselves, Who am I to be brilliant, gorgeous, talented, fabulous? Actually, who are you *not* to be? You are a child of God. Your playing small doesn't serve the world. There's nothing enlightening about shrinking so that other people won't feel unsure around you. We were born to make manifest the glory of God that is within us. It's not just in some of us; it's in everyone. As we let our own light shine, we unconsciously give other people permission to do the same. As we're liberated from our own fear, our presence automatically liberates others.[179]

Once a client is on board with the goal, change is still very slow. Giving up a lifetime attachment to perfectionism and replacing it with a continuous growth philosophy is easier to discuss than to achieve. This is one of the most common but difficult ongoing conversations that I have with my clients. To begin to change, one needs to make a major paradigm shift. The underlying concepts are abstract and complicated. The habits that need to be broken are deeply entrenched. It is not easy, but one of the most worthwhile steps you will ever take. It will set you free and positively change the course of your life. (For more on this, see a chapter entitled *Strive For Growth, Not Perfection* in the next section of the book, which is on the topic of values.)

RELATIONAL EMOTIONS: ANGER VS. AFFECTION

Negative and positive appraisals of other living beings, the environment or past events are expressed emotionally via the anger and affection clusters. The anger cluster subsumes such emotions as annoyance, contempt, disappointment, dislike, disgust, disrespect, frustration, hate, hostility, irritation, and rage. The affection cluster includes feelings that express approval, attraction, caring, liking, lust, love, etc. Given the nature of their work, lawyers tend to experience more of the emotions in the anger cluster than in the affection cluster. This raises their stress levels and creates greater risk for mental and physical health problems. Thus, it behooves you to pay close attention to these emotions.

ANGER IS AN OCCUPATIONAL HAZARD

Our adversarial system of justice encourages lawyers to be aggressive with each other. The practice of law is made even more adversarial by the fact that some of the people who are attracted to it actually thrive on conflict or at least are not averse to it. In addition, many legal work environments value productivity and financial success so much that they foster interpersonal competition and discourage camaraderie.

Thus, it is no surprise that, when compared to the general population, studies have shown lawyers to be more aggressive, cynical, authoritarian, dogmatic, and suspicious.[180] Compared to other lawyers, trial lawyers represent a particularly aggressive subgroup; they even tend to have higher testosterone levels than non-trial lawyers.[181]

The anger that lawyers experience at work is significantly correlated with their high stress levels and job dissatisfaction.[182] In addition, anger is harmful to their physical health.[183] Take, for example, the following 1985 study. A group of researchers contacted 118 lawyers who had been law students at the University of North Carolina in 1956 and 1957 and who had completed a personality test for another unrelated research project.[184] It turned out that their scores on a hostility scale many years earlier were very predictive of their mortality rates. Less than 5 percent of those with the lowest hostility scores had died by 1985. In contrast, lawyers with the highest hostility scores had a 20 percent mortality rate.

Does this mean that you should strive to never feel angry under any circumstances? Of course not. Short-term anger, when it is justified in specific instances and expressed properly, is both natural and healthy. Anger alerts you and others to the fact that there is a problem and motivates you and others to get it fixed. It can help you clarify issues, improve your relationships, and gain a sense of control over your life.

As with all negative emotions, the anger cluster is harmful when it is chronic and global. Some people justify their own chronic anger under the ancient assumption that it is cathartic. In reality, constant venting is not cathartic. Chronic anger begets more chronic anger and produces all of the damaging effects discussed above.

In dealing with your own anger, the first step you should take is determine whether yours is chronic. This task is made more difficult by the fact that many lawyers are so accustomed to their own hostility that they are unaware of it. They see themselves as realistic rather than cynical, and are not cognizant of how often they feel and act irritated and impatient. In some cases only something like a spouse's threat of divorce shocks them into awareness. Thus, before you reject anger as a problem for you, I suggest that you ask several people who care enough to tell you the truth whether they experience you as annoyed or hostile much of the time. Even if you are one of those people who tries to conceal your negative emotions, hostility reveals itself in so many ways that people who know you well will be able to tell whether it is a problem for you – often when you cannot.

If you decide that you do have a problem with hostility, you then need to decide whether you truly want to change. Make an honest assessment of how harmful your angry feelings are to your physical and mental health, as well as to your professional and personal life. Negative emotional habits are difficult to break. Without a serious commitment to do so, your attempts are doomed to fail.

Once you commit yourself to reducing your hostility, there are a number of concrete steps you can take.[185] The obvious ones are: avoid provocative situations, take time out when you are about to lose control, do relaxation exercises, eat properly, do physical exercise, get adequate sleep, ease your workload, improve your communication skills so that you can assert your legitimate needs without being antagonistic, and reduce your unrealistic or perfectionistic expectations. Since these strategies are discussed elsewhere in this book, I will not describe them here in any detail.

You should try one additional strategy that I have used to help many of my clients. When dealing with people who are chronically irritated, I start by carefully listening to all of their grievances. While many of the reasons they get annoyed have merit, hostile people tend to overreact to things and cannot seem to forget about them. Some of them recall unimportant negative incidents that occurred years earlier with a level of passion that is simply unjustified. Eventually I begin to wonder why they react to things so frequently and intensely, and cannot let go of them. I then pose a question that I recommend you should always ask yourself: What are you *really* angry about?

In answering this question, people often discover that the chronic anger they feel is really a lingering response to certain unhealed psychological wounds that were inflicted on them a long time ago. For example, some people hold on to the anger they experienced in response to feeling hurt, criticized, rejected or disrespected in some way by their parents. Whether their memories of the past are distorted or real, the effect is equally powerful. These are people who take too many things personally because they often misinterpret the actions of others as akin to what they experienced as kids. Once this connection is understood, it becomes easier for them to change. Sometimes it is helpful for them to reexamine the past and determine whether their memories are accurate in the first place. Either way, positive change usually occurs when they stop blaming everyone else for constantly feeling attacked and accept responsibility for raising their own self-worth.

AFFECTION IS A POWERFUL NEED

The affection cluster of emotions represents the fact that humans are group-oriented animals who have a social-biological need to relate and bond with others in positive ways. It is no accident that one type of affection or another (e.g., romantic love, friendship) is a core element of most novels, movies, and songs. Popular lyrics teach us that "people who need people are the luckiest people in the world" and that "all you need is love." Social and mental health scientists also agree that meaningful, positive relationships are a necessary element of happiness for most people.[186]

In case you remain unconvinced, consider this compelling fact: Recent scientific findings have shown that people who feel emotionally connected to others have a lower risk of developing such illnesses as cancer and heart disease, and a greater chance of surviving them.[187] Dean Ornish, the well known medical researcher and author on the topic of heart disease, concluded the following about affection:

> I am not aware of any other factor in medicine – not diet, not smoking, not exercise, not stress, not genetics, not drugs, not surgery – that has a greater impact on our quality of life, incidence of illness, and premature death from all causes..........If a new drug had the same impact, virtually every doctor in the country would be recommending it for their patients. It would be malpractice not to prescribe it – yet, with few exceptions, we doctors do not learn much about the healing power of love, intimacy, and transformation in our medical training. Rather, these ideas are often ignored or even denigrated.[188]

Unfortunately, the typical practice of law generally does not promote the expression of affectionate feelings. For all of the reasons I enumerated above, the anger cluster of emotions is what is often encouraged instead. The problem is that anger is harmful to both your mental and physical health.

So what is a lawyer to do about this? As I explained in the preceding section, the first thing you need to do is decide whether you really want to seriously commit yourself to a life in which you experience more affection than anger. If your answer is "yes," then you should first take the steps outlined earlier and reduce the amount of anger that you experience.

The next thing you can do is reevaluate your priorities. Your dedication to work productivity and financial achievement may have to be reduced a bit so that you can pay greater attention to your friends and family members. As a number of legal observers and scholars have suggested, also consider the option of practicing law with a greater emphasis on fostering positive relationships with your clients and colleagues and on promoting humanistic values.[189]

Finally, keep in mind that your ability to give and receive affection partly depends on whether you feel affection toward yourself (self-esteem). In other words, the less critical you are of your own imperfections, the less critical you will be of others. In turn, others will be more likely to be friendly toward you. Similarly, the more secure you are, the less afraid you will be to reveal yourself to other people and be intimate with them. Thus, the advice given in the preceding chapter on how to raise your self-esteem is also relevant to how you can develop more affectionate relationships with others.

ANTICIPATORY EMOTIONS: FEAR VS. HOPE

Fear and hope represent the anticipatory emotions. They express negative and positive expectations about the effects of future events on the self and others. The fear cluster includes such feelings as anxiety, apprehension, fear, hopelessness, panic, pessimism, worry, and terror. The hope cluster subsumes such emotions as confidence, faith, hope, optimism, sense of security, and trust.

In general, people who lean toward being hopeful, rather than fearful, perform better in their personal and professional lives and are healthier. That is, hopeful emotions are correlated with stronger immune systems, fewer infectious diseases, lower rates of cancer and cardiovascular illnesses, and fewer mental health problems.[190] The effects of hope and fear on lawyers, however, appear to be more mixed; even though chronic fear is unhealthy for them, it may help some lawyers function more effectively on the job.

For example, researchers have found that law students have stronger immune system functions when they are optimistic about their studies.[191] On the other hand, law students earn higher grades when they are pessimistic about their studies.[192] The most likely explanation for this unusual finding is that negative expectations must help law students prepare better for the Socratic method of teaching and do better at such tasks as critical analysis and fault finding in an adversarial context.

These research results remind me of something I learned a long time ago about the practice of law. Having listened to my opinion that it was unhealthy for him to be so negative about other people's motives, a lawyer-client of mine jokingly said to me once: "Doc, just because I'm paranoid doesn't mean that people aren't out to get me." He was right. In an adversarial legal system, it is natural to experience negative anticipatory feelings a great deal of the time. Such emotions help lawyers avoid or prevent costly mistakes and dangers.

Thus, many lawyers face a dilemma: What can they do about the fact that chronic fear helps them excel at the adversarial aspects of their jobs but also places them at greater risk for physical and mental health problems? To paraphrase an old English proverb, ideally a lawyer should hope for the best, but feel just enough fear to prepare for the worst. Obviously, achieving this type of balance is a challenge.

BEING FEARLESS IS NOT WISE

Scientists believe that because fear plays such a key role in energizing animals to evade danger, it is probably the oldest and most prevalent emotion in evolutionary history.[193] Fear has so much survival value that it is the emotion humans experience most often. Even brave people experience fear. What makes them brave is not that they are fearless; it's that they feel the fear and are able to overcome it.

To continually grow, you need to take risks. With risk comes fear. Its function is to energize you to evaluate matters. That is a good thing, and it should never be your goal to become fearless. The wise thing to do is to welcome your fears, assess their validity, make appropriate adjustments, and courageously conquer them.

Obviously, not all types of fear serve a useful purpose. Fear can be very dysfunctional when it is unduly strong or chronic. Besides causing unnecessary distress and health problems, unjustifiable fear can be very harmful in other ways. It can cause you to anticipate harm where there is none and thus distort your perceptions and judgments. In addition, it can cause you to avoid situations that you need to confront. Finally, it can cause you to feel guilty about your "cowardice," which in turn can lead you to experience low self-esteem and depression.

For example, I have known several lawyers who feared being humiliated so much that they developed a strong aversion to litigation. They fabricated elaborate justifications to make it appear as though important decisions about cases were based solely on facts. Secretly, however, many of their decisions were based on dysfunctional fears. Not only did they fear litigation, but they also dreaded the thought that someone would discover their fearfulness. Distress and low self-esteem were their constant companions. You can imagine how it affected their careers and personal lives.

If you suffer from dysfunctional fear, change can occur only if you recognize and confront it. This task is made more difficult, however, by the fact that many of our fears are triggered involuntarily. That is, our fear-like emotions have evolved in ways that allow them to be set off by multiple centers in our brains, including several that are more primitive and unconscious. These automatic triggers have adaptive advantage in emergency situations that demand speedy reaction times.[194] Unfortunately, since "quick and dirty" appraisals are also more likely to be wrong, they often arouse fears that are unreasonable and maladaptive. Given their involuntary nature, you may not be able to prevent many of your irrational fears from being aroused, but what you can do is use the conscious parts of your brain to extinguish them.

Start by learning how to identify your fears. Susan Jeffers, the author of an excellent book entitled *Feel The Fear And Do It Anyway*,[195] asserts that there are at least three levels of fears occurring in the everyday lives of most people: (1) fears about concrete occurrences, (2) fears about their inner psychological consequences, and (3) fears about not being able to handle it all.

For example, lawyers experience fear about such concrete negative possibilities as the loss of a case, a client, or income. Beneath these concrete worries are fears about the psychological consequences such losses evoke, such as feeling like a failure and feeling rejected. Finally, there is the overarching worry that you will not be able to endure either the concrete or the psychological consequences of what you fear. Dr. Jeffers calls it the "I can't handle it!" type of fear.[196]

Whenever you find yourself thinking and feeling as though you "can't handle it" all and would like to run away, offer yourself an alternative point of view. Consider telling yourself the following: "I *can* handle this. I have handled it in the past and will handle it in the future. Even if I am not successful with this challenge, I will feel better for having faced it. If I choose to run from it, I will feel like a helpless coward and die a thousand deaths. That's much worse." This is not just trite "happy talk." It happens to reflect the truth.

Once you have restrained the "I can't handle it!" type of fear, move on and apply your logic to your fears of rejection or failure, as well as to your more concrete fears. You will need to make three distinctions: (1) fears you cannot do anything about, (2) fears that you can do something about, and (3) fears that are overstated or irrational.

With regard to things you cannot do anything about, other than make the best of them, you need to get into the habit of telling yourself that they are not worth fearing. For example, we all know people who are impossible to please, no matter what we do. Similarly, sometimes the facts of a case are simply unfavorable. You are not responsible for such external realities and cannot do much about them, other than accept them without fear.

There are undesirable things that you can do something about, and those are worth fearing only if that energizes you to act. For example, being concerned about your actual income and your image as a rainmaker is helpful only if it stimulates you to do marketing. Once you begin to market, however, the fear has done its job, and it is best to let it go.

Finally, the thing to do with fears that are unjustified is to simply cross-examine them logically. For example, if you are constantly coming to the conclusion that your work products are inadequate, ask yourself to present some external evidence for it. If you rarely get anything but positive feedback, consider the possibility that your fears are unjustified and that you need to become less perfectionistic.

LEARN TO BE HOPEFUL

The hope cluster of emotions reflects a belief that one way or another things will turn out all right. Believing this makes you think and feel as though you can realize your goals. In turn, that motivates you to create goals, to develop a plan of action in furtherance of your goals, and to actually work toward achieving them. As a result, hopeful people tend to have higher self-esteem, as well as better physical and mental health.

Hopeful people tend to feel and appear to others as though they are lucky. The truth is that they experience the same good and bad luck that most of us do on average. What gives them the edge is that their hopeful stance makes them quicker and better at learning from the ill-fated events in their lives and seizing the opportunities that cross their paths.

Obviously, I don't mean to suggest that *all* you need to do in life is be optimistic. That is the kind of advice that is doled out to children by characters in fluffy musical comedies. As I discussed earlier, I am not an advocate of simplistic happy talk. Throughout this book, I advise you to confront your problems and fix them, because wishing them away usually does not work. I even assert that fear and pessimism, when justified, is adaptive and will help you prevent bad things from occurring. Here, I am just stating that adopting a modestly optimistic set of thoughts and feelings is one more choice you can make to notably improve your life.

Some people insist on maintaining a pessimistic attitude under the theory that it is more honest, modest and courageous to be gloomy. It is a free country and if you want to increase your likelihood of failure, then you should continue to adhere to the pessimistic philosophy. On the other hand, if your goal is to be more physically and psychologically healthy, and to succeed professionally and personally, then you should give optimism a try.

How does one develop a moderately optimistic, confident and secure stance in life? First, you have to understand the types of habitual thoughts that create hopeful emotions. In an excellent book entitled, *Learned Optimism: How To Change Your Mind And Your Life,*[197] Dr. Martin Seligman explains that optimists distinguish themselves by the way that they explain why good and bad things happen to them. Generally, optimists differ from pessimists along three explanatory dimensions: *permanence, pervasiveness, and personalization.*

With regard to the permanence dimension, optimists tend to presume that good things are stable, whereas bad things are temporary. Thus, when bad things happen, the optimist assumes that they will pass, whereas the pessimist assumes that they will persist. In other words, the optimist tends to use words like "always" in positive contexts, and words like "sometimes" in negative ones. The typical pessimist tends to do the opposite.

Similarly, the optimistic person is more likely to think that one's positive qualities are pervasive, and negative ones are not. When they don't perform well at a task, optimists tend to admit to their failure at something specific but don't generalize it to a more global level. For example, having missed a logical argument in a brief, an optimistic lawyer might confess to having made a mistake but will not conclude that he or she is therefore not smart enough to practice law. Pessimists tend to presume that their mistakes indicate something about their overall self-worth.

Finally, optimists tend to take credit for their successes and forgive their mistakes. Pessimists tend to blame themselves when things go wrong, but give other people or fate credit for their successes. When taken to an extreme, either view can distort reality too much and be harmful. However, a moderate bias in the direction of giving yourself credit for good things and forgiving yourself for bad things leads to greater success in life.

Understanding the habitual thoughts of the optimist is not enough to make you one. The next step you must take is to make a conscious and sincere choice that you want to think and feel like an optimist yourself. You have to come to grips with the fact that there is no such thing as absolute reality, and that how you choose to perceive it has significant consequences.

Luckily, optimism was ingrained in me very early. I have vivid memories of my mother philosophizing about the selectiveness of perception and advocating for how much healthier it is to create an inner reality that focuses on the positive. She did not argue that optimists are more accurate than pessimists – only that they are happier and therefore more successful. You must become your own parent and convince yourself that becoming an optimist will be very beneficial for you.

Finally, there is one more step you will need to take to complete your transformation: practice thinking and feeling like an optimist. As I explained in an earlier section of this book, the best way to start is to keep a diary of your pessimistic thoughts and emotions, and practice replacing them with optimistic ones. To use a computer metaphor, you will find that a lot of old programming will need to get erased before the new code becomes dominant and natural. It will take time.

COMPOUND EMOTIONS

The six clusters of emotions presented in the preceding chapters are like the primary colors of our emotional lives. Each cluster contains emotions that share a qualitative theme but differ in their intensity (e.g., dislike vs. hate), much like identical color hues differ in their brightness or saturation levels. Between clusters, the differences are qualitative and more distinct (e.g., anger vs. fear). What I want to focus on in this chapter is that each cluster is also a basic building block from which all other emotions are created. Since these other emotions are a mixture of two or more clusters, I call them the compound emotions.

The unhappy compound emotions involve a combination of two or more negative feelings from the guilt, anger, and fear clusters. These include depression, despair, envy, gloom, grief, jealousy, sadness, etc. Happy compound emotions involve a blend of positive feelings from the self-esteem, affection and hope clusters. They include such emotional experiences as joy, cheeriness, delight, euphoria, satisfaction, etc.

Why is knowing about compound emotions important? We all experience many compound emotions on a daily basis, and in order to understand them we need to be able to break them down into their component parts. For example, what does it mean when someone says that he or she is unhappy? Usually, it means that the person is experiencing some combination of negative emotions from the basic clusters I have outlined. You can determine which specific emotions are involved in a particular situation through questioning and analysis.

Imagine that someone in your office has a positive outcome on a case and gets a lot of praise for it, including some from you. Secretly, however, you find yourself feeling unhappy about it all. You begin to question yourself and soon discover that what you are really feeling in more precise terms is jealous. This bothers you, and you want to do something about it. Before you can do anything to improve matters, however, you will need to understand your jealousy.

Knowing that jealousy has to be some mixture of emotions from just three negative clusters will allow you to eventually come to the conclusion that what you are really feeling is: (1) an emotion from the anger cluster toward your colleague for appearing to be equal or better than you; (2) an emotion from the guilt cluster that reflects your sense of inadequacy in some way; (3) maybe an emotion from the fear cluster, because you are wondering whether your colleague's success will diminish your reputation in the eyes of others. To get rid of your jealousy and feel better, you will need to cross-examine the thoughts that give rise to each of these emotions. You will not be able to do that until you are able to identify each of them.

It is beyond my scope to give examples of every compound emotion that humans experience. However, I am certain that with an understanding of the six basic emotional clusters, you'll be able to break down any compound emotion into its elements. I have one more thought before leaving this subject: Remember that we also experience "mixed" emotions. These are nothing more than a conflicting combination of negative and positive feelings. The questioning and analysis required to break them down to their basic parts is the same.

UNDERSTAND, EVALUATE & IMPROVE EMOTIONS

As previously discussed, true emotional intelligence is the practical ability to *understand, evaluate and improve* our own and others' emotions. These three steps are comprehensively outlined in the preceding section of this book where I focus on improving one's thoughts. As I explain there, since thoughts are what trigger emotions, the two are intertwined; understanding one helps you understand the other. I go on to explain that once you comprehend your stress-producing thoughts and emotions, your next task is to evaluate their validity. Cross-examine them and consider replacing your dysfunctional interpretations with more constructive alternatives. When alternative interpretations are not the answer, I advise you to shift to solution-oriented thoughts such as, "What should I do about this?" Taking these three simple steps will decrease your negative emotions and stress levels significantly.

As an example, let us assume that you are a family lawyer, and one of your clients is giving you mixed signals regarding a pending divorce. One day he wants to finalize a proposed agreement, whereas the next day he makes new demands that cause negotiations to become acrimonious. Your client is very stressed himself, and he evokes stress in you, his wife and her lawyer. If you were to follow all of the techniques I have outlined in this and the preceding section of the book, you might do as follows.

Begin by getting an understanding of your own thoughts and emotions. Emotions are like pictures – they are often worth a thousand words. Thus, you can start by trying to identify your emotions. In this instance, you are probably feeling an emotion in the anger cluster; at the very least you are probably annoyed or irritated with your client and are probably thinking that his actions are wrong.

You also may be experiencing an emotion or two in the guilt cluster. For example, you may be feeling some remorse about your anger, since it is your obligation to represent the will of your client. You may be somewhat embarrassed by your client's changing demands and fearful of what the opposing counsel may think of your inability to control him. Additionally, you may be experiencing some guilt over the fact that part of you is pleased by your client's actions in that they result in more billable hours.

Once you understand your negative thoughts and emotions, it is time to evaluate their validity and ask yourself, "What *should* I be thinking and feeling?" After some deliberation you come to certain conclusions: Although it is only human to be pleased by the opportunity to bill additional hours, your guilt is somewhat justified in this instance because such an attitude is contrary to your core values. Furthermore, you decide that feeling embarrassed about what your colleague may think of your inability to control your client is unjustified; he has been there himself before, and your job is to focus primarily on your client's best interests.

Turning to your feelings of annoyance with your client, you decide that these emotions are inappropriate. You cannot expect yourself to like your client's actions, but staying angry with him is probably not helpful. Instead, you realize that some form of apprehension about your client's own best interests is probably more appropriate. That is, you realize that your client's actions are prolonging his own pain and could have a long-term negative effect on his relationship with his wife, whose cooperation he will need to raise their children.

After you evaluate all of your emotions, you come to the conclusion that you need to have one or more conversations with your client, in which you counsel him to bring the divorce negotiations to an end. In order to do that, however, you need to be emotionally intelligent about your client's thoughts and emotions as well as your own. You need to get a better understanding of what motivates him to prolong the divorce process. Could it be that he does not really want to get divorced and is still angry with his wife for wanting to sever their relationship? Could he be fearful that once the divorce is final, he will not be able to make it on his own emotionally? To be a true "counselor at law," you need to be able to help your client understand, evaluate, and improve his thoughts and emotions, and act in a more rational and solution-oriented manner.

"Wait a minute," you might ask, "are you telling me that I need to become a psychologist as well as a lawyer?" Obviously, you cannot expect yourself to be a mental health professional and may want to refer your client to one if the problem is serious enough. But, yes, if you want to be an emotionally intelligent lawyer who is optimally effective with clients, you need to become an amateur psychologist. That is what great counselors at law do.

EMOTIONAL INTERACTIONS

Among the significant factors that make the practice of law stressful is that lawyers frequently have emotionally difficult interactions with clients, adversaries, and colleagues. In some instances, what makes things difficult are the people (e.g., hostile, insecure), whereas in others, it is the subject matter (e.g., embarrassing, hurtful). Sometimes both are difficult. While it is beyond the scope of this book to teach you how to best deal with specific types of difficult people or stressful conversations, I will discuss the subject briefly. Should you want to learn more about this topic, know that there are several excellent books and tapes on it.[198]

The main point I want to make here is that the techniques already outlined in this and the preceding section will go a long way toward helping you deal with stressful interactions. The general steps are always the same: *understand, evaluate, and improve* your own and others' thoughts and emotions. So, whenever you are in an emotionally difficult conversation, start by getting a true understanding of everyone's thoughts and emotions. Then, evaluate them and determine how they can be improved.

In an excellent book entitled *Difficult Conversations*, Douglas Stone and his co-authors explain that the general characteristics of people's thoughts and emotions during an argument are actually very predictable.[199] That is, people on both sides of a stressful dispute often make one or more of the following assumptions about *truth, intent, and fault*: "There is only one truth, and my version of the facts is it. Your intentions are bad, while mine are good. It's all your fault, not mine."

These three types of assumptions elicit very predictable and familiar negative emotions: *guilt, anger and fear.* In fact, these three clusters of negative emotions are what make conversations difficult. Some of us express these emotions during our difficult conversations, while others repress them. We rarely deal with them in ways that are emotionally intelligent, however.

Once you understand the underlying thoughts and emotions that are making a conversation particularly difficult, it behooves you to evaluate them. A true evaluation begins by questioning your own and others' basic assumptions about truth, intentions, and fault. You might say to yourself and your opponent in a dispute: "Maybe there are several versions of the truth. Each of ours is an individual or partial version of the truth. Maybe neither of us have bad intentions. Maybe neither one of us is at fault, or there is enough fault to go around."

These types of revisions to our assumptions usually reduce the negative emotions in the air and create an atmosphere in which both sides seek to better understand the other and to be better understood themselves. When that happens, conversations shift from being difficult to being inquisitive and creative. At that point, constructive solutions to the disputes are only a matter of time.

SECTION VII: BE TRUE TO YOUR VALUES

I conceive that the great part of the miseries of mankind are brought upon them by false estimates they have made of the value of things.

Benjamin Franklin

Try not to become a man of success but rather try to become a man of value.

Albert Einstein

WHAT DO VALUES HAVE TO DO WITH STRESS?

Early in my career, I thought that the topic of values was outside of my area of professional expertise. My parents, who were immigrants and did not quite understand what a psychologist does, occasionally asked me whether my work was similar to that of a rabbi. My usual reply was that there were similarities, but that I focused on self-efficacy and mental health issues, not moral ones, and that there was a distinction between the two. Consequently, my clients' values were off-limits, and I did not delve into them. I was wrong.

Today, one of the most important things I do is help clients explore their values. I now realize that values, mental health, and peak performance are linked. People who suppress their values and behave in ways that are out of alignment with them tend to be stressed, unhappy, and less productive. Some even develop mental illnesses and substance abuse problems. And so, while I try to be nonjudgmental about my clients' values, I have to delve into them to be helpful.

The relationship between values and stress is very simple. When we do things that conform to our values we feel positive emotions (e.g., pride), and when we do not conform to our values we feel negative emotions (e.g., guilt). Since most people are wired to act in ways that result in pleasure rather than pain, one might predict that misaligned values and behaviors would not occur very often. Unfortunately, it is a very common problem in our society, and it causes much of our distress.

In conclusion, if you want to help yourself and your organization truly succeed, you need to pay a great deal of attention to values. This section will show you how.

WHAT ARE VALUES?

Although the word "values" has several meanings, I want to focus your attention on the one that refers to a person's beliefs about what is most important in life. There are at least two categories of such values: (1) our ideal behaviors (e.g., altruism) and (2) our preferred end-states of existence (e.g., financial security).[200] Within each of these categories there are many specific values, but I want to introduce you to seven core domains that I think are most important:[201]

- *Finance*– e.g., monetary achievement, material security, economic status, wealth, etc.

- *Work* – e.g., productivity, competence, strong effort, professional goals, ambition, advancement, etc.

- *Character* – e.g., trustworthiness, integrity, honesty, loyalty, responsibility, discipline, courage, etc.

- *Personal Growth* – e.g., intellectual and emotional fulfillment, continuous learning, expression of one's full abilities, creative freedom, adventure, etc.

- *Relationships* – e.g., social interactions, human bonding, group affiliation, friendship, family, love, etc.

- *Society* – e.g., social causes, human rights, altruism, justice, fairness, standing up for what is right, etc.

- *Religious Faith* – e.g., worshipping God, religious study and prayer, observation of religious traditions, faithfulness to religious principles, spirituality, etc.

Together, these themes subsume most of the basic principles or standards by which people in our culture measure success. Learn these seven categories of values, and you will better understand what makes you and others tick. Of course, you also need to know the relative importance that each person gives to these values. Some of us value social causes above financial success, while others value relationships above professional advancement.

WHAT ARE YOUR VALUES?

Identifying and becoming aware of what you truly value is one of the most important things you can do for yourself. Doing so gives you clear, firm, and enduring answers to some of life's most important questions, such as "Who am I, and what do I really want?" The next most important step you can take is to evaluate the extent to which you are living up to your own values. This gives you a highly meaningful measure of your own success in life. In addition, it helps you identify your goals for the future.

The questionnaire presented at the end of this chapter is designed to help you identify your most important values and determine the extent to which you are being true to them. My description of each value is meant to capture its essence, but the first thing you may want to do is play with the wording to make it all maximally meaningful to you. Then, rate each of the seven value domains on a ten point scale of importance. Unless two or more values are in fact equally important to you, try to give them different ratings so they can be ranked.

As a last step, rate the degree to which you are meeting your own expectations with regard to each value. Remember that most values consist of behaviors in furtherance of certain ideal goals and the ultimate fulfillment of such goals. For example, let us say that one of your goals is to achieve a particular level of wealth by the age of 60 and you are currently only 30 years old. The most valid measure of whether you are meeting your own expectations in this case is whether you are behaving in ways that are consistent with eventually achieving your concrete goal, not whether you have already attained it in the ultimate sense.

The column in the questionnaire that asks you to rate the importance of each value domain helps you define your ideal self. The other column helps you determine the extent to which are living a life that is in harmony with your ideal self. The more congruent your corresponding numerical ratings are, the more likely you are to be at peace. The more distance there is between them, the more likely you are to be experiencing low-self-esteem and stress.

On the surface, this exercise is very easy to do. While I have purposefully made it so, don't be fooled by its apparent simplicity. Take the time to think deeply about each of your ratings, as few other activities are more worthy of your time. Make sure that they accurately reflect what is truly important to *you*, not anyone else. There is more that I am going to ask you to do in the next few pages, but it requires you to complete this step thoughtfully and truthfully.

VALUES QUESTIONNAIRE

WHAT DO YOU VALUE? WHICH VALUES HAVE YOU LIVED UP TO? Each category of values below contains descriptors that try to capture its essence. Feel free to change some of the descriptors so that they represent you more accurately or insert additional values. Complete column (1) first and then column (2).	(1) Rate The Importance Of Each Value To You, On A 10-Point Scale 1=Not Important 10=Highly Important	(2) Rate The Degree To Which You Are Living Up To Each Value, On A 10 Point Scale 1=Failing Expectations 10=Meeting Expectations
Finance – e.g., monetary achievement, material security, economic status, wealth, etc.		
Work – e.g., productivity, competence, strong effort, professional goals, ambition, advancement, etc.		
Character – e.g., trustworthiness, integrity, honesty, loyalty, responsibility, discipline, courage, etc.		
Personal Growth – e.g., intellectual & emotional fulfillment, learning, using full abilities, creative freedom, adventure, etc.		
Relationships – e.g., social interactions, human bonding, group affiliation, friendship, family, love, etc.		
Society – e.g., social causes, human rights, welfare of others, altruism, justice, fairness, standing up for what is right, etc.		
Religious Faith – e.g., worshipping God, faithfulness to religious study, prayer, traditions and principles, spirituality, etc.		

STRESS PRODUCING VALUE CHOICES

Once you have completed the Values Questionnaire on the preceding page, take the time to assess the implications of your ratings. People who are by and large happy and satisfied tend to rate some values as more important than others, and conclude that they are generally living up to their own expectations. Since there is always room for improvement, few of us are completely satisfied across all value domains.

People who are less than satisfied with their lives generally exhibit their discontent through one or more of the following three rating patterns: (1) they rate important value domains as being significantly unfulfilled; (2) they rate too many values as being equally important; (3) they attribute too much importance to one or two values. Let us examine each of these patterns in some detail.

The first pattern is the one that I observe most often with my clients. That is, they perceive a significant disparity between their most important values and the extent to which they are living a life that is in harmony with them. Typical examples of this type of disparity include lawyers who value their family relationships the most but behave as though their work is much more important, who value intellectual creativity very highly but spend much of their time doing boring paperwork, or who value character highly but find themselves cutting ethical corners to meet their financial goals.

Lawyers like these, who do things that contradict their most important values, tend to be like "fish out of water." Internally, they suffocate on the fact that their actions and surroundings are incompatible with their true natures. Their thoughts are filled with "shoulds" and "oughts." Their emotions are characterized by guilt and regret. Consequently, their behaviors tend to be less than maximally effective. Ultimately, they experience negative self-esteem, a low sense of personal control, and pessimism about the future. There is only one way for them to find happiness, and that is to be true to their own values.

An additional problematic pattern I have observed with some clients is when too many value domains receive equally high ratings. Sometimes this signifies nothing more than a lack of thought when completing the Values Questionnaire. Often, however, it reflects a genuine but unrealistic desire to have it all. Lawyers who fall into this category tend to be perfectionistic and have a difficult time saying "no" to anything. They want to be super lawyers, super parents, super community leaders, super everything. In real life, you cannot have it all. Thus, eventually such people experience burnout. The way for them to find happiness is by developing a more realistic balance of wants and needs, and by learning to derive satisfaction from achieving less than perfect fulfillment ratings across some value domains.

Finally, some clients attribute too much importance to one or two values and have unrealistic expectations of them. For example, there are people who focus all of their energies on achieving wealth, expecting that it alone will bring them happiness. Oftentimes, what they are really seeking is self-respect and the affection of others, but they erroneously think that these goals can be achieved through the acquisition of wealth. The way for some of them to find happiness is to recognize their faulty logic, lower the importance they attribute to some values (e.g., money), and raise the importance of other values (e.g., relationships).

Another example of attributing too much importance to one value is the person who believes that hard work is the answer to everything - that the universe or God is fundamentally just and rewards all those who work extra hard. In reality, of course, the world is littered with unhappy people who work very hard but concentrate their efforts on the wrong things. The way for some of them to find happiness is to create a personal strategy that allows them to work smart rather than hard, and to concentrate some of their efforts on other activities.

My preceding example is not meant to suggest that all of us need perfect balance in our lives. There are people who absolutely love their work and are truly happier spending most of their energy on it. Secretly, they enjoy their work more than they enjoy spending time with their families and friends. Since this is not a socially acceptable stance to have in some circles, they are pressured often into pronouncing their remorse about having to work so much. Much of their unhappiness, however, stems from the expectations that others place on them, rather than from within. My usual advice starts with getting them to consider the possibility that honesty might be the best policy. Unfortunately, there are times when the consequences (e.g., divorce) of the absolute truth outweigh the benefits. Thus, not all internal conflicts about values are totally solvable and require some compromises.

THE VALUES ON WHICH
ALL SAGES AGREE

In my writings and seminars, I try very hard to present new ideas and insights on how to achieve success in life. Repeatedly, however, I find that the fundamental keys to success are not new. Parents, teachers, philosophers, religious leaders and many others have all said the same things over and over again. Their advice is usually straightforward, but difficult to implement. None of them offer short-cuts.

David G. Myers[202] reviewed thousands of psychological studies on what makes people happy in a book entitled *The Pursuit of Happiness*. He found that what is often said about money is true: once your basic needs are met, money does *not* buy you happiness. This has been proven in countless studies with people from all walks of life,[203] including lawyers.[204]

Myers also discovered that a great many people *are* happy with their lives – that happiness is not a rarity. In addition, he found that happiness is highly correlated with the following:

- physical health and fitness
- reasonable goals and expectations
- positive self-esteem and optimism
- feelings of competence and control
- challenging work balanced by leisure
- meaningful relationships and intimacy
- contributing to a community
- a good marriage and family

Several studies have uncovered that similar traits describe happy lawyers as well.[205] One of the primary characteristics that has been found to distinguish lawyers who do not feel as much of the strain that comes with the practice of law is a commitment to finding meaningful purposes in their daily professional and personal activities. Committed lawyers are more likely to be involved in the world around them and to have meaningful relationships with other people, including colleagues, family, friends, and members of their community.

The theme of finding meaning in your life is eloquently discussed in a number of excellent books written for lawyers.[206] One of these books, *Transforming Practices* by Steven Keeva, summarizes the problem with the field of law today as follows:

> What's missing? Caring, compassion, a sense of something greater than the case at hand, a transcendent purpose that gives meaning to your work – these are the legal culture's glaring omissions. It's not that they've been eliminated; in every city and town, there are lawyers who demonstrate the stubborn vitality of values and convictions that will not succumb to widespread aimlessness and cynicism. But to a great extent, such qualities are missing in the academy and in most law firms, and they are conspicuously absent from many lawyers' mental maps. Without them, only one criterion remains by which to measure success, one that has nothing at all to do with your need to do meaningful work or to belong to a profession that stands for something worthwhile: money. Where there is no meaning, at least there is money; where there is no joy, still there is money.[207]

In summary, they may use different words, but all of the sages both in law and in our general culture agree: Certain core values other than the obsessive pursuit of wealth are what lead most people to happiness. Consider the possibility that the same may be true for you.

To catch a glimpse of how some lawyers find meaning in their daily activities, consider how Oliver Wendell Holmes framed things for himself:

> Every calling is great when greatly pursued. But what other gives such scope to realize the spontaneous energy of one's soul? In what other does one plunge so deep in the stream of life - so share its passions, its battles, its despair, its triumphs, both as witness and actor? But that is not all. What a subject is this in which we are united - this abstraction called the Law, wherein, as in a magic mirror, we see reflected, not only our own lives, but the lives of all men that have been! When I think on this majestic scene, my eyes dazzle.[208]

I don't think that anyone has expressed it more eloquently than this, but allow me to put it another way: Above all, find the means by which to make your life's activities meaningful. That is what will give you the fuel to pursue them with passion, and passion is what you need to make your life vibrant.

STRIVE FOR GROWTH NOT PERFECTION

The value domains I have discussed so far will provide you with the foundational principles on which you can base most of your behaviors and goals in life. There is one more principle you need to decide on, however, which will underlie all of your values. This one is exceedingly important in that it is at the core of how you approach everything in life. In a nutshell, you need to decide whether you are going to place all of your faith and energy into achieving perfection or continuous growth.

Having observed the high levels of stress and failure that aiming for perfection causes, I have come to the conclusion that continuous learning, growth and improvement is a far superior goal. Upon hearing this, clients often ask me: "Aren't you just playing with words? Doesn't continuous improvement eventually lead to perfection? And, if there is a difference between these concepts, are you suggesting that I lower my standards?" My response to all three questions is "No."

By definition, perfectionists try to be flawless. To bring about their goal, they strive to avoid all errors. In part, they hope to produce perfect work products so that they can experience the pleasure of not feeling the fear and guilt associated with making mistakes. For example, consider the following excerpt from a commencement address given to the graduates of the University of Arkansas Law School in 1993:

> The reputation you develop for intellectual and ethical integrity will be your greatest asset or your worst enemy....Treat every pleading, every brief, every contract, every letter, every daily task as if your career will be judged on it.... I cannot make this point to you too strongly. There is no victory, no advantage, no fee,

no favor which is worth even a blemish on your reputation for intellect and integrity....Dents to the reputation in the legal profession are irreparable. [209]

At first, these words sound like good advice coming from someone who takes pride in his or her work and who values integrity. A closer look, however, reveals a value that may be misguided. The speaker advised the graduates to strive for perfection rather than lifelong learning.

What makes the goal of achieving perfection so unhealthy is its intolerance of human error. Since perfection does not exist, perfectionists are doomed to be perpetually frustrated. Their fear of mistakes tends to diminish their job satisfaction, makes them defensive, and can lead to depression. Paradoxically, eventually this reduces the quality of their work. Thus, believing in the achievability of perfection is a very costly illusion.

This point becomes poignant when one realizes that the commencement speech excerpted above was given by Vincent Foster, a very successful attorney who became President Clinton's deputy counsel in 1993. He gave that speech just a few months prior to his tragic suicide.

Whereas perfectionists try to achieve success in order to find happiness, a wiser and healthier thing to do is happily succeed. You do that by rejecting perfectionism and adopting a continuous learning philosophy. Unlike perfectionists, people who truly believe in the continuous growth model of life accept themselves as imperfect human beings who produce imperfect products. This is not seen as a failure on their part, just an acceptance of a universal reality. Notwithstanding their flaws, they experience higher self-esteem than do perfectionists.

Continuous learners accept the fact that there are always better ways of doing things and feel less fearful of making mistakes. Each new learning experience may remind them of their imperfections and even trigger some guilt. However, such thoughts and emotions are quickly replaced by the pride and joy that comes with getting better and better at something. They tend to enjoy the process as well as the outcome of their tasks. They believe that they can grow from both good and bad experiences. Because they know that the probability of everything going according to plan is zero, they don't react as negatively when things don't go exactly right. In their minds, mistakes and bad experiences are growth and improvement opportunities.

In similar fashion to the proverbial race between the hare and the turtle, perfectionists may be more likely to win sprints, whereas continuous learners are much more likely to win marathons. Think about which type of race best represents your life's goals. Compared to perfectionists, continuous learners get more pleasure and satisfaction out of their own work and are less critical of others. Thus, they are less likely to burn out and are more likely to leverage their talents through delegation and mentoring. Because they are much more open to feedback and continuous improvement, both the quality and volume of their lifetime accomplishments tend to be higher. (For more on this, see a chapter entitled *Self-Evaluative Emotions: Guilt Vs. Self-Esteem,* in the preceding section of the book, which is on the topic of emotions.)

DEFINE TRUE SUCCESS

"To laugh often and much; to win the respect of intelligent people and the affection of children; to earn the appreciation of honest critics and endure the betrayal of false friends; to appreciate beauty; to find the best in others; to leave the world a bit better, whether by a healthy child, a garden patch or a redeemed social condition; to know even one life has breathed easier because you have lived. This is to have succeeded."   *Anonymous*[210]

For many people in our society, the word "success" has become synonymous with financial achievement. There is, however, another type of accomplishment that I call *true success.* It embraces financial achievement but also includes providing excellent client service in an ethical and professional manner, being physically and mentally healthy, performing at your peak, enjoying meaningful personal and professional relationships, etc. Ultimately, I think it all comes down to a very simple proposition: *Unless you are happy, you can't really call yourself successful.*

And so, once you have thought deeply about your values, one of the most important steps you can take in life is to define true success for yourself. More specifically, I recommend that you write a one page essay entitled, "My Definition of Success: Who Am I? What Do I Want?" Some people call it a personal vision or mission statement. Regardless of the title you give it, what matters most is that the essay must contain a description of the real you and what you truly value. After you have written your definition of success, carry it around in your wallet or pocketbook, and read it to yourself at least once a day for a few weeks, until it becomes deeply ingrained in every part of your brain. After that, you can read it to yourself less frequently (i.e., once a month), just to keep it fresh in your mind. As you grow and things change, regularly ask yourself if your definition of true success needs to be updated, and rewrite it accordingly.

This exercise will help you map the overall direction of your life. It is based on the belief that while there are many events in life that we cannot predict or control, we do have some power to determine our futures. Once you have directional clarity, it becomes easier for you to make small and big choices – to say yes to opportunities that advance your goals and values and no to distractions that will delay or derail you. This exercise will not eliminate the unexpected events to which you will need to respond along your journey, but it will help you determine which alternate routes to take. Nothing about this exercise is incompatible with trial-and-error creativity, but it does reduce the likelihood of your behaving impulsively.

Clients inform me that even though writing their personal definition of success has a very powerful effect on them, it can be an emotionally arduous task. To make it easier for you to write yours, I have reproduced a sample in the next chapter. Use it as a guide but don't just copy it. Your definition of success has to be just that: yours and in your own words. Otherwise, it will have little meaning to you. Remember to keep it short, preferably to no more than one single-spaced, typed page, with small margins. This way it will be easy to carry in your wallet or purse and read in just two minutes. Whenever you are feeling lost or overwhelmed, use it as you would a compass.

MY DEFINITION OF TRUE SUCCESS: WHO AM I? WHAT DO I WANT?
by Anonymous

Given my personality, my work needs to be intellectually challenging and creative but without a lot of interpersonal conflict. Boredom and uninspired routine are my worst enemies. To be happy, I need to avoid work environments that are highly structured and put people under the constant pressure of deadlines. In addition to legal research and drafting, I need a moderate amount of contact with clients and colleagues. I'm also a person of integrity and a strong believer in ethics. Although I don't like to admit it, financial achievement is another of my moderately strong motives.

So, my best bet is a small law firm that offers me the ability to do interesting work which is moderately lucrative, in an informal atmosphere that attracts creative people who like and respect each other and enjoy interacting with clients. I know that this is much easier said than done, but such firms do exist. I need to find the one that is right for me. I certainly don't belong in a large law firm or corporate department, and being a solo is not for me either.

My wife and kids are extremely important to me, and I need to make sure that I spend enough time with them. If I don't do this, I'm sure to have strong regrets later in my life. I enjoy socializing with close friends, but I am not one to join social clubs or have an extended network of acquaintances. To be happy, I require a balance between time spent with others and quiet time spent by myself.

Let's face it, I'm a hedonist and like making a good income. Money allows me to send my children to better schools, surround myself with comfortable living spaces and great toys, go to the theater, etc. However, I need to slow down my spending and focus more on my family's long-term security. Because I'm an optimist, I tend to take more risks than I should with my investments and need to spend more time researching them.

While I am committed to human rights, try to help people in need and contribute to various social causes and charities, I'm not really an activist. I'm not sure whether I'm just too selfish or at a stage in my life where making a living and taking care of my family are all I can handle at the moment. For now I'm content with this aspect of my life, but I'll need to revaluate things at some point.

I get involved in too many activities and need to manage my time better. I need to keep trying to place my emphasis on doing things that are truly important in the long-term and stop trying to please everyone. Above all, I need to keep working on getting rid of the thought that I have to be perfect to succeed and replace it with a commitment to just keep growing, for as long as I live.

SECTION VIII: PUTTING IT ALL TOGETHER

The self is not something one finds, it is something one creates.

Thomas Szasz

A great flame follows a little spark.

Dante Alighieri

THE DISTINCTIVE TRAITS OF HAPPY LAWYERS

As discussed in a prior chapter, true success in life really comes down to whether you are generally happy or stressed. It's no coincidence that all of the stress management techniques contained in this book are at their core designed to answer this question: How do I achieve happiness? The short answer is: Do what happy people do. And so, in this chapter I want to help you put it all together by summarizing what happy lawyers do.

Lawyers who are generally content with their lives over the long-term tend to share certain personality traits and habits that are very instructive. Like all people who achieve lasting contentment, happy lawyers know that most things are created twice, once in the mind and once in reality. Thus, one of the things they have in common is a set of clear and concrete goals that are free of mixed emotions. Knowing what they want, they also develop concrete plans to fulfill their goals. These plans are then broken down into small steps that are achievable and do not appear overwhelming. They try to build fun into their plans because pleasurable tasks are more likely to get done and bring greater satisfaction.

Obviously, happy lawyers also follow through on their plans. When going into action they experience fear, but are courageous enough to accept their own fallibility as normal. They recognize that the probability of everything going exactly according to plan is almost zero. Thus, they constantly seek feedback and make adjustments. For them, there is no such thing as failure, only opportunities for growth and improvement.

Another trait that distinguishes lawyers who are satisfied is a feeling that they are competent. Such lawyers do not believe in fate as much as in their own ability to influence the world.

They perceive life's stresses as predictable consequences of logical events and themselves as capable of controlling, or at least influencing, such events. They confront their problems rather than run from them. Instead of chronically complaining about their problems, happy lawyers focus on finding solutions to them. They analyze the past - but only en route to thinking about the future and how it can be improved.

Finally, contented lawyers are also characterized by such personality traits as good will and friendliness. They have a generally positive view of people and try to treat others with kindness and respect. They act out of their own sense of integrity and expect others to act accordingly. When others don't meet their expectations, they are willing to forgive but are also not hesitant to be assertive about their own needs and rights. They don't get overly disappointed when things don't go exactly their way; that is just to be expected.

In a highly popular book entitled *The 7 Habits of Highly Effective People*, Stephen R. Covey[211] outlined the fundamental keys to success another way:

- Be Proactive
- Begin With The End In Mind
- Put First Things First
- Think Win/Win
- Seek First To Understand, Then To Be Understood
- Synergize (Harmonize All Habits)
- Sharpen The Saw (Keep Improving)

To learn more about these habits, read Covey's book. The audio version is one of the best self-help CDs ever produced, and I recommend it highly.

TIME MANAGEMENT

"I wasted time, and now doth time waste me."
William Shakespeare

Since time pressures are a major concern for most lawyers,[212] I am going to devote a few pages to teaching you the essential principles of effective time management. My most basic point throughout this chapter is this: Surface level time management advice, which gives you a list of do's and don'ts, is simply ineffective for most people. Like many of the other issues I have discussed in this book, becoming an excellent time manager often requires you to understand, evaluate, and improve the thoughts, emotions, and values that cause you to mismanage your time in the first place.

DO THE IMPORTANT THINGS FIRST

Experts agree[213] that the most significant time management step any of us can take is to habitually *do the important things first.* Most people do just the opposite. They get into the office and say to themselves: "First, let me clean up some (less important) loose ends. Then, when my desk is clear, I'll be able to concentrate on the important things." Of course, all tasks take more time than expected, and there are always additional unanticipated projects that arise as well. By the end of the day, there is a realization that the important matters will have to wait until the next day. This scenario repeats itself many times until the important things become so urgent that they must get done first.

How can we put an end to this stressful style of working? This problem is most fully explored in a book by Stephen Covey and two colleagues, entitled *First Things First.*[214] The authors point out that effective time managers symbolically keep their eye on two instruments: a compass and a clock. That is, they monitor their direction in life as well as their speed. To do this, effective time managers learn to categorize all activities along two dimensions: *importance and urgency*. Furthermore, they try to fill their days with activities that are *important but not urgent*.

The adage that instructs "first things first" is easy to comprehend, but difficult to follow. To start with, it requires us to know what is important. How many of us truly know what is important? Even when we do, how many of us march to our own drumbeat? When I discuss this issue with my clients, I often encounter strong resistance. Some lawyers actually tell me that they are too busy to figure out what is important. In reality, most of them are afraid to face some unpleasant truths, such as that they are not truly focusing on what is most important in their lives.

Spending time on tasks that you do not consider important creates stress. When you clarify what is most important (what you value) and do as many important things as are possible every single day, your life changes in a profound way. The immediate effect is a great sense of satisfaction that results from living the life you want to lead and accomplishing the things that matter. Later, in the autumn of your life as you sit in a rocking chair and ponder what it was all about, you will have fewer regrets.

Another reason so many lawyers experience stress is that too often their days are absorbed by activities that are urgent. Although some urgent activities in law are inevitable, many of them are caused by an assortment of time-wasters. In one of the best time management books I have read, entitled *The Time Trap*, Alec Mackenzie[215] identifies the twenty biggest time wasters as follows:

1. Management by Crisis	11. Meetings
2. Telephone Interruptions	12. Paper Work
3. Inadequate Planning	13. Unfinished Tasks
4. Attempting Too Much	14. Inadequate Staff
5. Drop-in Visitors	15. Socializing
6. Ineffective Delegation	16. Confused Authority
7. Personal Disorganization	17. Poor Communication
8. Lack of Self-Discipline	18. Inadequate Controls
9. Inability to Say "No"	19. Incomplete Information
10. Procrastination	20. Travel

To boost your efficiency, you first need to identify your primary time-wasting habits. The best way is to keep a precise two-week time log that will answer the age-old question, "Where does my time go?" For each of ten working days, keep a diary of everything you do. Briefly describe each activity, note when it started, the total time it took, and whether it was important and/or urgent. I have provided a form you can use for this purpose on the next page.

Once you have made a list of your time-wasting habits, choose one or two that you think would be easiest to break. Try changing your behaviors, and keep score of how well you do. The chances are that your bad habits will be more difficult to break than you thought. If that is the case, you will need to delve into the thoughts, emotions, and values that drive your behaviors. Allow me to illustrate this technique, using several time-wasters that are very difficult to conquer: *interruptions, procrastination, and ineffective delegation.*

TIME LOG FOR _____(DATE)

DESCRIBE ACTIVITY (e.g., phone with Tom, dictated brief, coffee & read newspaper)	START TIME (e.g., 9:30am)	ELAPSED TIME (e.g., 10 minutes)	IMPORTANT (I) vs. NOT IMPORT. (NI) ------------ URGENT (U) vs. NOT URGENT (NU)

END OF DAY REFLECTIONS (e.g., name big time wasters, give yourself suggestions)

INTERRUPTIONS

Interruptions are among the most difficult time-wasters that lawyers experience. It is very difficult to resist a ringing phone or a colleague who pops into your office and asks, "Got a minute?" Seldom does it take only a minute. Not only do interruptions take you away from important work, but afterward there is a significant time-lag in regaining your previous level of concentration.

The usual advice given to solve this problem is very simple: Whenever possible and without hurting your ability to serve clients or perform leadership functions, do not allow important work to be interrupted. Unfortunately, following this advice is not that easy. Although behavioral tips on reducing interruptions are the subject of many books[216] on time management, they are difficult to effectuate until you recognize the psychological changes you will need to make first. That is, people who cannot control interruptions commonly have unconscious motives that pull them in the opposite direction. Until you confront these motives, nothing will change.

For example, some people are reluctant to stop others from interrupting them because they are afraid of being offensive and, in turn, of being rejected. In addition, there are those who allow themselves to be interrupted regularly because they cannot stand the suspense of not knowing what other people want and have a difficult time resisting the pull of curiosity. Interruptions make some of us feel important, and they help justify another major time-waster, namely procrastination.

To uncover your hidden motives, try disallowing yourself to be interrupted a few times, and record your resulting thoughts and emotions. Once you fully understand the psychological dynamics involved, try to evaluate their validity. For example, you might ask yourself: "Is it really true that if I don't respond to every interruption immediately, people will reject me?" After you recognize the illogic of your habitual thoughts and emotions, you can work on replacing them with more adaptive ones. Only then will you will be in a position to apply the behavioral tips given by time management experts.

For example, in the case of telephone interruptions, it may require training a skilled secretarial assistant to say the right things: "I'm very sorry, but Ms. Smith is not available right now. However, may I make a telephone appointment at a time that she can call you back?" Most people say yes, and this gives the attorney immediate control over the timing of the telephone conversation.

Prior to actually making the telephone appointment, the assistant should ask the caller: "May I tell Ms. Smith what this is about so that she can prepare herself prior to returning your call?" At this point, the assistant makes a determination as to whether the matter can be handled by someone else, including herself/himself. He or she might say something like: "I think that I can get that information for you out of the file. May I call you right back?" On the other hand, if the judgment is made that the matter requires the attorney's immediate attention, he/she might say: "Oh my! This sounds urgent. Let me see if I can interrupt/find Ms. Smith to see if she can call you as soon as possible. One of us will call you back in a few minutes."

If the matter requires the attorney's attention but is not urgent, the assistant can go ahead and make a telephone appointment during pre-designated blocks of time, preferably times that tend to match your energy levels. For example, some people do their best writing in the morning, and phone-calling later in the day.

Drop-in visitors can be handled with equal finesse. For example, after determining the nature of the issues to be discussed, you can say something like: "I really do want to talk to you about this and think that I can be of help. However, right now I must finish this work. Can we make an appointment, at a time when I can give you my full attention?" Then, when you make an appointment, schedule it at a time that meets your needs.

Nothing I have suggested is meant to imply that you be unresponsive to your clients or colleagues. In fact, lack of attention is the single biggest complaint that clients and associates have about lawyers, and their number one reason for seeking a change. From a client's perspective, there is nothing more frustrating than a lawyer who does not return phone calls. From an associate's standpoint, it is very disappointing to have a supervisor or mentor who is rarely available. This is *not* what I am suggesting. My message is that you should just get greater control of when you attend to phone calls and visitors.

PROCRASTINATION

Procrastination is such a common habit that some people have actually come to consider it an adaptive trait. (A few lawyers I know think of it as an art form.) This faulty logic is expressed when some of us say, "I work better under pressure." In reality, it would be more accurate to say: " I work more efficiently when time runs out, and I have no choice but to stop procrastinating. I wish I could stop procrastinating before I find myself under pressure." Do you see the difference?

By definition, you work more efficiently and think more clearly when you do not procrastinate. Time pressure does not improve your performance; it simply forces you to stop procrastinating. Your peak performance, however, is likely to occur when you do not procrastinate and are *not* under time pressure either. Not only is this preferable for health reasons, but it is also more likely to prevent mental errors and increase creativity.

As with other time-wasters, procrastination has underlying psychological causes. Generally, the reason we avoid something is that we think it will lead to emotional pain. A common emotion that procrastination avoids is fear of failure. For example, a typical scenario might proceed as follows: You look at a file and say to yourself, "This is a difficult case." The underlying implication is that you are going to fail - and that triggers fear. Instead of confronting your original premise and all of its corollaries (e.g., "I'm not a good lawyer."), you get rid of the emotional pain by avoiding the task.

Another common reason people procrastinate is out of a genuine lack of interest in the work. You say to yourself, "This is going to be boring!" In turn, this leads to thoughts about your whole identity and whether your life is fulfilling. Such thoughts may trigger a variety of negative emotions, including anger and guilt. Again, instead of confronting your thoughts and emotions in a constructive manner, you reduce the emotional pain by simply avoiding the boring task.

When you realize and begin to deal with the psychological issues that underlie your procrastination, there are a number of behavioral tips you can follow. The most effective step you can take is to break projects down to smaller and smaller units, until you can honestly say, "Individually each of these steps are very doable and painless." Then take each step in turn, spreading them out as much as is necessary. Having done this exercise a few times, you will find that it becomes easier and easier to procrastinate less and less.

INEFFECTIVE DELEGATION

Ineffective delegation can be a most debilitating and time-wasting habit as well. It means that you cannot maximize your achievement through the efforts of others, which in turn means that you are limiting the extent to which you can leverage your talents. In short, you will find it difficult to manage other people and will be doomed to being a worker bee. That is, you are more likely to work longer hours and less likely to earn the higher levels of income.

Once more, the underlying causes of this disability are psychological. They include perfectionism (fear of mistakes), excessive feeling of responsibility for everything, lack of confidence in others, need for control, fear of being controlled, and fear of competition from employees. As with the other time-wasters, you need to develop an understanding of the thoughts and emotions that prevent you from delegating effectively. Then, evaluate their validity, and replace them with thoughts and emotions that are more adaptive.

There are a number of books on the market that can teach you how to delegate.[217] The main thing you need to change is the belief that for things to be done right you have to do them yourself. Learn to live by a different rule: anything that can be done by others should be done by others. Of course, you must hire the right people, be clear in your instructions, and create a supportive psychological environment.

Effective managers accept the fact that everyone is imperfect and capable of making mistakes. They create an atmosphere in which mistakes are expected. Thus, they anticipate errors and build them into their scheduling. Staff are expected to grow and learn from their mistakes.

The effective manager provides moral support, coaches, and teaches the staff but does not do its work. People are entrusted to continuously learn and improve. When staff members realize achievements and advance their status, the effective manager does not feel jealous or fearful but rejoices in how well it reflects on his or her department.

QUANTITATIVELY SPEAKING

Assuming that you are able to become a more efficient time manager, imagine what it would mean if you could gain one extra hour per day- just one! That is, suppose that you could work more efficiently, so as to be finished one hour earlier each day. The cumulative effect on your productivity would be astounding. For example, assuming that you work a modest 5 days a week for 48 weeks of the year, you would have an additional:

- 5 hours per week
- 20 hours per month
- 6 forty-hour weeks per year

To achieve these gains, all you need to do is waste a little less time, as per the suggestions outlined above. Most of us imagine that once we acquire extra time we will become more productive and successful in both our professional and personal lives. Having the extra time certainly makes it more possible for you to achieve additional professional goals, seek personal adventures, express your creativity, contribute to your community, and relate better to your family and friends. However, it is naive to assume that you will automatically use your extra time wisely. How you use your extra time is a separate challenge.

QUALITATIVELY SPEAKING

"We tend to slip into an attitude toward time
which is rather like that of a passenger who sits
backward on a speeding train." *Robert Grudin*

Most people think about time management in quantitative terms: doing things faster and getting more done. However, time management can have a qualitative meaning as well: doing things that truly matter or that you enjoy. With this distinction in mind, think about who is the better time manager. Is it the person who spends time on endeavors that are enjoyable and meaningful, or the person who is efficient and can do a great many tasks? Although these are not mutually exclusive options, pitting them against each other may lead to several insights about the kind of time manager you really want to become.

Once you begin thinking of time management in both quantitative and qualitative terms, everything you do will take on new meaning. You will think about what your calendar truly represents: a diary of how you are choosing to spend your life. The number of things you accomplish will be weighed against their importance and meaningfulness. The results or products of your efforts will be evaluated in the context of the extent to which you enjoyed the process.

To become an optimally effective time manager, the first thing you should do is explain to yourself why you want to manage your time more effectively in the first place. Take out a sheet of paper and list your goals. Start with the most abstract goals (e.g., self-esteem, love, security, adventure, creativity) and proceed to the most concrete (e.g., argue before the Supreme Court, more time with kids, earn more money, travel).

Without a set of strong motives, your attempts at time management will fail. You might try a few techniques and temporarily improve your productivity. However, unless this leads to greater job or life satisfaction, you will become less and less motivated to use them. To succeed, you must be clear about the personal and professional goals that time management will help you achieve.

Consider one more thing about the quality of your time: You cannot always schedule it. For example, some lawyers I know claim that even though they spend less time with their children than they would like, they make up for it by scheduling them in for high quality time. In my own experience as a parent,

I found that some of my most important interventions occurred at totally unexpected times and lasted only several minutes. Thus, while I do agree that it is important to schedule in your quality time, quantity matters as well because the opportunities for quality experiences often come at you when you least expect them – out of the blue and not according to your schedule.

THE CURE FOR OVERWORK

Finally, as a recovering workaholic myself, I would like to share with you an important insight that took me years to discover: The cure for overwork is called *less work*. Right about now, you may be saying to yourself, "Simplification is fine up to a point, but this borders on insulting!" Nevertheless, I find it necessary to state the obvious because many intelligent people I know just don't get it.

That is, most people do not realize that time management strategies are designed to make people work more efficiently, not to work less. Efficient time management is only temporarily effective as a stress management tactic. Armed with greater skill for efficiency, the typical workaholic lawyer, working in a workaholic law firm, soon takes on more tasks than before and ends up just as stressed as ever. It is like consolidating your loans; the temporary effect is to reduce payments, but it usually does little to change spending habits. Many of us know this at an intuitive level and resist becoming good time managers. We anticipate that our only reward will be even more work.

A common suggestion given to overburdened lawyers is to spend more time getting involved in alternative activities, such as pro bono work or community service.[218] These activities do add variety to an attorney's day and they promote philanthropy and compassion, all of which are important. What they do not do, however, is reduce lawyers' workloads. For example, pro bono cases are as stressful and can take as much time as other cases.

Beware of remedies that sound easy. Restructuring your major priorities is difficult. Professional success is a powerful motivator, especially when it is linked to psychological needs such as security, esteem, power, and autonomy. Untangling these thorny connections and replacing them with a healthier balance of activities is intricate work. Even the help of a psychotherapist does not guarantee success. To fit treatment into their schedules, workaholic lawyers tend to choose workaholic therapists. Generally, this is not a good match.

Again, real change will require you to undergo a major reexamination of your basic values. Workaholism does speed up professional advancement and does result in greater income. What it does not do is allow you to reinforce close social and family bonds, or give you the time to engage in other personally fulfilling activities that contribute to a balanced and contented life. The kind of change that is required often involves breaking through much resistance, guilt, fear and social pressure. It is not an easy process and requires a great deal of courage, but the goal is very worthwhile.

LAW PRACTICE MANAGEMENT

If you examine law firm mission statements, you will find that most of them come down to the same basic goals, namely achieving excellence in three areas: *client service, work environment, and financial security.* Of course, each of these goals is related to the other; a very negative work environment eventually hurts client service, which in turn hurts finances, etc. The problem with too many mission statements, however, is that their goals are just words on a piece of paper. Attaining such goals is difficult. Part of the reason for this is that running a law firm effectively requires more than pure legal or business skills. It also requires those same psychological skills discussed throughout this book. Allow me to explain.

RECRUITMENT AND RETENTION
OF GOOD PEOPLE

Most business managers will tell you that recruiting and retaining good people is one of their most critical management challenges. Within law firms, prestige and money are the currencies that are most often used to accomplish this task. Take the example of how many large law firms typically go about recruiting and retaining associates. They look for law graduates from the most prestigious schools with the highest rankings and offer them high starting salaries and signing bonuses. If and when first-rate associates try to leave, law firms typically offer them more money to persuade them to stay.

This management strategy is often ineffective an misguided. Just look at the high attrition rate of associates. The National Association for Law Placement has found that in mid-size to larger firms about 40 percent of new associates leave by their 3rd year, and over 60 percent leave by their 5th year.[219] Given the fact that it takes most associates about 3-4 years to become profitable,[220] a high turnover rate is costly and affects a firm's profitability very significantly.[221] It's not that prestige and money don't matter to associates. It's just that they are not the only factors that matter.

On the recruitment end, most law firms make the mistake of failing to take into account whether the personalities and values of its new people are well-matched to the firm's general culture. I will never forget the first time I recognized this fact. I was called in to help four young partners work out a management problem. They had formed their firm several years earlier and had achieved a great deal of success growing their business. Yet, the morale at the firm was low, and they admitted that they needed to improve their management style. During my interviews with the partners individually, I had them recall how they came together. Before becoming partners, they had known each other only by reputation. All of them were fine lawyers, had complementary areas of expertise, and wanted to form their own firm. These were the criteria they used in deciding to join forces. It did not occur to them to consider such touchy-feely questions as: "Do we like each other?"

After meeting with the partners individually, I met with them as a group to present my findings. I hypothesized that one of their core problems was that they did not care for one another. Maybe it was because they had different personalities and values or because they had not taken the time to worry about such matters. I went on to explain that this might be the reason why there was not much joy in the hallways of their firm and why buying a filing cabinet required a partnership meeting for them. They did not have to be best friends outside of work, but they did have to become friendlier with each other and develop a greater feeling of trust for one another.

You know that look you get when a dog tilts its head as it observes something curious? That is the look they gave me as they listened in silence. I am sure that all of them experienced some regrets at hiring a psychologist instead of a traditional business consultant. Finally, one of them said: "Dr. Elwork, we respect each other's professional skills. Isn't that enough? Do we have to like each other? Forming a partnership is not the same as getting married, is it?"

As we proceeded to explore these questions, I came to certain conclusions that I know to be true. Joining a law firm *is* like getting married. Lawyers spend a lot more time with their immediate colleagues than they do with their spouses. Thus, the compatibility of personalities and values is a very important factor to consider during the recruitment process. These elements cannot be uncovered by reading lawyers' resumes, assessing their professional competence, or knowing what schools they attended. The way to assess someone's personality and values is to get to know him or her a little bit, and that takes time. Law firms that do not take the time to do this initially pay dearly for it in the end.

Many law firms make similar mistakes in their efforts to retain their good attorneys. That is, they focus on financial incentives and fail to address three major psychological reasons that many lawyers leave their firms or even law altogether: being overwhelmed by work, not having enough time for a meaningful personal life, and working in an environment that lacks collegiality or mentoring. Effective firm managers focus on both financial and psychological incentives and know that the latter require them to have emotional intelligence.

SUPERVISION & MENTORING

Another important aspect of managing a firm is providing effective supervision and mentoring. Observers of the legal profession believe that many law firms have stopped providing the type of supervision and mentoring that they once did for their associates. The reason for this shift is that nowadays partners are focused on their own short-term bottom lines rather than the long-term futures of their firms. Current compensation systems generally do not explicitly value time spent by partners on supervision or mentoring. If you ask most partners across the country what their compensation is based on, they will tell you that it is primarily their billable hours or fees. They will also tell you that it would diminish their income to expend much energy on supervision and mentoring.

Unfortunately, inadequate supervision and mentoring leads to a reduction in loyalty and a higher rate of attrition among associates, less leadership development from within the firm to take over for the older generation, and lower quality of services. In the long run, supervision and mentoring is what assures a firm's survival. To do it effectively, senior members of a firm have to value interpersonal relationships, be good at managing their own psychological states of mind, and have good people skills. In addition, law firms need to reward people for their supervision and mentoring.

COMPENSATION SYSTEMS

Many compensation systems within law firms reflect basic misunderstandings of what motivates people. For example, I often hear managing partners or practice group leaders say the following: "Our people are unhappy, but I don't know what to do because we can't afford to pay them any more money." I usually ask, "How do you know that they're unhappy about the money?" That is when they usually give me this look that makes me imagine what they are thinking: "Isn't it always about money? What planet are you from?"

Then, we do a survey to try to uncover what people are in fact unhappy about and often find that it is not the money at all. Oftentimes it is the sense people have of being unappreciated, or of working in a cold and unfeeling environment that pays them well but treats them like replaceable commodities. Throwing money at these types of problems is not only a waste of money, but it also serves to worsen the problem by reinforcing the employees' negative perceptions of the firm.

Another fact that many managers fail to appreciate is: When you reinforce some behaviors with money and not others, those things that are not reinforced are much less likely to get done. One would think that this is a simple psychological principle to understand, but all you need to do is look at how compensation is distributed in many firms to know that it must *not* be clearly understood. For example, if you want lawyers to serve on committees and complete important administrative functions, you need to value and reward these activities by allocating billable hour equivalent (BHE) credits to them. When the only behaviors to get measured and rewarded are billable hours, but you expect your people to do other things as well, those other things will simply not get done or not get done well.

CLIENT SATISFACTION AND MARKETING

No amount of advertising, brochures, or any other form of publicity even come close to the marketing effectiveness of keeping your clients satisfied. Having clients come back to you time and time again, having them expand the services they purchase from you, and having them talk about you positively to others should be your number one marketing goal. Nearly every experienced lawyer I know understands this simple truth. Yet, a great many lawyers do not know quite what to do in order to satisfy their clients. What is missing often is an appreciation of marketing psychology.

In a nutshell, you need to understand what experts refer to as *client centered marketing*. As the term implies, the marketing plans emerge when you view the world through your clients' eyes, not your own. If you do that, the first thing you will learn is that what clients want most are lawyers they can trust. What criteria do they use to decide whether a lawyer is *trustworthy*? It all comes down to three elements:

- *professional competence*
- *ethical and personal integrity*
- *interpersonal skills and caring for others*

Most lawyers recognize the first two elements as being necessary to trustworthiness, but they often fail to recognize the importance of the third one. Because so many lawyers are thinkers as opposed to feelers, it is difficult for them to fully appreciate the power of interpersonal skills and caring. You may not like to hear it or accept it, but the following is true: No matter how competent or ethical you are, unless your clients believe that you care about them, your trustworthiness will be questioned.

What leads clients to think that you do not care? Making promises that you do not keep and not returning phone calls are among the actions viewed by clients as clear signs that you do not care enough. When you charge them for that 6 minute phone call, they get the sense that your relationship with them is purely about money. Being insensitive to how such actions make clients feel is the single biggest marketing mistake you can make.

I have sat in on many marketing meetings where the topic of cross-marketing gets raised. That is, everyone in the room gets excited about the idea of bringing in more business to the firm by going to existing clients and introducing them to the firm's other services. The benefits to the firm of having clients buy more services are obvious. Seldom do the lawyers at such meetings ask a very important client-centered question: How would our *clients* benefit from purchasing more services from us? Naturally, they also fail to ask a follow-up question: Unless we have a real answer to the first question, will our clients not see right through the fact that we are more interested in our needs than theirs, and be offended by it? Effective rainmakers tend to be client-centered and do ask such questions.

MONITORING PROFITABILITY

Many firms monitor gross rather than net revenues. The more effective thing to do is to monitor both gross and net revenues. The rationale for doing this is simple: It is one of the best ways to measure the profitability of specific departments or lawyers. One department may be bringing in much larger gross revenues than another, but be much less profitable when you subtract their costs (gross revenues minus costs = profits). Since the only thing you can spend is what is left over after the bills are paid, tracking gross revenues alone is uninformative. Thus, monitoring true profitability (net revenues) is an important law practice management task.

Even when they understand these simple concepts, getting law firm leaders to monitor profitability is not always easy. I have often encountered tremendous resistance to it. All kinds of reasons are given for why it has not been done (e.g., "the firm is doing well, and we don't have time for fancy bookkeeping"). The real reasons, however, are mostly psychological in nature: fear of being discovered to be unprofitable, fear that it will cause conflict, fear that tough management decisions will need to be made and people will be hurt by them, etc. Despite being critical to the long-term financial health of the firm, law firm leaders often struggle with monitoring profitability unless they appreciate the psychology of it.

Incidentally, what I am addressing may sound like it applies to larger firms only, but that is not true. Monitoring profitability is critical for law practices of any size. Yet, many small firms and even solo practitioners fail to do it, for the same reasons as large law firms (e.g., fear of what they will discover).

When profitability at a law firm *is* measured, unfortunately it is often done in ways that are not emotionally intelligent. For example, one of the issues that arises is how the profitability data on each practice group or individual attorney should be disseminated. Many firms distribute this type of information to all partners, under the misguided psychological theory that it will help create healthy internal competition. The idea is that sinners will feel punished, learn a painful lesson, and become more motivated to do better. In reality, this strategy only humiliates people, lowers everyone's morale, makes them less loyal, and creates a culture of fear, hostility, and divisiveness.

The most effective way to reveal detailed profitability data is to have them distributed only to a few key individuals who can use them for constructive strategic business planning. When used this way, profit monitoring can gain wide acceptance and will not be seen as divisive.

ADAPTING TO CHANGE

Finally, all businesses need to monitor the competitiveness of their products or services. Depending on the types of legal services you offer and the kinds of clients you serve, you will be competing against other lawyers or law firms across one or more of the following three dimensions: *innovation, quality, and cost.* You cannot afford to stand still because your competitors will not, and your clients will eventually be drawn to at least consider the services of other lawyers. Thus, whether you are a solo practitioner or a large firm, your best long-term survival strategy is to create a mindset of *continuous improvement.*

Unfortunately, the concept of continuous improvement is easy to explain but not to implement. It requires continuous change, and change is difficult for a variety of psychological reasons. Continuous change requires you to repeatedly confront the idea that something you are doing now is not good enough any longer. Many lawyers are perfectionists, and perfectionists have a hard time with continuous improvement because it forces them to confront feelings of guilt a great deal of the time. For those who overcome the guilt, it also means struggling with the fear that they may fail at doing something new and different.

And so, it is too often the case that people just choose to stay the same. The way to overcome this type of maladaptive resistance to change is to become adept at the psychological skills discussed elsewhere in this book.

If you want to delve more deeply into law practice management skills, I highly recommend a series of books written by David Maister, such as *Managing the Professional Service Firm*[222] and *True Professionalism.*[223]

FAMILY LIFE

Staying happily married to anyone takes effort, but having a lawyer as a spouse presents some special problems.[224] Lawyers tend to work very long hours within an adversarial atmosphere that breeds hostility, cynicism and paranoia. They tend to be perfectionistic and critical. In addition, lawyers are professional debaters who are trained to present one-sided arguments and always prevail. If this is not a formula for marital challenges, I do not know what is.

While research on this topic is scant, the available data support the idea that the practice of law is tough on family life. For example, one survey of close to 2600 lawyers in North Carolina revealed that among those who had been divorced or separated, 36 percent reported that the "stresses of professional life were major causes of their marriage failing."[225] Of the attorneys who had not been married, 46 percent reported that the "pressures of their professional life had been a major deterrent to getting married." In a national survey of about 2,200 lawyers, 31 percent of the men and 37 percent of the women who were married but had no children reported that the demands of their work were behind their decision to be childless.[226]

THE TIME FACTOR

Lack of time together is a common topic of discussion among many couples. This problem is certainly not limited to families of legal professionals, but it does arise more often in those families than it does in many others. Workaholism is rampant in the legal community. Lawyers commonly eat dinners without their families, bring work home, go into the office on weekends, and fail to take vacations. Working exceedingly long hours may benefit one's career, but it is generally harmful to one's family life and is correlated with higher divorce rates.[227]

One national survey of lawyers in private practice showed that over 44 percent complain that they do not have enough time with their families.[228] Another survey suggested that young attorneys find it particularly difficult to balance the practice of law with family life.[229] Young attorneys (both males and females) who hope to marry one day are in the stage of life where they need personal time to find a mate. Those who are married need time to spend with their newly formed families. Too often, young attorneys find that they cannot get the personal time they need without jeopardizing their careers.

Female attorneys, regardless of age, face special challenges regarding time management. Although we have come a long way in terms of women's rights in our country, it is still more socially acceptable (though, of course, unhealthy) for men to neglect their families. Women are expected to be the primary caretakers of children and elderly parents. As a result, busy female professionals experience the highest levels of work-family conflicts. Not surprisingly, with the exception of high school dropouts, women (not men) with graduate level degrees have the highest divorce rates.[230]

Because the legal profession is not family friendly, female lawyers experience significant role conflicts. Eventually, many female attorneys find a socially acceptable and healthy balance between work and family life. Others, however, wind up feeling forced to give up something, either some of their career goals or some aspects of their family life. One study has shown that compared to female physicians and female college professors, female attorneys are less likely to marry or have children, more likely to get divorced, and less likely to re-marry after a divorce.[231] A similar pattern has emerged when female lawyers are compared to male lawyers.[232]

Family discussions about this topic generally follow a very familiar pattern. One family member usually accuses the lawyer of spending too many hours at work and expresses feelings of rejection. "You love your work/clients more than you do me/your family," says the rejected spouse or child. "No I don't," says the lawyer. "I am doing it for you, so that you/we can live more comfortably and have financial security. I've got enough pressures without you adding to them."

By the time a couple or family sees a counselor, there is a great deal of anger in the air. But if enough love still resides underneath the anger, there is hope. Therefore, it is helpful if all parties first express the love they feel for each other.

The spouse or child who is demanding more time is really saying, "I love you and want to spend more time with you." The defensive lawyer is generally saying, at least in part, "It hurts me to be accused of not loving you because the truth is that I do. My anger is in part based on the fear that I could lose you, and that in turn is based on my love for you ."

Once their love for each other is established and explicitly expressed, the couple or family can then explore ways to spend more time together. Given the demands of a typical law practice, it is helpful to first discuss ways in which the *quality* of everyone's time together can be improved. Regularly scheduled special time needs to be set aside for both the couple and the children, doing things that all enjoy. With few exceptions, this special time together needs to be given high priority and adhered to religiously.

Planning quality time together is not the only answer. There is a limit to how much of our important daily interactions can be scheduled. Yes, it is a great idea to reserve a weekend afternoon for family fun time. But families are not just families on weekends. Helping your family members live through life's daily and unexpected little crises requires you to be available when needed. This is an issue of quantity, not just quality.

Ultimately, making a decision to spend more time with your family does require you to examine your values and answer some tough questions. Imagine yourself in your senior years sitting on a rocking chair and reflecting on your life. Which will you regret more, not taking on another case or not spending enough time with loved ones? If the latter choice is your answer, why are you not acting accordingly?

REASON AND PASSION

As a group, lawyers tend to be characterized by their expertise at solving legal problems on the basis of reasoned logical analysis. Unfortunately, they are not quite as good at solving personal emotional difficulties. In fact, lawyers' inclination to emphasize reason makes them less likely to understand passion. Consequently, many lawyers tend to be somewhat unaware of their own and others' emotions and the role these play in stimulating thinking and behavior.

This is less of a problem for female attorneys because, as a group, women are more in touch with their emotions than men are, and female lawyers are more emotionally aware than male attorneys.[233] Compared to other women in our country, however, female attorneys still tend to overemphasize reasoned logic and suffer some of the same consequences as their male colleagues.[234]

Obviously, dispassionate logic alone is not the best foundation on which to build a marriage and a family. Spouses and children require a great deal of unfettered love. The degree to which affection exists and is freely expressed at home is a good predictor of successful marriages. In addition to loosening up their expressions of love, many lawyers could benefit from learning better ways of handling negative emotions when they arise either within themselves or their family members. A good place to start is to become adept at the emotional intelligence skills discussed in this book.

CYNICISM, PARANOIA AND PERFECTIONISM

Lawyers are exposed to a great deal of cynicism about human nature and often develop some paranoia as a necessary survival skill. While is not uncommon or surprising that many lawyers bring this cynicism and paranoia home with them, nothing could be more harmful to a relationship. Among the several signs of a troubled marriage is the prevalence of distrust and disrespect. Lawyers and their spouses must be constantly on guard to prevent negative emotions generated by events at the office from bleeding into the marital relationship.

Because legal mistakes can be costly, lawyers pay great attention to detail. This raises performance anxiety and encourages perfectionistic thinking. Perfectionists tend to like being in control and have trouble being spontaneous. They also tend to be critical and demanding. Not only are these traits harmful to relationships at work, but they are also exceedingly unhealthy for family relationships. When a spouse or the children feel as though they are constantly criticized and that nothing they do is good enough, this is another sign that family relationships are in trouble. It behooves lawyers to leave their perfectionism at the courtroom steps.

LEGAL ARGUMENTS VS. FAMILY DISCUSSIONS

Another hazard of being a lawyer is the tendency to speak with family members as if they are people at the office. Your spouse or child should never hear phrases like, "Tell me that fact pattern again." This type of language makes your loved ones feel as though they are nothing more to you than witnesses, clients, or professional colleagues.

Do not use professional debate tactics with family members. Children and spouses of lawyers often report that they find it impossible to win an argument with their "in-house counsel." At the end of these lost arguments, the lawyer's family members may feel hurt and hopeless about resolving future arguments. Such outcomes chip away at their love for the lawyer and diminish their desire to communicate with him or her. Neither result is healthy for the relationship.

What is a lawyer to do? In many instances, fighting fairly with your loved ones means doing just the opposite of what you might do as a litigator. Whenever possible and warranted, accept responsibility – do not deflect it. Most family arguments are at least two-sided. Feel free to represent both sides. Be a zealous advocate of your relationship, not just yourself.

To foster trust within a relationship, think of the truth as the whole truth and nothing but the truth. Don't craft a series of half-truths that are favorable to your argument. It will result in the charge of perjury every time. In addition, you do not have to win every argument. In fact, purposefully losing a few will help you become a winning spouse and parent.

BOTTOM LINE

Excelling in the practice of law and in family life is challenging. The personality traits and behaviors that make you a good lawyer may interfere with your ability to be a good spouse and parent, and vice-versa. Nevertheless, many lawyers do manage to succeed both at work and at home.

Their success starts with a deep desire to make it all work and a strong commitment to themselves, their work, and their families. In addition, they realize that meaningful and positive relationships at home bolster their ability to withstand the many stresses encountered in their legal careers. These lawyers find that their family life does not interfere with their work. On the contrary, it helps them succeed at work.

If you would like to delve more deeply into how to improve your family life, I recommend that you start by reading a book by Fiona H. Travis, entitled *Should You Marry A Lawyer?*[235]

CAREER DECISIONS

When individual lawyers seek the help of a counselor with their career decisions, it is not unusual for the conversation to start with: "I have been thinking about quitting my job or law altogether and need some help making up my mind." My usual response is "slow down." I say this because by the time most lawyers seek professional help about their careers, they are often so burned out that they are ready to make radical changes. Because they are driven by desperation rather than inspiration, their thinking often lacks clarity. While quitting their jobs or the law may in fact be the right thing to do, given the risks and costs involved, these should be options to consider only after they have taken the time to fully understand their situation.

People who are burned out often exhibit the symptoms of at least a mild form of depression, such as emotional exhaustion, feelings of inadequacy, and a sense of hopelessness. Before helping my clients make important career changes, I first want to make sure that I understand exactly what is causing these symptoms.

While it is uncommon, I consider the possibility that there is a physical illness behind their burnout symptoms. The list of possible physical causes is too long and complex to discuss fully here, but examples include the following: side effects of blood pressure medicines, brain tumors, lyme disease, etc. Not being an expert on these matters, one of my first questions is: "When was the last time you had a complete physical?"

A common response to such a question is "been there, done that." That is, lawyers do not tend to start with a mental health professional and then go to a physician; the sequence is usually the reverse. Many lawyers who seek counseling have already been to their physicians, gotten a physical, been diagnosed with either depression or anxiety, and are on a psychotropic drug. It is only when the drugs do not work that many succumb to the possibility that psychological counseling may help.

Once I eliminate the possibility of a physical explanation for the symptoms of burnout, I explore the psychological ones. Although not all burnout symptoms that lawyers experience can be blamed on their line of work, the fact that they experience them at high rates suggests that the environmental stressors discussed earlier in this book may have at least a contributory effect. If this is a possibility in your case, first you should consider improving your current work environment. For example, if you are constantly being put under the stress of unreasonable deadlines, go to the person(s) involved and attempt to change the timelines. Or, if you do not have enough support in the office, ask for additional support.

One would think that such advice is obvious, but I find that too many lawyers do not even try these simple steps because they suffer from the illusion that it is a sign of weakness to do so. Their thought is that a "real lawyer can handle anything and that if I can't take what is handed to me, I must not be good enough for this job." This type of logic is usually misguided.

As outlined previously, there are also several personality traits common to lawyers that can cause burnout. The most significant one is perfectionism. For perfectionists, being just plain human is equivalent to being an incompetent failure. Obviously, this belief system is a recipe for tremendous self-imposed pressure and unhappiness. Since you take yourself wherever you go, getting another job does not necessarily solve this problem. Thus, working on your maladaptive personality traits is another intervention you should try before making important career moves.

As also discussed earlier in this book, another reason that some lawyers experience burnout is that their core values are not aligned with their work life. Some misalignments are caused by internally-conflicted personal values (e.g., high ambition vs. family). Other misalignments are created by the fact that there is a conflict between a lawyer's values and those of the people with whom he or she works (e.g., financial success at any cost vs. ethical behavior).

If your value misalignments are internal, they must be resolved internally. Again, leaving your job or the law will usually not resolve such conflicts. If, on the other hand, your values conflict with those of your colleagues, then you are "a fish out of water," and a separation may be in order. Make sure that your values are aligned with those of any new organization that you join, however. Too many lawyers who leave one job for another make the same mistake over and over again, by working for organizations in which they do not belong (e.g., law firms that value billable hours above all else).

In summary, before you make a career change you should deeply examine why you are unhappy in your current position and then consider all of the alternatives. Your first impulse may be to run from your job, but taking the time to truly evaluate your predicament and explore a variety of options is certainly a more sensible approach. You may still decide to leave your job or the law altogether, but at least it will be for valid reasons and with more clarity about what you want to do instead.

As you critically consider your career options, you may want to seek the help of a professional. I ask my clients to complete several questionnaires that assess their values, personality traits, interests, and skills. When all of the measures I take converge to point in one direction, what they suggest is usually highly valid and helpful. Sometimes lawyers need to simply take the steps discussed above (e.g., make internal personal changes or improve the current environment in which they work). For others, the changes may include switching specialty areas, leaving for another law firm that is more aligned with their values, practicing law in a different context (e.g., government or corporation), or finding another line of work that uses their professional skills (e.g., real estate development).

In addition to or instead of consulting an expert for help with your career choices, you may want to read one or more of the career books that are written specifically for lawyers. Here is a sample list:

> Deborah Arron, *What Can You Do With A Law Degree: A Lawyer's Guide To Career Alternatives Inside, Outside & Around The Law* (5th ed., 2003).

> Deborah Arron, *Running From The Law: Why Good Lawyers Are Getting Out Of The Legal Profession* (3rd ed., 2003).

> Hindi Greenberg, *The Lawyer's Career Change Handbook: More Than 300 Things You Can Do With A Law Degree* (1998).

> Gary A. Munneke & William D. Henslee, *Nonlegal Careers For Lawyers* (4th ed., 2003).

> Gary A. Munneke, *Careers In Law* (3rd ed., 2003).

> Deborah Schneider & Gary Belsky, *Should You Really Be A Lawyer? A Guide To Smart Career Choices Before, During & After Law School* (2005).

> Heidi McNeil Staudenmaier (ed.), *Changing Jobs: A Handbook For Lawyers In The New Millennium (*3rd ed., 1999*).*

SECTION IX: ADVICE FOR IMPAIRED LAWYERS

Although the world is full of suffering, it's also full of the overcoming of it.

Helen Keller

It is with disease of the mind, as with those of the body; we are half dead before we understand our disorder, and half cured when we do.

Charles Caleb Colton

CONFRONT YOUR MENTAL HEALTH DISORDERS

"The mass of [people] lead lives of quiet desperation."
Henry David Thoreau

As detailed elsewhere in this book, the data on mentally impaired lawyers are very alarming. They indicate that lawyers are at a significantly higher risk for developing depression or problem drinking than the general population. Obviously, these ailments damage lawyers and their families. In addition, they diminish lawyers' ability to serve clients and often lead to violations of professional practice standards and malpractice.

Unfortunately, the stigmas associated with mental illnesses and substance abuse disorders make these ailments difficult to confront. As a result, many lawyers deny that they have a mental health problem and just try to endure it. Unfortunately, denial does not make things go away. It often makes things get much worse and exacts a heavy price - emotionally, professionally, and financially.

This section is intended to introduce the reader to some of the issues that mentally impaired attorneys commonly face and make suggestions for how they can get professional help. The introductory information presented here is meant only for general educational purposes and is not intended to take the place of professional help. Thus, if you even suspect that you have a mental health disorder of any type, do not rely on this or any other book - consult a health professional.

Like most other groups, lawyers experience a wide range of mental health disorders. While it is beyond our scope to even introduce most of them, depression and alcohol abuse are singled out for discussion as they are the most common mental health problems that lawyers experience. Note that two of the chapters in this section have been authored by my colleague, Douglas B. Marlowe, who is both a lawyer and a psychologist, and a highly respected researcher on the topic of substance abuse and public policy.

LEGAL QUESTIONS FACING IMPAIRED LAWYERS

**by Douglas B. Marlowe, Ph.D., J.D.,
and Amiram Elwork, Ph.D.**

Lawyers with psychological problems are often hesitant to get help partly because they worry about such issues as confidentiality, liability and job security. To some extent, the types of concerns they have depend on whether their treatment is purely voluntary or is mandated by disciplinary authorities. Not surprisingly, greater protections exist for individuals who are in the former category. For this reason it is always advisable to seek help proactively, before an impairment has had a significant effect on one's professional functioning.

This chapter addresses the most common legal questions facing lawyers in either elective or mandated treatment. A final section deals with what colleagues and employers of impaired attorneys are obligated to do. This is only an introductory outline of the issues. Lawyers with serious concerns regarding any issues covered here will require a more thorough review of the law in their jurisdictions. Local Lawyer Assistance Programs (LAPs) or the American Bar Association's Commission on Lawyer Assistance Programs are good resources for this type of information.

THE ELECTIVE TREATMENT CONTEXT

Is Treatment Confidential?

Voluntary substance abuse and mental health treatments receive strict privilege and confidentiality protections. These protections are derived from professional ethical standards, state licensing laws for mental health professionals, testimonial privileges that attach in many states to communications with licensed mental health professionals, and the "privacy rule" within a federal law entitled *Health Insurance Portability and Accountability Act of 1996* (HIPPA).[236] The United States Supreme Court has held that a psychotherapist-patient privilege also exists under federal common law and that it applies at least to communications with licensed clinicians.[237]

Federal and state laws also provide broad content-based protections for substance abuse and mental health records held in regulated treatment facilities, regardless of the professional identity of the service provider. Without the written informed consent of the client, substance abuse and mental health treatment information may be disclosed only to other treatment providers in an emergency, third party payers or financial auditors, judicial officials in the course of civil commitment and similar types of legal proceedings, or pursuant to a court order on a showing of good cause. There are also provisions for non-consensual disclosure of such information to proper authorities when patients are a danger to themselves or others, or when it is necessary to report child abuse or neglect.

Court sanctioned Lawyer Assistance Programs (LAP) are now available in most jurisdictions to help provide impaired lawyers with peer support and professional intervention. Generally, communications between an impaired lawyer and LAP staff or volunteers are strictly confidential, either by virtue of laws that protect all substance abuse or mental health treatment information, or through separate statutes or court rules that apply specifically to LAPs in a given jurisdiction. For more information on your local LAP, access the website for the ABA's Commission on Lawyer Assistance Programs, which at this writing is at: www.abanet.org/legalservices/colap/.

Informed consent forms for the release of substance abuse or mental health information should clearly specify who is permitted to release and to receive the information, the purpose of the disclosure, and how much and what kind of information may be disclosed. They should indicate that consent is revocable at-will, and specify a date, event, or condition upon which consent automatically expires. Consensual disclosure to one party does not imply that disclosure is permitted to other parties, nor does it reduce the confidential nature of the information. When governed by federal laws, substance abuse treatment information cannot be used to initiate a criminal investigation or to substantiate criminal charges against a patient.

Must I Acknowledge My Impairment On A Bar Application?

Rule 8.1 of the ABA's Model Rules of Professional Conduct[238] requires Bar applicants to respond truthfully and completely on admissions materials. This duty may be difficult to honor on questions relating to mental illness and substance abuse, but that is the expectation. Admissions Boards do have a right and a duty to inquire about impairments that might affect an applicant's fitness to practice law. If a pattern of impairment emerges in the application that raises questions about fitness, the Admissions Board is required to inquire further about possible substance abuse or mental illness, and to make necessary referrals for further assessment.[239]

As a way of striking a balance between the public's right to be protected from unfit lawyers and applicants' rights to be protected from discrimination or to feel safe getting mental health treatment, Bar application questions are generally narrowly tailored to focus on an applicant's *current* fitness to practice law. Several courts[240] have found that narrowly tailored questions on Bar applications conform with the protections accorded to mentally impaired individuals under the *Americans with Disabilities Act* (ADA).[241]

Given My Impairment, Can I Be Admitted To The Bar, Get A Job And Be Supported In Overcoming My Limitations?

The *Americans with Disabilities Act* (ADA)[242] provides broad anti-discrimination protections for individuals with disabilities. The term "disability" encompasses any physical or mental impairment that substantially limits one or more major life activity. It extends protections contained in Section 504 of the *Rehabilitation Act of 1973*[243] to public employers, private employers of 15 or more people, and professional regulatory boards. The Board of Bar Examiners is a public entity within the meaning of the ADA,[244] and in most states protections therefore apply to Bar admissions determinations.

Disabled lawyers are entitled to "reasonable accommodations" that assist them in meeting employment demands. Employers are excused from making accommodations that impose an "undue hardship," requiring excessive effort and expense in light of the financial and other resources of the employer. Accommodation is also not required if the employee poses a significant risk to the health and safety of other individuals. Although employers do not have an obligation to eliminate stresses that are inherent in the job, accommodations may include part-time or modified work schedules to reduce job-related stress or facilitate attendance in treatment.[245] Note that accommodation is not required if it is not requested.

Current users of illegal drugs are exempted from ADA protections.[246] Discrimination is prohibited, however, if the individual has completed or is enrolled in a drug abuse rehabilitation program, and there is significant evidence to show that he or she has achieved abstinence. To verify abstinence, employers may institute drug-testing programs for identified substance abusers. There is no protection for relapse during the course of rehabilitation, even if the relapse is of short duration and does not affect job performance. Protections are unavailable if a lapse occurred recently enough to justify a reasonable belief that drug use may be intermittent or on-going.[247]

The Equal Employment Opportunity Commission (EEOC) has opined that the stresses associated with family and employment problems are not covered by the ADA unless they are of sufficient severity to meet diagnostic criteria for a recognized mental disorder.[248] Thus, to avail oneself of the protections accorded by the ADA, proper diagnosis and treatment by a mental health professional is often required.

If I Am Mentally Impaired, What Are My Responsibilities To Clients?

Rule 1.16(a)(2) of the ABA's Model Rules of Professional Conduct[249] states that when a "lawyer's physical or mental condition materially impairs the lawyer's ability to represent the client," he or she should either refrain from accepting a new case, withdraw from a preexisting case or seek the assistance of a co-counsel. This is also an established principle in both state rules of professional conduct and several state supreme court decisions. Failure to act in accordance to this principle provides a cause for suspension, loss of license, and malpractice.

RIGHTS AND RESPONSIBILITIES IN THE DISCIPLINARY CONTEXT

If impairment has already contributed to professional misconduct or unfitness, the status of being mentally ill or substance dependent does not shield the attorney from the consequences of his or her actions. It may, however, trigger a set of procedural safeguards and dispositional options that permit the attorney to receive appropriate treatment and resume the competent practice of law once he or she recovers from the impairment.

Are Impairments Disclosed At Disciplinary Proceedings Confidential?

In a number of states, complaints submitted to a lawyer disciplinary board can become a matter of public record at an early stage of the process, soon after the initial investigations are completed. Once it is determined that there has been a violation of a professional standard, the state's highest court may order a public censure or public reprimand of an attorney, or may post a public notice that the attorney has been placed on inactive status. In particular, disciplinary matters that are predicated upon an attorney's conviction of a crime are generally not confidential. Similarly, if an attorney is declared to be incapacitated from practicing law due to mental illness, infirmity, or addiction to drugs or alcohol, the state disciplinary board is normally required to post a public notice of the attorney's transfer to inactive status. A notice of public discipline or transfer to inactive status is also transmitted to the ABA National Discipline Data Bank.

If My Infractions Are Caused By Mental Impairments, Will I Retain My License?

Most jurisdictions offer some variant of probation or short-term suspension for attorneys who are convicted of relatively minor infractions of professional rules of conduct. This requires a showing that the continued practice of law by the respondent is unlikely to harm the public or to cause the courts or legal profession to fall into disrepute. In most jurisdictions, evidence of substance abuse or mental illness is considered a mitigating factor, and counseling for such problems is an ordinary condition of probation or reinstatement.

For the mental impairment to be considered a mitigating factor in disciplinary actions, lawyers are generally required to demonstrate a causal link between it and the professional misconduct. Some jurisdictions require a demonstration that "but for" such impairment, the misconduct would not have occurred. The impairment does not have to be the sole cause of the misconduct, but it must be a substantial factor. Other jurisdictions only require showing that the impairment be "a factor" in causing the misconduct. The opportunity to reinstate a license is offered in most jurisdictions if there is evidence of a sustained recovery from the impairment, and the recovery has arrested the misconduct.

Is Treatment And Related Types Of Information Shared With Disciplinary Authorities?

A common condition of probation requires the impaired attorney to execute any written authorization that is necessary for the Disciplinary Board to verify compliance with treatment. For example, substance abuse probationers are typically required to abstain from all classes of mood-altering or mind-altering chemicals, to regularly attend Alcoholics Anonymous (AA) or another designated treatment program, to undergo any treatment procedure prescribed or recommended by a physician or addiction counselor, and to authorize verification of attendance and compliance with treatment. Similarly, lawyers who are diagnosed as mentally ill may be required to take psychotropic drugs as prescribed by a psychiatrist, attend psychotherapy sessions, and submit periodic progress reports to the Disciplinary Board. The permissible scope of disclosure is generally limited to a brief description of the treatment program as well as a brief statement regarding the client's attendance, prognosis, and progress in treatment.

A "practice monitor" or "financial monitor" may be appointed to temporarily oversee an attorney's practice, to secure client funds, or to control financial decisions. In most states, a "sobriety monitor" may also be appointed for attorneys placed on substance abuse probation.

When an attorney's impairment leads to criminal liability, the release of treatment information may also be a condition of criminal probation. For example, an addicted lawyer might be charged with possession of a controlled substance. Federal regulations permit substance abuse information to be disclosed to criminal justice authorities who have made participation in a treatment program a condition of probation, parole, or a similar disposition.[250] Disclosure must be limited to those individuals having a specific need for the information in connection with their duty to monitor the client's progress, and must be limited in scope to that which is necessary to permit adequate monitoring. As noted earlier, this information may not be used to substantiate or initiate criminal charges against the client. It may only be used to verify compliance with probationary conditions. Unfortunately, state laws are often silent with regard to disclosure of mental health information in criminal justice contexts.

DEALING WITH IMPAIRED COLLEAGUES

ABA Ethics Committee Formal Opinions 03-429[251] and 03-431[252] outline the duties of lawyers who have knowledge of a colleague, either inside or outside their own firm, who is mentally impaired. In a nutshell, lawyers must take reasonable steps to make sure that the impairment of a colleague does not cause a breach of the ABA Model Rules of Professional Conduct. Regardless of one's feelings of empathy and loyalty toward an impaired colleague, a lawyer's overarching obligation is to take affirmative steps to protect the rights of clients and the integrity of their own profession.

If the intervention occurs before any breach has occurred, the first appropriate step may be to simply confront the impaired attorney about the mental impairment and the noticeable signs of incompetent behaviors. The second step is to help the impaired attorney get professional help and take reasonable steps to protect his or her own clients. A local LAP is usually an excellent source for confidentially protected help and advice regarding such interventions.

If it is determined that a mental impairment of a colleague has resulted in a violation of any rules of professional conduct, and depending on the specific circumstances, a report to a professional authority may be required. The partners of an impaired attorney who has violated clients' rights may be required to disclose such breaches to the affected clients as well. A resignation or dismissal of a lawyer from a firm does not eliminate the partners' reporting obligations.

As discussed earlier, The *Americans with Disabilities Act* (ADA)[253] requires all public employers and all private employers of 15 or more people to make "reasonable accommodations" that assist the mentally impaired in meeting employment demands. However, employers do not have to make accommodations that impose an "undue hardship" on their resources. In addition, accommodation is not required in cases where an impaired employee poses a significant risk to the health and safety of other individuals. Employers are not required to eliminate stresses that are an integral part of the job, but under some circumstances they may be required to offer part-time or modified work schedules as a way of reducing job-related stress or facilitating attendance in treatment.[254] No accommodation is required unless it is requested.

ALCOHOLISM: SYMPTOMS, CAUSES & TREATMENTS

by Douglas B. Marlowe, Ph.D., J.D.

Alcoholism exacts an exorbitant toll on lawyers, the legal system, and consumers of legal services. In a 1990 study[255] conducted by the North Carolina Bar Association, a staggering 17% of the 2,600 attorneys surveyed admitted to drinking 3-5 alcoholic beverages per day. In the state of Washington, another study[256] found that 18% of the 801 lawyers surveyed were problem drinkers. It is estimated that the number of lawyers in the United States actively abusing alcohol and drugs is twice that of the general population.[257] Approximately 40% to 70% of attorney disciplinary proceedings and malpractice actions are linked to alcohol abuse or a mental illness.[258]

Yet despite this high incidence, lawyers suffering from alcoholism often feel painfully alone. Fearing discovery or retribution, they are reticent to ask questions or attempt to learn more about their problem. Very often, they fail to seek help before the problem has escalated to serious proportions. The purpose of this chapter is to introduce the impaired lawyer to the symptoms and causes of alcohol dependence and the large menu of treatment options that now exist. This information also should be of help to colleagues, friends and family members of alcohol-dependent attorneys.

THE SYMPTOMS

Denial is a common feature of alcoholism.[259] There are widely differing opinions about whether denial is an unconscious psychological defense mechanism, a misguided effort to conceal the shame of addiction, or simply an understandable reaction to accusations or punitive actions by other people. Regardless, it is clear that those who are addicted to alcohol are often the last ones to recognize or acknowledge the existence of a problem. As an unfortunate result, they may not seek help until they are faced with serious medical, legal, financial, or social repercussions.

The official diagnostic criteria for alcoholism or alcohol dependence focus on the compulsive use of alcohol despite the significant negative consequences of that use.[260] Some alcoholics will exhibit symptoms of physical dependence, including a need for significantly increasing amounts of alcohol to achieve the desired effect (tolerance), or withdrawal symptoms (e.g., nausea, tremor, insomnia, rapid heart beat, sweating) when levels of alcohol in the blood decline.

For a large proportion of alcoholics, however, dependence is manifested only by a behavioral or psychological compulsion to use alcohol, without any noticeable accompanying physical symptoms. This may include recurrent episodes of binge drinking, unsuccessful efforts to quit or to reduce the use of alcohol, persistent concerns about one's alcohol use, excessive involvement in alcohol-related activities, reduced involvement in productive social and occupational activities, or the continued use of alcohol despite significant physical or psychological ill effects.

In addition to alcohol *dependence*, there is also a diagnostic category known as alcohol *abuse*. Alcohol abusers may not experience a physical or psychological compulsion to use alcohol, but they do engage in a maladaptive pattern of alcohol use under dangerous or inappropriate circumstances. For example, repeated alcohol use may result in a failure to fulfill major role obligations such as going to work or taking care of children. Alcohol abuse may also lead to recurrent interpersonal conflicts with family members or significant others, legal problems, physical injury or medical illness. Under such circumstances, it is not productive to debate whether the person is truly addicted. Regardless, he or she may be in serious need of assistance before irreparable damage is done. Moreover, although not everyone who abuses alcohol will go on to becoming dependent on it, needless to say, the risk becomes unacceptably greater with increasing usage.

A number of mnemonic devices have been developed by addiction professionals to rapidly assess whether someone may have a serious alcohol problem. The most commonly used interview technique is called the CAGE:[261] (1) "Has anyone ever recommended that you **C**ut back or stop drinking?" (2) "Have you ever felt **A**nnoyed or **A**ngry when someone commented on your drinking?" (3) "Have there been times when you've felt **G**uilty about or regretted things that occurred because of your drinking?" (4) "Have you ever used alcohol as an **E**ye-opener to help you get started in the morning or to steady your nerves?" A positive answer to three of these four questions is generally believed to be strongly suggestive of alcohol dependence. However, *any* positive answer is considered cause for further inquiry.

In addition to focusing on these direct symptoms of alcoholism, it is often very instructive and productive to focus on the loss of functions or competencies that typically accompany addiction.[262] Efforts to confront an alcoholic with positive evidence of his or her addiction (e.g., black-outs, binges, or the smell of liquor on the breath) typically invoke excuses, manipulations, or angry counter-attacks. It is much harder, however, to deny the existence of a problem when one's accomplishments have fallen far short of one's goals and abilities. More importantly, rather than increasing defensiveness and resistance to change, focusing on missed opportunities and lost goals tends to have the positive effect of mobilizing one's intrinsic motivation to make positive changes.

THEORIES OF CAUSATION

Theories about the causes and treatment of alcoholism are generally more reflective of personal philosophies and belief systems than of scientific or clinical evidence. Historically, the Moral Model of Addiction viewed alcoholism as a sign of a weak character or moral turpitude. As such, treatment, if any, was designed to confront the alcoholic with the consequences of his or her behaviors and force or shame him or her into making improvements.

The Disease Model of Addiction views alcoholism as mainly a medical illness. This model, which came to prominence in the middle part of the 20th century, found some support from recent discoveries about the genetic, biochemical, and neurological aspects of addiction. Treatments based upon the Disease Model sometimes emphasize the individual's relative powerlessness over the illness. This philosophy has attracted a great deal of support from the self-help movement because of its de-emphasis on issues of blame and morality.

Most recently, a Habit or Behavioral Model of Addiction has been proposed, particularly in the fields of psychology and education. This model views addiction as a learned behavior in part, resulting from faulty problem solving, ineffective role modeling, or a complicated system of rewards and punishments which sustains the alcohol usage.[263] Rather than viewing the individual as powerless in the face of a disease process, the Behavioral Model seeks to increase the individual's sense of efficacy and potential control over the problem. A distinction is made between moral blameworthiness regarding the past and behavioral accountability in the future. People may not choose to be addicted, but it is assumed that they have ultimate control over changing their behavioral patterns.

Philosophies aside, no one really knows for certain what causes alcoholism, and it is highly unlikely that any single causal agent will ever be identified. Alcoholism appears to be a result of many different processes. For any particular individual, it may stem from a genetic predisposition, an environmental stress or trauma, learning history, or a complex combination of any of these.

It is useful to think about alcoholism in light of the Diathesis-Stress Model of Illness.[264] Some individuals have a strong genetic loading (diathesis) for a particular disease, which may be activated with minimal environmental influence. For example, some people are genetically predisposed to develop cancer, which may manifest itself almost irrespective of diet, exercise, or other habits. Other individuals, in contrast, are genetically heartier and do not develop the disease unless they are exposed to potent environmental carcinogens. In a similar vein, individuals vary in their genetic vulnerability to alcoholism. Some people can apparently drink steadily without becoming dependent or socially maladapted. Others are less fortunate.

Given the current state of medical science, it is difficult to know with certainty who is or is not vulnerable to developing alcoholism. However, a look at your family tree may shed light on your own risk liability. Rates of alcoholism are significantly higher within some families than in the general population.[265] It is uncertain whether this is due to an inherited familial vulnerability to alcoholism, or to role modeling or social learning. Children of alcoholics may simply be exposed to alcohol at a younger age, or they may be negatively affected by concomitant family dysfunction.[266] Most likely, a positive family history reflects both learned and genetic factors, in which biological and environmental forces combine to increase one's risk exponentially.

Compared to the general population, alcoholics suffer from significantly higher rates of psychiatric disorders such as depression and anxiety. This has led to some speculation that alcoholics might be self-medicating their uncomfortable emotional state.[267] In fact, part of the chemical effect of alcohol is to dull the emotions. It is difficult, however, to disentangle cause and effect because of alcohol's depressant influence on the central nervous system.[268] Chronic alcohol use may bring about long-term brain changes, leading to the development of depressive or anxious states. It is also possible that some individuals have a generalized vulnerability to stress which, depending on the specific circumstances, may manifest itself as alcoholism, depression, anxiety, or some combination of these and other emotional disturbances.

Regardless of the actual cause and effect between psychiatric illness and alcoholism, it seems clear that these disorders can reciprocally exacerbate each other. A resumption of psychiatric symptoms has been shown to lead to a greater risk of relapse and more alcohol use among alcohol abusers. Conversely, more alcohol use has been shown to lead to an exacerbation of psychiatric symptoms.[269] For this reason, it is very important for treatment to include a two-pronged approach for clients with both substance use and psychiatric problems. It is no longer acceptable to treat the two disorders independently.

TREATMENT OPTIONS

Regardless of the counseling option one chooses, it is always highly advisable to first undergo a thorough evaluation by a physician. A number of complicating medical conditions often accompany chronic alcohol abuse which, paradoxically, may be exacerbated by withdrawal from or sudden reduction in alcohol use.[270] In addition, a physician can address other related difficulties such as vitamin deficiencies that may contribute to a more difficult recovery.

For clients who are experiencing physical dependence on alcohol (tolerance and withdrawal), the initial stage of treatment often involves some degree of detoxification from alcohol. Recent research suggests that detoxification can often be accomplished on an outpatient basis. However, patients who have a history of alcohol-related seizures or delirium tremens (DTs), and those who arrive for their initial detoxification session intoxicated, may still require detoxification in a medically managed hospital-based setting.[271]

For clients who experience significant symptoms of anxiety and withdrawal during detoxification, treatment often includes the use of benzodiazepines (or comparable medication if there are heart or liver problems), vitamin therapy, and, in some instances, measures to correct electrolyte imbalances resulting from dehydration or poor nutrition. Benzodiazepines are generally effective for anxiety, but they present a substantially lesser risk than barbiturates (an older class of anti-anxiety medications) for developing tolerance or dependence and for having dangerous interactions with alcohol. Although many practitioners may be hesitant to risk substituting one drug for another, research has shown that physically dependent patients treated without medication have more severe withdrawal symptoms over time, and they also may have greater incidences of seizures and cognitive problems. As a result, they have a substantially greater risk of relapse.

Unfortunately, many individuals with alcohol problems have a history of going through multiple short-term detoxifications, without receiving follow-up care. A 1998 report by the Institute of Medicine of the National Academy of Sciences[272] has now confirmed what clinicians have known for years: *detoxification is not enough.* Alcoholism is a chronic, recurring disorder, just like diabetes, heart disease, or hypertension.[273] As such, it typically requires relatively long-term maintenance care, up to a year or more.

Importantly, there appears to be a direct relationship between how long one remains in addiction treatment and how well one does in the future.[274] Longer treatment generally leads to better outcomes. In fact, a national study of drug abuse treatment in the United States found that there may be a minimum threshold of at least three months for effective outpatient substance abuse treatment.[275] Prior to three months, outcomes may not be appreciably better than having no treatment. After three months, however, outcomes may get steadily better with longer tenure in treatment. Although this national study focused mostly on drug abuse, the same principles appear to apply to alcohol treatment as well.

A dizzying array of different treatment options are available for alcohol dependence. Many practitioners tout their particular program as being most effective for most clients under most circumstances. Unfortunately, these superlatives tend to confuse consumers and cause needless dissension within the addictions field. The consumer of addiction services should attempt to find the best match for his or her needs and comfort level. Just like shopping for a suit, not all styles are an appropriate fit. If you are uncomfortable with or disillusioned by one treatment choice, do some additional research and consider other options. Several books are available which provide fairly balanced appraisals of different treatment options, including synopses of empirical evidence (if any) supporting the efficacy of these programs.[276]

Treatment programs differ along many dimensions, including: their causal and treatment philosophies; whether they are conducted in an inpatient, outpatient or residential setting; whether they are administered by licensed professionals or by peers who are themselves in recovery; and whether they are performed in an individual, group, or family therapy format.

Traditionally, alcoholism was treated in an inpatient or residential setting. The first week or so was generally dedicated to detoxification, followed by a structured routine of group and recreational therapies. The emphasis was generally placed on preventing the individual's contact with alcohol or alcohol-related stimuli, and generating curative interactions with fellow peers in recovery through a process known as milieu therapy.

Although this may be an effective mode of intervention for some clients in the short term (ranging from 28 days to up to 6 months), it may not adequately prepare an individual for returning to life in the real world, with all of its associated stressors and triggers for relapse. Being away from the familiarity of family, friends, and job may itself cause additional stress and feelings of loneliness. Social and occupational demands continue to pile up during this absence, and family tensions may be intensified. These and other considerations such as economic pressures from third party payers, have led to a greater reliance on outpatient treatment for those individuals who do not have severe medical or psychiatric complications accompanying their alcohol use.[277] In fact, a few studies have found no differences in outcomes for clients with moderate degrees of alcoholism who were treated in either a residential or outpatient setting.[278]

Outpatient treatment enables the individual to practice strategies and skills learned in therapy in the real world and to bring new material and actual experiences into the therapy sessions.[279] For individuals with more severe addictions, this may be accomplished in a day or partial hospital program, in which therapeutic services are provided for several hours during the day or evening, after which the individual returns home for the night.

In either a residential or outpatient setting, medication may be prescribed as one part of the treatment regimen.[280] There are now four broad classes of medications that are approved in the United States for the treatment of alcohol dependence. The oldest medication, called Disulfiram (Antabuse), produces unpleasant physical effects, including headache, nausea, and anxiety, when combined with alcohol. To ensure compliance with this aversive regimen, it is sometimes necessary to have a family member or significant other of the individual monitor daily ingestion.

Another medication called Naltrexone acts as an opioid antagonist. Many of alcohol's pleasant effects are caused by triggering the release of natural chemicals in our brains called endorphins that invoke feelings of euphoria and sedation. Naltrexone acts to partially block this process, thus preventing alcohol from fully achieving its desired effect. Several rigorous research studies have confirmed Naltrexone's ability to reduce rates of relapse and overall amounts of drinking.[281]

A third class of medication that is showing some promise for alcohol treatment is called serotonergic agents. These medications generally increase levels of a chemical in the brain called serotonin, which in turn reduces feelings of depression, impulsivity, and anxiety. It is possible that these medications work most effectively for alcohol-dependent clients who are also suffering from depression or anxiety.

A fourth medication called Acamprosate or Campril, is believed to correct an imbalance between glutamate and GABA, the brain's primary excitatory and inhibitory neurotransmitters. Theoretically, regulation of the GABA-glutamate system as well as other neurotransmitters could lead to better modulation of one's emotions, and thus could reduce self-medication via alcohol. Unfortunately, a large-scale study published in 2006 compared the effects of several medications for alcoholism and found that acamprosate performed no better than placebo.[282] The best outcomes were achieved from naltrexone.

Some patients and treatment providers are very resistant to pharmacological treatment for alcoholism because they fear that it merely replaces one drug with another. It is important to recognize, however, that these medications do *not* have the same intoxicating or addictive effects as alcohol or other addictive drugs. Particularly in cases involving physical dependence, or those with severe psychosocial or medical complications, adjunctive pharmacotherapy may be very helpful, at least in the short run. It is therefore advisable to seek consultation with a physician during the course of addiction treatment.

At the same time, however, it is very important to recognize that pharmacological treatment alone is rarely sufficient. For instance, the positive effects of Naltrexone have been shown to be greatly increased and extended over time by combining it with a particular form of counseling called cognitive-behavioral therapy.[283] Therefore, a multi-pronged approach using both medication and counseling may be the most beneficial route for many clients.

Historically, the content of addiction counseling focused on early life experiences and intrapsychic conflicts which were hypothesized to later result in addiction. However, empirical evidence has failed to identify common psychological conflicts or personality structures among alcoholics.[284] Therefore, more modern approaches focus to a greater extent on alcohol-specific cognitions rather than on unconscious psychological forces. For example, the goal may be to correct illogical or maladaptive thoughts related to alcohol (e.g., Whisky is my best friend.) or dysfunctional attitudes about oneself in relation to drinking (e.g., I'm a worthless person, so I might as well get drunk.).[285]

Behavioral strategies utilized in the treatment of alcoholism typically involve identifying triggers or risk factors for alcohol use and teaching the person to avoid them. Therapy sessions may be spent practicing alcohol-refusal strategies and planning ways to minimize exposure to alcohol or alcohol-related stimuli. Group or family interventions may be particularly well-suited for developing and practicing these strategies.[286] Significant others, for example, are frequently reliable reporters about alcohol-related triggers and events. Similarly, in a group setting, the individual may learn about common triggers and coping strategies that have been identified or employed by other people.

To the extent that counseling utilizes these types of approaches, it is most likely to be effective. Treatments such as cognitive-behavioral therapy (CBT), relapse prevention (RP), behavioral marital therapy, self-control training (for less serious alcohol problems), social skills training, and stress management training (for less serious alcohol problems) have been shown to be effective in at least two or more controlled scientific studies.[287] In contrast, approaches such as confrontational interventions, drug abuse resistance education (DARE), educational lectures and films, insight-oriented psychotherapy, supportive psychotherapy, and residential milieu therapy have been shown *not* to be effective. It also appears that acupuncture, while generally liked by clients and apparently helpful for reducing physical pain, has little effect in the treatment of alcoholism.

Another form of treatment called motivational interviewing or motivational enhancement therapy (MET) has been shown to be quite effective with resistant or unmotivated clients. This approach helps to build a desire for change by underscoring the negative effects of alcohol use on the client's life in a non-confrontational manner. It also helps the client gain confidence in his or her ability to change and assists in mobilizing internal and external resources toward the initiation of abstinence.

By far the most common intervention for alcoholism is a self-help, twelve-step group, such as Alcoholics Anonymous (AA). These programs generally focus on the goal of abstinence as opposed to reduced or controlled drinking.[288] Participants receive group support, repeated reminders about the consequences of alcohol use, and straightforward advice about methods for maintaining abstinence. AA is a spiritual (not necessarily religious) program that requires some belief in a power beyond oneself, and an acknowledgment of one's relative powerlessness over addiction in the absence of spiritual or communal support.

Although anecdotal testimonials to its efficacy abound, the scientific evidence for its superiority over other treatment approaches is largely lacking or contradictory.[289] Nevertheless, one of the most promising components of AA is the appointment of a sponsor for each participant, who is available to provide guidance and assistance 24 hours a day. Another advantage of AA is that, in many geographic regions, open group sessions are available without prior appointment most days or evenings of the week. Finally, AA uses a peer group approach to instill a number of psychologically healthy values, such as sincerity, forgiveness, tolerance, gratitude, humility, self-care, and affiliation.[290]

Studies indicate that continued involvement with AA following a course of professional treatment is associated with better outcomes over the long run.[291] It is possible that AA helps to maintain and consolidate the gains that were made during professional treatment. This may be a result of staying involved with a sober support network, or of continued practicing of alcohol-refusal or alcohol-avoidance strategies. Alternatively, it is possible that continued involvement with AA is simply a marker of a greater commitment to recovery on the part of some people. If so, then perhaps on-going involvement with various types of peer-based support networks could help to extend the effects of professionally-administered treatment.

Presently, there do not appear to be noteworthy differences in outcomes between professionally administered interventions that have been demonstrated to be effective. The National Institute on Alcohol Abuse and Alcoholism (NIAAA) conducted an eight-year national study called Project MATCH,[292] which was designed to compare cognitive-behavioral therapy (CBT), motivational enhancement therapy (MET) and 12-Step facilitation therapy. The latter treatment is an individualized, professionally-administered intervention designed to familiarize clients with the principles of AA and prepare them to enter AA following professional counseling. More importantly than simply comparing these three treatments, Project MATCH was designed to determine whether certain types of interventions might be better suited for certain types of clients.

The results of Project MATCH were both encouraging and disappointing. The good news was that all three treatments appeared to bring about significant improvements for clients. This suggests that treatment can work for many people. On the other hand, there was no evidence that one treatment was any more or less effective for particular types of clients presenting with different levels of motivation, different demographic characteristics, or different degrees of severity of alcoholism.

For now, the best advice we can give clients is to choose from among those interventions reviewed above, both pharmacological and behavioral, which have been shown to be effective. From within that list, trust your intuition, and pick the treatment that feels most comfortable and appropriate to you. If you become uncomfortable or disillusioned with a particular treatment after giving it a fair chance, then try another one until you are reasonably satisfied. Remember that, once you find a reasonable treatment for your needs, stick with it. Longer treatment often brings better gains, and a minimum of three to twelve months seems to be required.

Importantly, most successful programs share common core ingredients that appear to be essential for recovery. These include an opportunity to share feelings with others, be heard, be reinforced for abstinence, reduce resistance in an atmosphere of trust, reduce withdrawal symptoms and manage cravings, and realize that you are not alone with the problem of alcoholism. Regardless of the specific program you choose, you are highly likely to receive some symptom relief simply by taking a measurable first step.

DEPRESSION: SYMPTOMS, CAUSES & TREATMENTS

If you are a lawyer who is suffering from depression, you are not alone. Several studies in the early 1990s have demonstrated that lawyers have among the highest rates of depression in the nation. For example, the North Carolina Bar Association[293] surveyed close to 2,600 attorneys and found that about 37% of them admitted to being depressed, approximately 25% reported physical symptoms of depression (e.g., appetite loss, lethargy), and over 11% reported suicidal ideation at least 1-2 times per month in the past year. Another study in the state of Washington[294] surveyed 801 lawyers and found that 19% of them reported symptoms of clinical depression, a rate that was twice the national average for the general population. Finally, a Johns Hopkins University study[295] found that of 28 occupational groups across the country, lawyers were the most likely to suffer from depression and 3.6 times more likely than average.

THE SYMPTOMS

Depression is commonly felt across several experiential domains. The most characteristic emotional symptoms include sadness, fear, guilt and anger. Mentally, a depressed person is likely to express a sense of pessimism and hopelessness, low self-esteem and helplessness. In more severe cases, depression is also characterized by suicidal ideation.

These thoughts and emotions are often accompanied by some degree of cognitive impairment, such as a significant inability to concentrate or remember. Such symptoms can have a destructive effect on a lawyer's ability to work. Where attention to detail and logical analysis are crucial, mental impairment often reduces the speed and quality of a lawyer's work and increases the likelihood of administrative and substantive errors. That can lead to malpractice.

Depression is also characterized by a number of behavioral or physical symptoms, such as a sad facial appearance, crying, slowness of speech and movement, agitation, loss of appetite, sleep disorders, lowered interest in sexual activities, and various bodily complaints (e.g., stomachache).

Some symptoms of depression are also symptoms of other ailments, both psychological and physical. For example, several of the behavioral and physical signs listed above can be indicative of alcoholism or depression. Depressed people also often develop a common symptom of an anxiety disorder, which is to obsess about things. A number of physical ailments such as viral infections, brain tumors, post-menstrual syndrome, lyme disease, or the side effects of blood pressure medicines can cause symptoms of depression as well. Thus, especially in the more serious cases of what appears to be depression, comprehensive assessments should be sought from a qualified mental health professional and a physician.

THE CAUSES

Current professional diagnostic methods presume that there are different types of depression, each of which have some distinctive features (e.g., intensity, duration). After many years of research, however, there is still no consensus on the causes of depression. There are those who believe depression is caused by genes or malfunctioning brain chemistry. Others think that environmental stressors and psychological habits are what cause depression. These disagreements are not purely academic, in that they result in differences of opinion on how depression should be treated.

As with all controversies of this type, there is a "chicken-or-egg" problem. Undoubtedly, depression involves both the mind and the body, but either one can cause the other. For example, it has been demonstrated that depression is both predictive of (cause) the onset of cardiovascular disease, as well as a common reaction to (effect) the onset of cardiovascular disease.[296] Thus, more and more experts are coming to the conclusion that there are various types of depression and that none of them can be explained by a single biological, biochemical, social, environmental, or psychological factor.[297]

Obviously, some of the mental health problems lawyers experience have little to do with their vocation. On the other hand, the fact that lawyers experience higher rates of depression than average indicates that certain aspects of being an attorney may contribute to the problem. The most likely agent to explain the higher rates of depression among lawyers is occupational stress, which is caused by the discrepancy between the demands of being a lawyer and the capacity of lawyers to manage them. Such demands are magnified by the high level of perfectionism among lawyers. A complete discussion of what makes the practice of law so stressful is covered elsewhere in this book.

TREATMENT CHOICES

The majority of people with a depressive disorder do not seek professional help. This is sad in itself because depression happens to be a disorder that responds well to treatment in most cases. In severe instances of depression, such as when there is a high risk of suicide, hospitalization may be necessary. Most often, however, depressed patients are treated on an outpatient basis. Typically, treatment involves either psychotherapy, medications, or a combination of the two.

Psychotherapy

There are numerous schools of thought about how psychotherapy should be conducted with depressed patients. Some proponents of each approach claim that theirs is the best one. The truth is that most reputable psychotherapies have something valuable to offer, but none represents the ultimate answer. Here are the most common types of psychotherapy, in alphabetical order:

Behavioral Therapy - This type of treatment applies learning principles to systematically transform a person's current self-destructive behaviors into adaptive behaviors. For example, a person who is prone to procrastination is taught concrete behavioral techniques to overcome this destructive habit. This brings about more positive or reinforcing real life experiences, which in turn lead to more optimistic thoughts and feelings.

Cognitive Psychotherapy - The aim of cognitive therapy is to correct dysfunctional thinking patterns. For example, people who are depressed tend to anticipate the worst and react to negative events by overgeneralizing and personalizing their effects. A cognitive therapist will attempt to make a client aware of and question the logical validity of these thought patterns, and consider alternative points of view.

Couple, Family, and Group Psychotherapies - There are a variety of approaches that involve more than just one person in treatment. These approaches will differ somewhat as a function of the therapist's underlying theoretical points of view. What they share in common, however, is the idea that people grow through relating, learning from, getting support from and giving support to others.

Humanistic Psychotherapy - This category of counseling emphasizes the creation of a warm, supportive, and non-judgmental therapeutic environment, in which the client feels free to engage in self-exploration and self-expression. It focuses on conscious thoughts, feelings, and current experiences. Change occurs because the positive therapeutic relationship encourages the client to experiment and grow.

Psychodynamic Psychotherapy - Sometimes referred to as psychoanalytically oriented psychotherapy, the primary focus of this type of treatment is the examination of key relationships and experiences in a person's past and present, and how these are related to current problems. Change occurs through insight into previously unresolved conflicts and unconscious motives, which frees the person to make new choices.

Which type of psychotherapy should you choose? In numerous scientific studies, cognitive therapy has been shown to be particularly effective with depression. The approach is called "cognitive" in part because it requires clients to exercise logical reasoning in solving life's problems. Since lawyers are trained practitioners of rational analysis applied to practical problems, I find this approach to be one with which they resonate, and I have borrowed heavily from it in this book.

When seeking professional help, however, my advice is to look for a psychotherapist who appreciates the perspectives of several schools of thought and is able to integrate them. In my experience, the most effective psychotherapists recognize the following: Patients do better with psychotherapists whom they perceive to be understanding, non-judgmental, caring, and trustworthy. It is important to help patients understand how their current problems are often related to earlier life experiences. It is also important to help patients focus on the "here and now" and work on their currently dysfunctional beliefs and emotions. Working on their self-esteem is often critical for depressed patients, and helping them improve their personal relationships is also very important. Finally, in addition to psychotherapy, an anti-depressant medication can be a most useful tool.

Medications

Turning to the topic of medications, there are a number of highly effective anti-depressants available today that, unlike the medications of years ago, are safe and have very manageable side effects. It is beyond our scope to discuss them in-depth here, but there are number of widely available books on this topic.[298] The most popular type of anti-depressant being prescribed today is known as a selective serotonin reuptake inhibitor. SSRIs, as they are known, help restore the brain's chemical balance by increasing the supply of serotonin, a neurotransmitter that has been found to affect mood and behavior. This type of medication is sold under such brand names as Lexapro, Prozac, Paxil, Zoloft, etc. It is best to have them prescribed and their side effects monitored by a psychiatrist. Nevertheless, most family physicians are familiar with these drugs and commonly prescribe them in less severe cases of depression.

As was mentioned earlier, people who have depressive symptoms often also experience a form of generalized anxiety, which is typically characterized by obsessive thinking. The anti-depressants mentioned above effectively treat this form of anxiety as well. These anti-depressants are preferable to certain other drugs that are specifically designed for anxiety disorders, as the latter tend to be habit-forming.

Stay away from the over-the-counter alternatives to anti-depressant medications. The research on their efficacy is weak at best, and they are not covered by most prescription plans. Except for the illusion that taking pills manufactured by a relatively unregulated industry is somehow less stigmatizing, there is absolutely no advantage to them. At the same time, as discussed elsewhere in this book, proper nutrition and even some supplements such as calcium and fish oils have been shown to reduce depressive symptoms. If you need to do more, however, seek the advice of a medical doctor and take real prescription medications.

There are times when all that a depressed patient needs is an anti-depressant medication. When the cause is biochemical (e.g., pre-menstrual syndrome) or a mildly-traumatic recent event (e.g., an automobile accident that could have seriously injured people but did not), an anti-depressant pill may be all that is needed. Medications take the edge off of negative emotions, increase patients' ability to ease back into life's daily activities, and help clarify thought processes.

At the same time, anti-depressants alone are not effective in all cases. Medications do not help people correct their core dysfunctional beliefs and habits that they have developed over their lifetimes, and they do not provide them with the insights and courage necessary to align their lives with their values. Making these types of changes often requires more than just medications. Thus, if you are depressed because you are simply in the wrong profession, practicing the wrong type of law in the wrong type of firm, or surrounded by the wrong type of people who do not share your values, no pill will solve your problems. In such cases, medications may still be helpful, but only when they are taken in combination with psychotherapy.[299]

SELF-HELP FOR MILD SYMPTOMS

If your symptoms of depression or alcoholism are chronic or acute, the best advice I can give you is to seek professional help. However, let's say that you find yourself feeling down or drinking a little more often than you would like, and you are getting concerned that these symptoms may turn into something more serious. Short of getting professional help, there are a number of steps you can take on your own, and most of them are detailed throughout this book. Here are several reminders.

DEALING WITH THE "BLUES"

The first thing to do when you are feeling "blue" is to improve your eating, drinking, exercise and sleep habits. These steps will help lift your emotions by affecting certain mood-altering brain chemicals. Unfortunately, people who are feeling down tend to do just the opposite; they disregard their diets, increase their alcohol or drug intake, stop exercising, and do not adhere to a normal sleep schedule. You need to resist such urges.

Similarly, you need to pay particular attention to certain external or environmental factors that contribute to the way you feel. For example, resist the urge to isolate yourself and become idle. As much as possible, surround yourself with people you like, and keep yourself busy. If you cannot seem to do your important work effectively, do the less important work or even your chores. Make an effort to schedule experiences that will raise your spirits or make you laugh. You will be surprised by how difficult it is to stay low under the influence of uplifting environmental forces.

Ultimately, however, you will need to confront the negative thoughts that are causing your negative emotions. The first thoughts you may need to face are: "I can't do anything about my feelings. Nothing will work." Ask yourself to only imagine doing some of the things that are recommended throughout this book. Then, ask yourself to try implementing just one or two of them. Once you shift from a passive to an active mode and begin to actually work on solving your problems, you will find that some of your gloomy feelings may start to be replaced by glimmers of hope.

Once you delve into your thoughts, you may discover a number of mental habits that are very dysfunctional. For example, you may find that you tend to assume the worst, discount the positive, personalize events, blame yourself, overgeneralize, and magnify things. These habits are embedded in statements like the following: "Unless I get a few more cases soon, this practice is doomed; people are not calling because I must not be that good." Thoughts like these need to be brought into conscious awareness, cross-examined, and revised.

Another mental habit that you may discover is that you tend to be perfectionistic about what you expect of yourself, what you think others expect of you, and what you expect of others.[300] Such expectations evoke a great many "should" statements, which in turn trigger guilt, fear of failure, and fear of rejection. Using the techniques described elsewhere in this book, become aware of your perfectionistic thoughts and revise them.

DEALING WITH EXCESSIVE DRINKING

When it comes to excessive alcohol consumption, the first and best thing you can do is admit to it. Most people who drink too much deny it. If a little voice inside of you or someone who cares about you says that you are drinking too much, you probably are. There is an easy experiment that you can conduct to prove to yourself that you do not have a problem: See if you can stop all alcohol consumption for two consecutive weeks.

People who do not have a drinking problem may find it inconvenient to abstain from alcohol for two weeks, but they are able to do it without much difficulty. If you cannot abstain from drinking alcohol, find it difficult to do, or get irritated at the thought of it, then it is very likely that you do have a problem. Unless your condition is truly minimal, the best self-help advice I can offer you is to seek the aid of a professional or a self-help group that specializes in this area. If yours is a minimal problem, however, you can attempt to confront it yourself.

First, get a better understanding of why you find it difficult to abstain from alcohol. Determine the psychological role alcohol plays in your life, objectively measure the amount and frequency of your alcohol intake, and think about the negative effects that this has on you. Although it does take a little extra effort, you will get more insight into your drinking behaviors if you keep a daily diary of them. By way of further evaluating your drinking problem complete the following check list of alcohol dependency signs:

- ☐ Do you rely on alcoholic drinks to help you relax or be comfortable in social situations?
- ☐ Do you rely on alcoholic drinks to help you think better, be more creative, or work harder?
- ☐ Do you rely on alcoholic drinks to help you manage your moods, feel less depressed or tense, or forget your problems?
- ☐ Do you find yourself thinking about or having an urge to get an alcoholic drink at different times of the day?
- ☐ Do you often find yourself drinking more than others around you?

☐ Do you often experience regret about your drinking patterns?

☐ Do you find yourself lying or giving excuses about your alcohol intake?

☐ Do you often drink alone or hide liquor?

☐ Do you get intoxicated and have hangovers or memory blackouts?

☐ Is your drinking affecting your daily activities, such as being on time or getting your work done?

If your answer to any of these questions is a yes, delve into uncovering the psychological dynamics involved. Once you have done that, try to abstain from alcohol use for two weeks again. Before doing so, remember what I have explained elsewhere in this book, namely that all human experiences can be viewed as being composed of the following sequence of elements:

Stimulus > Thought > Emotion > Behavior

Since what you are trying to reduce is behavior, one way to proceed is to gain better control of the elements that precede it. For example, one thing you can do is get control of the stimuli or environmental factors that trigger your drinking behaviors. This may include disposing of the liquor that you have at home or in the office, or refraining from going to places where liquor is readily available. You will find it much easier to reduce your drinking urges and behaviors when less liquor is available.

Similarly, you will need to control any drink-inducing thoughts and emotions that get triggered by external stimuli. Let us say that you have gone out to lunch with a client who orders an alcoholic drink. When the waiter turns to you, you may find yourself thinking: "My client will be offended if I don't order one as well. Besides, the alcohol will make me feel less anxious." These thoughts will trigger such emotions as fear of rejection and hope that tension will be reduced. The emotions will impel you to say: "I'll have a martini, please." If you learn to interrupt such thoughts and emotions and practice replacing them with healthier ones, your drinking patterns will change for the better. Using the methods of analysis described elsewhere in this book, you can systematically root out the thoughts and emotions that trigger your drinking behaviors.

Obviously, if the advice I have given you in this chapter and throughout the book does not work, get professional help. Depression and problem-drinking are fully treatable, and there is no reason for you to continue to suffer in silence or wait until things are much worse.

HOW TO GET HELP

In 1988, the American Bar Association created the Commission on Lawyer Assistance Programs (CoLAP; formerly known as the ABA Commission On Impaired Attorneys) and charged it with the task of educating the profession on both legal and treatment issues related to substance abuse and mental illness. In addition, the Commission supports the development of lawyer assistance programs throughout the United States, Canada, and Great Britain. It publishes a Directory of State and Local Lawyer Assistance Programs, educational materials, pamphlets, audiotapes and videotapes. For further information contact:

Commission On Lawyer Assistance Programs
American Bar Association
541 North Fairbanks Court
Chicago, Illinois 60611-3314
Phone: (312) 988-5359; Fax: (312) 988-5280
http://www.abanet.org/legalservices/colap/home.html

In addition to contacting CoLAP, you can locate local organizations, self-help groups, and professionals who provide helpful services to lawyers by referring to your local legal directory, contacting your local bar association, or reading the relevant ads and articles in your local legal publications. Lawyer Assistance Programs (LAP) are now available in most localities. Their purpose is to help prevent and treat lawyer impairments through education and intervention. Most LAPs have toll-free hotlines. They take great care to protect the confidentiality of all communications, and are excellent resources for getting both legal and treatment information.

If you would rather not contact your local LAP to find a mental health professional, follow the same type of advice you would give for finding a lawyer. Most people think that it is best to get a personal recommendation from a family member, friend or physician. Alternative methods include looking in the local telephone directory or seeking referrals from professional organizations, universities, and hospitals. In addition, there is the option of calling someone whose name appears in the media.

In the main, there are three types of licensed mental health professionals: psychologists, psychiatrists and social workers. At times, each of these professions claims to have superiority in certain domains. For example, some psychiatrists claim that their ability to prescribe drugs and administer psychotherapy makes them uniquely qualified to treat all mental illnesses. Some psychologists claim that their greater reliance on psychotherapy than on drugs and their special expertise in psychological testing and assessment makes them better diagnosticians and psychotherapists.

In truth, however, such generalizations are simply not useful in finding someone to help you with your specific set of problems. It is the actual expertise of the particular professional that makes the difference, not the claims of his or her profession. Interview several mental health professionals before making a choice. The initial meeting, often granted at no cost, can help you establish the individual's credentials, experience, treatment preferences, and personality.

Liking and trusting your counselor is critical. Since much of the treatment will require your collaboration, the treatment strategy needs to be made explicit and make sense to you. I prefer mental health professionals who have successfully integrated several schools of thought into the way they conduct treatment and have experience treating lawyers. Remember that it is possible for you to work with more than one provider. For example, a psychologist or social worker can act as your therapist, while your physician or psychiatrist can monitor your medications if they become necessary.

SECTION X: EPILOGUE

There is a curious paradox that no one can explain
Who understands the secret of the reaping of the grain
Who understands why spring is borne out of winter's laboring pain
Or why we must all die a bit before we grow again

> *By lyricist Tom Jones,*
> *from the musical play "The Fantasticks"*

I find the great thing in this world is not so much where we stand, as in what direction we are moving. To reach the port of heaven, we must sail sometimes with the wind and sometimes against - but we must sail, and not drift, nor lie at anchor.

> *Oliver Wendell Holmes*

STILL ONLY THE THINGS I HAVE LEARNED SO FAR

I was lucky growing up. Although neither of my parents took a single course on the psychology of success, they taught me important lessons about it. Whenever I brooded over making a mistake, my father would say: "I am glad you have the courage to admit your error, but the important thing for you to think about now is what have you have learned and what you are going to do the next time." Similarly, when I felt sad about how difficult life is sometimes, my mother would say: "Meaning comes from within. You have the ability to create beauty or ugliness, happiness or unhappiness. It's up to you."

Experience has taught me an additional lesson: Usually, there are no shortcuts! I do not mean to suggest that the difficult paths we choose for ourselves are always desirable. Indeed, I have often gone in the wrong direction altogether or made things much more tedious than necessary. I just mean that whenever I have overcome important challenges, they have generally required a great deal of effort, perseverance, patience, and courage. Normally, the shortcuts I have attempted have lead me to dead-ends.

Another meaningful lesson I have learned is that life should be a continuous growth-experience. For example, I realize that this book is imperfect, for it reflects only the things I have learned so far. However, this edition is better than the last one, and I plan to continue refining my recommendations. My hope is that you too will consider the stress management techniques you have learned from this book as only one step in your efforts to continuously improve your life. If you do that, then both of us will have truly succeeded.

ENDNOTES

[1] American Bar Association, At The Breaking Point: The Report Of A National Conference On The Emerging Crisis In The Quality Of Lawyers' Health And Lives, And Its Impact On Law Firms And Client Services (1991).

[2] American Bar Association, The State Of The Legal Profession - 1984: Report Of The Young Lawyers Division (1985).

[3] American Bar Association, The State Of The Legal Profession - 1990: Report Of The Young Lawyers Division (1991).

[4] Larry R. Richard, Psychological Type And Job Satisfaction Among Practicing Lawyers In The United States (1994; Ph.D. dissertation, Temple University, Philadelphia, available through University Microfilms International Dissertation Services.)

[5] Aric Press, *The Good Life,* The American Lawyer, June 1999, at 79.

[6] North Carolina Bar Association, Quality of Life Survey of North Carolina Attorneys: Report of Quality of Life Task Force (1991).

[7] Dianne Molvig, *1999 Bench-Bar Survey: Lack of Civility Still A Major Concern Among Respondents,* The Wisconsin Lawyer, Dec. 1999, at 10.

[8] Dennis W. Kozich, Stress is Taking its Toll on Wisconsin Attorneys, Wisconsin Lawyer, Apr. 1989, at 12.

[9] John Sonsteng & David Camarotto, Minnesota Lawyers Evaluate Law Schools, Training and Job Satisfaction, 26(2) William Mitchell Law Review 327 (2000); John Sonsteng, Attorney Satisfaction High in Minnesota, Bench & Bar of Minnesota, Dec. 2000, at 31; *But see*, J.P. Heinz, K.E. Hull, & A.A. Harter, Lawyers and Their Discontents, 74 Indiana Law Journal 735, 736 (1999); Heintz et al., surveyed Chicago lawyers and found that only 6 percent reported being dissatisfied, a proportion that is much lower than the norm. One possible reason for these contradictory findings is that Heinz et al. used face-to-face interviews, as opposed to anonymous paper surveys. That is, it's possible that when it comes self-revelations that are private and perceived to be risky, lawyers are less likely to be honest in face-to-face interviews.

[10] Mathew M. Dammeyer & Narina Nunez, Anxiety and Depression Among Law Students: Current Knowledge and Future Directions, 23(1) Law and Human Behavior 55 (1999).

[11] G.A.H. Benjamin, A. Kaszniak, B.D. Sales & S.B. Shanfield, *The Role Of Legal Education In Producing Psychological Distress Among Law Students And Lawyers*, American Bar Foundation Research Journal 225 (1986).

[12] G.A.H. Benjamin, E.J. Darling & B.D. Sales, *The Prevalence of Depression, Alcohol Abuse, And Cocaine Abuse Among United States Lawyers,* 13 International Journal of Law and Psychiatry 233 (1990).

[13] W.W. Eaton, J.C. Anthony, W. Mandel & R. Garrison, *Occupations And The Prevalence Of Major Depressive Disorder,* 32 Journal Of Occupational Medicine 1079 (1990).

[14] James W. Grosch & Lawrence R. Murphy, *Occupational Differences in Depression and Global Health: Results From a National Sample of U.S. Workers,* 40(2) Journal of Occupational and Environmental Medicine 153 (1998).

[15] Laura Gatland, Dangerous Dedication: Studies Suggest Long Hours, Productivity Pressures Can Cause Serious Health Problems and a Higher Suicide Rate for Attorneys, American Bar Association Journal, Dec. 1997, at 28.

[16] *See,* A. Elwork & G.A.H. Benjamin, *Lawyers In Distress,* 23 The Journal of Psychiatry and Law 205 (1995).

[17] *See, e.g.,* Handbook of Health Psychology (Andrew Baum et al. eds., 2001); Edward P. Sarafino, Health Psychology: Biopsychosocial Interactions (4th ed. 2001); Health Psychology (Derek W. Johnson et al. eds., 2000); Shelley E. Taylor, Health Psychology (5th ed. 2002); Bruce S. Rabin, Stress, Immune Function, and Health: The Connection (1999).

[18] *See, e.g.,* Amiram Elwork, *Married To A Lawyer,* Trial, February 1999, at 87; Sharon K. Houseknecht et al., *Marital Disruption Among Professional Women: The Timing Of Career And Family Events,* 31 Social Problems 273 (1984); Teresa M. Cooney & Peter Uhlenberg, *Family-Building Patterns of Professional Women; A Comparison of Lawyers, Physicians, and Postsecondary Teachers,* 51 Journal of Marriage & Family 749 (1989); Bryan E. Robinson, *The Workaholic Family: A Clinical Perspective,* 26 American Journal of Family Therapy 65 (1998); Clarence Hibbs, *Attorneys: High Performance And Family Relationships,* in High Performing Families: Causes, Consequences and Clinical Solutions 71 (Bryan E. Robinson & Nancy D. Chase ed., 2001); Aric Press, *The Good Life,* The American Lawyer, June 1999, at 79.

[19] R. Klein, *The Relationship Of The Court And Defense Counsel: The Impact On Competent Representation And Proposals For Reform,* 29(3) Boston College Law Review 531 (1988).

[20] R.B. Allan, *Alcoholism, Drug Abuse and Lawyers: Are We Ready to Address the Denial,* 31 Greighton Law Review 265, 268 (1997); ABA Commission On Impaired Attorneys, An Overview Of Lawyer Assistance Programs In The United States 1 (1991); C.P. Anderson, Survey Regarding Impairment and Attorney Misconduct in Illinois (1993) (unpublished statistics available through the Attorney Registration and Disciplinary Commission of the Supreme Court of Illinois); M.R. Ramos, *Legal*

Malpractice: The Profession's Dirty Little Secret, 47 Vanderbilt Law Review 1657, 1698 (1994); Standing Committee On Lawyers' Professional Liability, The Lawyer's Desk Guide To Legal Malpractice 105 (1992);

[21] Aric Press, *The Good Life,* The American Lawyer, June 1999, at 79.

[22] D. E. Conner, *Depressed Employees Get Big ADA Awards,* Lawyers Weekly USA, A1 (Sept. 25, 1995); *Reasonable Accommodation,* 14 (9) Mental Health Law Reporter 65 (September, 1996).

[23] National Association for Law Placement, Keeping the Keepers: Strategies for Associate Retention in Times of Attrition (1998); National Association for Law Placement, Beyond the Bidding Wars: A Survey of Associate Attrition, Departure Destinations, and Workplace Incentives (2000); D. Margolick, *Alienated Lawyers Seeking-And Getting-Counsel In Making The Transition To Other Careers,* New York Times B7 (Feb.10, 1989); M.R. Ramos, *Legal Malpractice: The Profession's Dirty Little Secret,* 47 Vanderbilt Law Review 1657, 1715 (1994); John Sonsteng & David Camarotto, Minnesota Lawyers Evaluate Law Schools, Training and Job Satisfaction, 26(2) William Mitchell Law Review 327 (2000).

[24] M.R. Ramos, *Legal Malpractice: The Profession's Dirty Little Secret,* 47 Vanderbilt Law Review 1657 (1994).

[25] Mary Ann Glendon, A Nation Under Lawyers 15 (1994).

[26] This chapter contains many conclusions that are based on the same multiple books, articles and reports. To avoid excessive repetition of citations, allow me to simply state that the conclusions in this chapter are based on a review of the following literature: M.A. Altman, Life After Law (1991); American Bar Association, The State Of The Legal Profession - 1990: Report Of The Young Lawyers Division (1991); D.L. Arron, Running from the law: Why good lawyers are getting out of the legal profession (1991); J.C. Barefoot, K.A. Dodge, B.L. Peterson, W.G. Dahlstrom & R.B. Williams, *The Cook-Medley Hostility Scale: Item Content And Ability To Predict Survival,* 51 Psychosomatic Medicine 46 (1989); Susan Swaim Daicoff, Lawyer, Know Thyself (2004); Connie J.A. Beck, Bruce D. Sales, & G. Andrew H. Benjamin, *Lawyer Distress: Alcohol-Related Problems And Other Psychological Concerns Among A Sample Of Practicing Lawyers,* 10(1) Journal of Law and Health 1 (1995-96); G.A.H. Benjamin, A. Kaszniak, B.D. Sales & S.B. Shanfield, *The Role Of Legal Education In Producing Psychological Distress Among Law Students And Lawyers,* American Bar Foundation Research Journal 225 (1986); S. Benson, *Why I Quit Practicing Law,* Newsweek, November 4, 1991, at 10; Canadian Lawyer, *The 1999 Canadian Lawyer Law Firm Associates Survey: An Annual Review of Associates Lives at Their Mid-sized to Large Firms,* 23(11) Canadian Lawyer 41 (1999); Commission on Women in the Profession (ABA), Lawyers and Balanced Lives: A Guide to Drafting and

Implementing workplace policies for Lawyers (1990); Kenneth G. Dau-Schmidt, *The Fruits of Our Labor: An empirical Study of the Distribution of Income and Job Satisfaction Across the Legal Profession,* 49(3), Journal of Legal Education 342 (1999); Janet Stidman Eveleth, *Decade of Difference: Quality of Life Improves for Maryland Lawyers,* 32(1) The Maryland Bar Journal 50 (1999); M.C. Fisk, *A Measure Of Satisfaction,* 12(38) The National Law Journal, S2-S12 (1990); R. Frances, G. Alexopoulos, & V. Yandow, *Lawyers' Alcoholism,* 4(2) Advances In Alcohol And Substance Abuse 59 (1984); E.H. Friedman & H.K. Hellerstein, *Occupational Stress, Law School Hierarchy And Coronary Artery Disease In Cleveland Attorneys,* 36 Psychosomatic Medicine 72 (1968); S. Goldberg, *Satisfaction,* 75(4) ABA Journal 40 (1989); B.S. Gould, *Beyond Burnout,* 10(3) Barrister 4 (1983); E.H. Greenebaum, *Lawyers' Relationship To Their Work,* 53 Legal Education 651 (1978); M.D. Gupta, *Machiavellianism Of Different Occupational Groups,* 18(2) Indian Journal of Psychometry and Education 61 (1987); Karen Hall, *Take the Money and Run: 2000 Midlevel Associate Survey,* American Lawyer, October 200 (Supplement 7), at 10; J.P. Heinz & E.O. Laumann, Chicago Lawyers: The Social Structure of the Bar (1984); R.L. Hirsch, *Will Women Leave The Law,* 16(1) Barrister 22 (1989); R.L. Hirsch, *Are You On Target?,* 12(1) Barrister 17 (1985); S.E. Jackson, J.A. Turner & A.P. Brief, *Correlates Of Burnout Among Public Service Lawyers,* 8(4) Journal of Occupational Behavior 339 (1987); S.C. Kobasa, *Commitment And Coping In Stress Resistance Among Lawyers,* 42(4) Journal of Personality and Social Psychology 707 (1982); L.J. Landwehr, *Lawyers As Social Progressives Or Reactionaries: The Law And Order Cognitive Orientation Of Lawyers,* 7 Law And Psychology Review 39 (1982); G.W. LaRussa, *Portia's Decision: Women's Motives For Studying Law And Their Later Career Satisfaction As Attorneys,* 1 Psychology of Women Quarterly 350 (1977); J.S. St. Lawrence, M.L. McGrath, M.E. Oakley, & S.C. Sult, *Stress Management Training For Law Students: Cognitive-behavioral Intervention,* 1(4) Behavioral Sciences And The Law 101 (1983); Maine Bar Association, *Snapshot From the 1996 Survey of Maine Attorneys,* 12(3) Maine Bar Journal 160 (1997); Hilde Mausner-Dorsch & William F. Eaton, *Psychosocial Work Environment and Depression: Epidemiologic Assessment of the Demand-Control Model,* 90(11) American Journal of Public Health 1765 (2000); Kirsten McMahon, *The 2000 Canadian Lawyer law Firm Associates Survey: Annual Review of Associates' Lives at Their Mid-sized to Large Firms,* 24(11) Canadian Lawyer 27 (2000); P. Miller, *Personality Differences And Student Survival In Law School,* 19 Journal Of Legal Education 460 (1967); Dianne Molvig, *1999 Bench-Bar Survey: Lack of Civility Still A Major Concern Among Respondents,* 72(12) The Wisconsin Lawyer 10 (1999); D.C. Moss, *Lawyer Personality,* 77(2) ABA Journal 34 (1991); Martha Neil, *Toil Taking Toll,*

Lawyers Tell Surveyors, Chicago Daily Law Bulletin, August 22, 2000, at 1; Aric Press, *The Good Life,* 21(5) The American Lawyer 79 (June, 1999); P. Reidinger, *It's 46.5 Hours A Week In Law,* 72(9) ABA Journal 44 (1986); J.M. Rhoads, *Overwork,* 24 Journal of the American Medical Association 2615 (1977); D.L. Rhode, *The Profession and Its Discontents,* 61(4) Ohio State Law Journal 1335 (2000); Lawrence Richard, *The Lawyer Types,* 79(7) ABA Journal 74 (1993); H.I. Russek & L. Russek, *Is Emotional Stress An Etiological Factor In Coronary Heart Disease?,* 17 Psychosomatics 63 (1976); R.E. Sheeny, *Effects of Stress Inoculation Training for First-year Law Students,* 61(6-A) Dissertation Abstracts International Section A: Humanities and Social Sciences 2188 (2000); R.S. Smith, *A Profile Of Lawyer Lifestyles,* 70(2) ABA Journal 50 (1984); N. Solkoff & J. Markowitz, *Personality Characteristics Of First Year Medical And Law Students,* 42 Journal Of Medical Education 195 (1967); R. Tomasic, *Social Organization Amongst Australian Lawyers,* 19(3) Australian and New Zealand Journal of Sociology 447 (1983).

[27] Deborah L. Arron, Running From The Law 27, 39(1991); Walt Bachman, Law v. Life 100 (1995); Mary Ann Glendon, A Nation Under Lawyers 29 (1994); Anthony T. Kronman, The Lost Lawyer 300 (1993); Sol M. Linowitz & Martin Mayer, The Betrayed Profession: Lawyering At The End Of The Twentieth Century 107 (1994); Benjamin Sells, The Soul of the Law 71 (1994).

[28] John W. Wright, The American Almanac Of Jobs And Salaries 236 (1993).

[29] To be precise, the American Bar Association's market research department reported that, based on information provided by licensing authorities in each state, as of December 31, 2000, there were 1,049,000 lawyers in the United States.

[30] This is an excerpt from an invited address Will Rogers gave to the legislative body of the State of California, in response to a bill that had just been passed, which was designed to curb the dishonest behaviors of lawyers. *See,* 1 The Coolidge Years, 1926-1929, Will Rogers' Daily Telegrams, at 67 (James M. Smallwood & Steven K. Gragert, eds., 1978). My thanks to Pat Lowe of the Will Rogers Memorial Museum Library for helping me find the cite and understand its historical context.

[31] Public defenders report that their biggest stressors include work overload, dealing with angry clients and families, having to go to trial with little preparation or with a bad fact pattern, and arguing with zealous prosecutors. *See,* David Richard Lynch, *The Nature of Occupational Stress Among Public Defenders,* 57(8-A) Dissertation Abstracts International Section A: Humanities & Social Sciences 3689 (1997).

[32] Susan Swaim Daicoff, Lawyer, Know Thyself (2004).

[33] Lawrence R. Richard, *The Lawyer Types*, 79(7) ABA Journal 74 (1993); Lawrence R. Richard, Psychological Type And Job Satisfaction Among Practicing Lawyers In The United States (1994; Ph.D. dissertation, Temple Univ., Philadelphia, available through University Microfilms International Dissertation Services.); Susan Swaim Daicoff, Lawyer, Know Thyself (2004); *See also,* Jean Stephanie and Richard Delgato, How Lawyers Lose Their Way: A Profession Fails Its Creative Minds (2005).

[34] Mary Ann Glendon, A Nation Under Lawyers (1994); George W. Kaufman, The Lawyer's Guide To Balancing Life And Work (1999); Steven Keeva, Transforming Practices: Finding Joy And Satisfaction In The Legal Life (1999); Anthony T. Kronman, The Lost Lawyer (1993); Sol M. Linowitz & Martin Mayer, The Betrayed Profession: Lawyering At The End Of The Twentieth Century (1994); Mike Papantonio, In Search Of Atticus Finch: A Motivational Book For Lawyers (1996); Benjamin Sells, The Soul of the Law (1994).

[35] National Association for Law Placement (NALP), Dearth of Women and Attorneys of Color Remains in Law Firms, December 3, 2001, at http:www.nalp.org; Sharyn R. Anleau, Women In Law: Theory, Research And Practice, 28(3) Australian And New Zealand Journal Of Sociology 391 (1992); Fiona M. Kay & John Hagan, The Persistent Glass Ceiling: Gendered Inequalities In The Earnings Of Lawyers, 46(2) British Journal Of Sociology 279 (1995); Fiona M. Kay & John Hagan, Cultivating Clients in the Competition for Partnership: Gender and the Organizational Restructuring of Law Firms in the 1990s, 33(3) Law & Society Review 517 (1999); Patricia MacCorquodale & Gary Jensen, Women In The Law: Partners Or Tokens?, 7(4) Gender And Society 582 (1993); D.L. Rhode, The Profession and Its Discontents, 61(4) Ohio State Law Journal 1335, 1348 (2000); Janet Rosenberg, Harry Perlstadt & William Phillips, Now That We Are Here: Discrimination. Disparagement And Harassment At Work And The Experience Of Women Lawyers, 7(3) Gender And Society 415 (1993).

[36] American Bar Association, The State Of The Legal Profession - 1990: Report Of The Young Lawyers Division (1991); American Bar Association, ABA Young Lawyers Division Survey: Career Satisfaction (1995); North Carolina Bar Association, Quality of Life Survey of North Carolina Attorneys: Report of Quality of Life Task Force (1991); *See also,* preceding two chapters.

[37] *See, e.g.,* Report of the Boston Bar Association Task Force on Professional Challenges and Family Needs, Facing the Grail: Confronting the Cost of Work-Family Imbalance (1999); Bryan E. Robinson, Chained To The Desk: A Guidebook For Workaholics, Their Partners And Children, And The Clinicians Who Treat Them (1998); Christina Maslach & Michael P. Leiter, The Truth About Burnout: How Organizations Cause Personal Stress And What To Do About It (1997); Dianne Fassel, Working

Ourselves To Death: The High Cost Of Workaholism And The Rewards Of Recovery (2000); Jonathan Lazear, The Man Who Mistook His Job For A Life: A Chronic Overachiever Finds The Way Home (2001); Anne W. Schaef & Diane Fassel, The Addictive Organization (1990); Karen C. Seybold and Paul R. Salamone, *Understanding Workaholsim; A Review Of Causes And Counseling Approaches*, 73(1) Journal of Counseling and Development 4 (1994).

[38] *See, e.g.,* Christina Maslach & Michael P. Leiter, The Truth About Burnout: How Organizations Cause Personal Stress And What To Do About It (1997).

[39] Aric Press, *The Good Life,* The American Lawyer, June 1999, at 79. In this survey of 624 partners at the nation's largest law firms, whose average incomes are over $500,000, 31 percent said that their workload was too great, 17 percent reported being less than content, and 12 percent said their careers had a significant negative effect on family life.

[40] Maine Bar Association, *Snapshot From the 1996 Survey of Maine Attorneys,* 12(3) Maine Bar Journal 160 (1997). This survey found that even though the vast majority of law firms in Maine are small (15 lawyers or less), more than 60 percent reported a work week that is at least 45 hours, 40 percent reported working 45-54 hours per week, 18 percent said they worked 55-64 hours per week, and 5 percent worked over 65 hours per week.

[41] *See, e.g.,* J.E. Wallace, *It's About Time: A Study of Hours Worked and Work Spillover Among Law Firm Lawyers*, 50(2) Journal of Vocational Behavior 227 (1997).

[42] J.M. Satterfield, J. Monahan, and M.E.P. Seligman, *Law School Performance Predicted By Explanatory Style,* 15(1) Behavioral Sciences and the Law 95 (1997).

[43] See, e.g., D.L. Rhode, *The Profession and Its Discontents,* 61(4) Ohio State Law Journal 1335 (2000).

[44] *See, e.g.,* Tim Kasser, The High Price Of Materialism (2002); David G. Myers, The Pursuit Of Happiness: Who Is Happy And Why (1992).

[45] Kenneth G. Dau-Schmidt, *The Fruits of Our Labor: An Empirical Study of the Distribution of Income and Job Satisfaction Across the Legal Profession,* 49(3) Journal of Legal Education 342 (1999).

[46] *See, e.g.,* Canadian Lawyer, *The 1999 Canadian Lawyer Law Firm Associates Survey: An Annual Review of Associates Lives at Their Mid-sized to Large Firms,* 23(11) Canadian Lawyer 41 (1999).

[47] Excerpted from a famous sentence, "The mass of men lead lives of quiet desperation." Henry David Thoreau, Walden (1854).

[48] *See, e.g.,* Cameron Stracher, Buried Alive: Why Do So Many Associates Hate Their Jobs? The American Lawyer, Oct. 1998, at 34.

[49] American Bar Association, The State Of The Legal Profession - 1984: Report Of The Young Lawyers Division (1985).

[50] American Bar Association, The State Of The Legal Profession - 1990: Report Of The Young Lawyers Division (1991); *See also*, C. Chiu, *Do Professional Women Have Lower Job Satisfaction Than Professional Men? Lawyers As A Case Study*, 38(7-8) Sex Roles 521 (1998).

[51] *See, e.g.*, Andrew R. Dunn, *Associate Attrition: Departure Rates Are Not Always Related To Salary*, New York Law Journal, November 28, 2000, at 5; John Flynn Rooney, *1200 Lawyers Quit Practicing Law Over 2 years, State Report Shows*, Chicago Daily Law Bulletin, April 29, 1996, at 1.

[52] National Association for Law Placement, Keeping the Keepers: Strategies for Associate Retention in Times of Attrition (1998); National Association for Law Placement, Beyond the Bidding Wars: A Survey of Associate Attrition, Departure Destinations, and Workplace Incentives (2000).

[53] *See, e.g.*, Pal Braverman, *Midlevel Survey: Prestigious Firms High On Misery*, New York Law Journal, Oct. 13, 2000, at 24; National Association for Law Placement, Keeping the Keepers: Strategies for Associate Retention in Times of Attrition (1998); National Association for Law Placement, Beyond the Bidding Wars: A Survey of Associate Attrition, Departure Destinations, and Workplace Incentives (2000).

[54] *See, e.g.*, Wendy Davis, *Mid-level Associates Express Dissatisfaction*, New York Law Journal, Oct. 2, 2000, at 1; Monica Bay, *Life, Law And The Pursuit of Balance*, 20(4) Barrister Magazine 4 (1994); Canadian Lawyer, *The 1999 Canadian Lawyer Law Firm Associates Survey: An Annual Review of Associates Lives at Their Mid-sized to Large Firms*, 23(11) Canadian Lawyer 41 (1999); Kirsten McMahon, *The 2000 Canadian Lawyer law Firm Associates Survey: Annual Review of Associates' Lives at Their Mid-sized to Large Firms*, 24(11) Canadian Lawyer 27 (2000); Martha Neil, *Toil Taking Toll, Lawyers Tell Surveyors*, Chicago Daily Law Bulletin, August 22, 2000, at 1.

[55] American Bar Association, ABA Young Lawyers Division Survey: Career Satisfaction (1995).

[56] Steve Mendelsohn, *The Ideal Law Job, in* Success Briefs For Lawyers: Inspirational Insights On How To Succeed At Law And Life 157, 161 (Amiram Elwork & Mark R. Siwik eds., 2001)

[57] *See,* Canadian Lawyer, *The 1999 Canadian Lawyer Law Firm Associates Survey: An Annual Review of Associates Lives at Their Mid-sized to Large Firms*, 23(11) Canadian Lawyer 41 (1999).

[58] Jeremy Blachman, Anonymous Lawyer: A Novel (2006).

[59] Robert Kurson, *Who's Killing The Great Lawyers From Harvard*, Esquire, Aug. 2000, at 82.

[60] Report of the Boston Bar Association Task Force on Professional Challenges and Family Needs, Facing the Grail: Confronting the Cost of Work-Family Imbalance (1999).

[61] North Carolina Bar Association, Quality of Life Survey of North Carolina Attorneys: Report of Quality of Life Task Force (1991).

[62]*Employee Retention Is Major Challenge For Law Firms*, Lawyers Weekly USA, March 20, 2000, at B2; other less popular strategies include flexible schedules, training and casual dress.

[63] Catalyst, Beyond a Reasonable Doubt: Building the Business Case for Flexibility (2005); Karen Hall, *Take the Money and Run: 2000 Midlevel Associate Survey,* American Lawyer, October 2000 (Supplement 7), at 10; Sara C. McManus and Ellen B. Barker, *Attrition: What Do Associates Want?* 158(12) New Jersey Law Journal 31 (1999); Elaine McCardle, *Gen-X Associates*, Lawyers Weekly USA, November 15, 1999, at B10.

[64] Karen Hall, *Take the Money and Run: 2000 Midlevel Associate Survey,* American Lawyer, October 200 (Supplement 7), at 10.

[65] Catalyst, Beyond a Reasonable Doubt: Building the Business Case for Flexibility (2005); Sara C. McManus and Ellen B. Barker, *Attrition: What Do Associates Want?* 158(12) New Jersey Law Journal 31 (1999); Karen Hall, *Take the Money and Run: 2000 Midlevel Associate Survey,* American Lawyer, October 200 (Supplement 7), at 10; Elaine McCardle, *Gen-X Associates*, Lawyers Weekly USA, November 15, 1999, at B10.

[66] National Association for Law Placement (NALP- Report of the Foundation for Research and Education), Beyond the Bidding Wars: A Survey of Associate Attrition, Departure Destination and Workplace Incentives (2000); Sara C. McManus and Ellen B. Barker, *Attrition: What Do Associates Want?* 158(12) New Jersey Law Journal 31 (1999); Elaine McCardle, *Gen-X Associates*, Lawyers Weekly USA, November 15, 1999, at B10.

[67] *See*, B. Berger, *Prisoners of Liberation: A Psychoanalytic Perspective on Disenchantment and Burnout Among Career Women Lawyers,* 56(5) Journal of Clinical Psychology 665 (2000).

[68] Lawrence R. Richard, *The Lawyer Types*, 79(7) ABA Journal 74 (1993); Lawrence R. Richard, Psychological Type And Job Satisfaction Among Practicing Lawyers In The United States (1994; Ph.D. dissertation, Temple Univ., Philadelphia, available through University Microfilms International Dissertation Services.); Contrary to a viewpoint that is prevalent among lawyers, people who are more sensitive to emotional issues are not less intelligent. In fact, as I argue later in this book, just the opposite may be true.

[69] *See*, B. Berger, *Prisoners of Liberation: A Psychoanalytic Perspective on Disenchantment and Burnout Among Career Women Lawyers,* 56(5) Journal of Clinical Psychology 665 (2000).

[70] F.M. Kay, *Flight From Law: A Competing Risks Model of Departures from Law Firms,* 31(2) Law & Society Review 301 (1997).

[71] See, e.g., Rand Jack & Dana C. Jack, Moral Vision and Professional Decisions: The Changing Values of Women and Men Lawyers (1989); Susan Daicoff, *Making Law Therapeutic for Lawyers: Therapeutic Jurisprudence, Preventive Law, and the Psychology of Lawyers,* 5(4) Psychology, Public Policy, and Law 811 (1999); Susan Swaim Daicoff, Lawyer, Know Thyself (2004); J. White and C. Manolis, *Individual Differences In Ethical Reasoning Among Law Students,* 25(1) Social Behavior and Personality 19 (1997).

[72] American Bar Association, The State Of The Legal Profession - 1984: Report Of The Young Lawyers Division (1985); American Bar Association, The State Of The Legal Profession - 1990: Report Of The Young Lawyers Division (1991); *See also,* C. Chiu, *Do Professional Women Have Lower Job Satisfaction Than Professional Men? Lawyers As A Case Study,* 38(7-8) Sex Roles 521 (1998); *But see,* K.E. Hull, *The Paradox of the Contented Female Lawyer,* 33(3) Law & Society Review 687 (1999). This researcher did not find a significant gender difference in job satisfaction among lawyers and reached a conclusion that contradicts many other studies. However, the data on which the findings are based are also reported by J.P. Heinz, K.E. Hull, & A.A. Harter, Lawyers and Their Discontents, 74 Indiana Law Journal 735, (1999). Heintz et al., surveyed Chicago lawyers and found that only 6 percent reported being dissatisfied, a proportion that is much lower than the norm for both men and women. One possible reason for these contradictory findings is that Heinz et al. used face-to-face interviews, as opposed to anonymous paper surveys. It's possible that when it comes self-revelations that are private and perceived to be risky, lawyers are less likely to be honest in face-to-face interviews.

[73] F.M. Kay, *Flight From Law: A Competing Risks Model of Departures from Law Firms,* 31(2) Law & Society Review 301 (1997).

[74] National Association for Law Placement, Keeping the Keepers: Strategies for Associate Retention in Times of Attrition (1998); National Association for Law Placement, Beyond the Bidding Wars: A Survey of Associate Attrition, Departure Destinations, and Workplace Incentives (2000).

[75] F.M. Kay, *Flight From Law: A Competing Risks Model of Departures from Law Firms,* 31(2) Law & Society Review 301 (1997).

[76] *Id.*

[77] John Sonsteng & David Camarotto, *Minnesota Lawyers Evaluate Law Schools, Training and Job Satisfaction,* 26(2) William Mitchell Law

Review 327 (2000); *See also*, John Sonsteng, *Attorney Satisfaction High in Minnesota*, Bench & Bar of Minnesota, Dec. 2000, at 31.

[78] Sharon K. Houseknecht et al., *Marital Disruption Among Professional Women: The Timing Of Career And Family Events,* 31 Social Problems 273 (1984).

[79] Report of the Boston Bar Association Task Force on Professional Challenges and Family Needs, Facing the Grail: Confronting the Cost of Work-Family Imbalance (1999).

[80] Rosslyn S. Smith, *A Profile of Lawyer Lifestyles,* American Bar Association Journal, Feb. 1984, at 50.

[81] Teresa M. Cooney & Peter Uhlenberg, *Family-Building Patterns of Professional Women: A Comparison of Lawyers, Physicians, and Postsecondary Teachers*, 51 Journal of Marriage and the Family, 749 (1989).

[82] Marc B. Schenker, Muzza Eaton, Rochelle Green, & Steven Samuels, *Self-Reported Stress and Reproductive Health of Female Lawyers,* 39(6) Journal of Occupational and Environmental Medicine 556 (1997); Laura Gatland, *Dangerous Dedication: Studies Suggest Long Hours, Productivity Pressures Can Cause Serious Health Problems and a Higher Suicide Rate for Attorneys,* American Bar Association Journal, December 1997, at 28.

[83] American Bar Association, The State Of The Legal Profession - 1990: Report Of The Young Lawyers Division (1991); Lawrence R. Richard, Psychological Type And Job Satisfaction Among Practicing Lawyers In The United States (1994; Ph.D. dissertation, Temple Univ., Philadelphia, available through University Microfilms International Dissertation Services).

[84] American Bar Association, The State Of The Legal Profession - 1990: Report Of The Young Lawyers Division (1991).

[85] American Corporate Counsel Association, In-House Corporate Attorneys: A Profile Of The Profession (1998), at http://www.acca.com/news/press/survey.html.

[86] Isaiah M. Zimmerman, *Stress And The Trial Lawyer,* 9(4) Litigation 37 (1983).

[87] J.M. Dabbs, Jr., E.C. Alford, & J.A. Fielden, *Trial Lawyers and Testosterone: Blue-collar Talent in a White-collar World,* 28(1) Journal of Applied Social Psychology 84 (1998).

[88] Deborah Eisel, *How Do You Spell Relief: Family Lawyers Share Their Best Stress-Reduction Secrets*, 16(3) Family Advocate 16 (1994).

[89] This model of stress is based on the ideas of a number of theorists and researchers. *See, e.g.,* Aaron T. Beck, Cognitive Therapy And Emotional Disorders (1976); Edward A. Charlesworth & Ronald G. Nathan, Stress

Management (1991); Handbook Of Stress, Medicine, And Health (Cary L. Cooper ed., 1996); Cary L. Cooper, Philip J. Dewe, & Michael P. O'Driscoll, Organizational Stress: A Review And Critique Of Theory, Research, And Applications (2001); Albert Ellis, Reason and Emotion In Psychotherapy (1962); J.J. Hurrell, L.R. Murphy, S.L. Sauter, & C.L. Cooper, Occupational Stress: Issues and Developments in Research (1988); R.L. Kahn, & P. Byosiere, Stress in Organizations, In Handbook of Industrial and Organizational Psychology 571 (Vol.3, 2nd ed. 1992); R.S. Lazarus, Emotion And Adaptation (1991); R.S. Lazarus & S. Folkman, Stress, Appraisal and Coping (1984); Richard S. Lazarus & Bernice N. Lazarus, Passion and Reason (1994); Hans Selye, History and Present Status of the Stress Concept, In Handbook of Stress 7 (1982); K.T. Strongman, The Psychology Of Emotion (4th ed. 1996); James C. Quick, Lawrence R. Murphy and Joseph J. Hurrell, Stress And Well-Being At Work: Assessments And Interventions For Occupational Mental Health (1992).

[90] Actually, at times even the first element of the stress response comes from within, in that our own thoughts, memories, emotional reactions and behaviors can themselves become stimuli.

[91] *See, e.g.,* Antonio R. Damasio, Descartes' Error: Emotion, Reason, And The Human Brain (1995); Joseph Ledoux, Synaptic Self: How Our Brains Become Who We Are (2002); Bill Moyers, Healing and the Mind 177 (1995).

[92] *See, e.g.,* Handbook of Health Psychology (Andrew Baum et al. eds., 2001); Edward P. Sarafino, Health Psychology: Biopsychosocial Interactions (4th ed. 2001); Health Psychology (Derek W. Johnson et al. eds., 2000); Shelley E. Taylor, Health Psychology (5th ed. 2002); Bruce S. Rabin, Stress, Immune Function, and Health: The Connection (1999).

[93] Martin E. P. Seligman, Learned Optimism (1992); Martin E.P. Seligman, What You Can Change And What You Can't: The Complete Guide To Self-Improvement (1994); Christopher Peterson, Steven F. Maier and Martin E.P. Seligman, Learned Helplessness: A Theory For The Age Of Personal Control (1993).

[94] *See, e.g.,* Handbook of Health Psychology (Andrew Baum et al. eds., 2001); Edward P. Sarafino, Health Psychology: Biopsychosocial Interactions (4th ed. 2001); Health Psychology (Derek W. Johnson et al. eds., 2000); Shelley E. Taylor, Health Psychology (5th ed. 2002); Bruce S. Rabin, Stress, Immune Function, and Health: The Connection (1999); Bill Moyers, Healing and the Mind (1995).

[95] *See, e.g.,* Herbert Benson & Miriam Z. Klipper, The Relaxation Response (2000); Martha Davis, Mathew McKay & Elizabeth Robbins Eshelman, The Relaxation & Stress Reduction Workbook (2000).

[96] *See, e.g.,* American Bar Association, At The Breaking Point (1991); Commission On Women In The Profession, Lawyers And Balanced Lives:

A Guide To Drafting And Implementing Workplace Policies For Lawyers (1990).

[97] National Association for Law Placement (NALP), Trends Report: Part-time Schedules Remain Widely Available but Rarely Used by Attorneys (November 27, 2000).

[98] K. J. Klein, L.M. Berman, M.W. Dickson, *May I Work Part-time? An Exploration of Predicted Employer Responses to Employee Requests for Part-time Work.* 57(1) Journal of Vocational Behavior 85 (2000).

[99] Gail Diane Cox, *Litigator 'Disabled' If Can't Work Long Day; Court Finds Trial Lawyers must Be Healthy Enough To Work 16-20 Hour Days*, The National Law Journal, March 13, 2000, at 29, A9.

[100] C.F. Epstein, *The Part-time Solution and the Part-time Problem,* 46(2) Dissent 96 (1999).

[101] Scott Turow, Pleading Guilty 54 (1993).

[102] *See, e.g.,* Catalyst, Beyond a Reasonable Doubt: Building the Business Case for Flexibility (2005); Keith H. Hammonds, *Balancing Work And Family: Big Returns For Companies Willing To Give Family Strategies A Chance,* Business Week, September 16, 1996, at 74; Robert Levering & Milton Moskowitz, *The 100 Best Companies To Work For: Introduction,* Fortune, February 4, 2002, at 60; Lori-Ann Rickard & M. Diane Vogt, Keeping Good Lawyers: Best Practices To Create Career Satisfaction (2000).

[103] See, Catalyst, Beyond a Reasonable Doubt: Building the Business Case for Flexibility (2005).

[104] Steve Mendelsohn, *The Ideal Law Job, in* Success Briefs For Lawyers: Inspirational Insights On How To Succeed At Law And Life 157, 163 (Amiram Elwork & Mark R. Siwik eds., 2001).

[105] *See, e.g.* Isaiah M. Zimmerman, *Stress And The Trial Lawyer,* 9(4) Litigation 37 (1983).

[106] Christa Zevitas, *Courts Give Lawyers Guaranteed Vacation Time,* Lawyers Weekly USA, August 23, 1999, at B17.

[107] *See, e.g.* Isaiah M. Zimmerman, *Stress And The Trial Lawyer,* 9(4) Litigation 37 (1983).

[108] *See, e.g.*, Steven Keeva, Transforming Practices: Finding Joy And Satisfaction In The Legal Life 37-48 (1999); George W. Kaufman, The Lawyer's Guide To Balancing Life And Work (1999); Samuel P. Guyton, *Practicing Law While Living Within The Wheel Of Life, in* Success Briefs For Lawyers: Inspirational Insights On How To Succeed At Law And Life 61 (Amiram Elwork & Mark R. Siwik eds., 2001); Mark R. Siwik, *Lawyers From The School Of Athens, in* Success Briefs For Lawyers: Inspirational Insights On How To Succeed At Law And Life 189 (Amiram Elwork & Mark R. Siwik eds., 2001); Jenny B. Davis, *Life In Question: How Five*

Lawyers Worked Out Answers On Their Own, ABA Journal, May 2001, at 52; Debra Baker, *Dream Weavers,* ABA Journal, June 1998, at 54; Lori-Ann Rickard & M. Diane Vogt, Keeping Good Lawyers: Best Practices To Create Career Satisfaction (2000).

[109] *See, e.g.,* Sara C. McManus and Ellen B. Barker, *Attrition: What Do Associates Want?* New Jersey Law Journal, December 1999, at 31; Catalyst, Beyond a Reasonable Doubt: Building the Business Case for Flexibility (2005).

[110] Monica C. Higgins & David A. Thomas, *Constellations and Careers: Toward Understanding the Effects of Multiple Developmental Relationships*, 22(3) Journal of Organizational Behavior 223 (2001).

[111] Jean E. Wallace, *The Benefits of Mentoring for Female Lawyers*, 58(3) Journal of Vocational Behavior 366 (2001).

[112] George W. Kaufman, The Lawyer's Guide To Balancing Life And Work (1999).

[113] George W. Kaufman, *True Mentoring, in* Success Briefs For Lawyers: Inspirational Insights On How To Succeed At Law And Life 167, 169 (Amiram Elwork & Mark R. Siwik eds., 2001).

[114] *See, e.g.,* Walt Bachman, Law v. Life 100 (1995); Mary Ann Glendon, A Nation Under Lawyers (1994); Anthony T. Kronman, The Lost Lawyer (1993); Sol M. Linowitz & Martin Mayer, The Betrayed Profession: Lawyering At The End Of The Twentieth Century (1994); Benjamin Sells, The Soul of the Law (1994).

[115] See, e.g., Susan E. Davis, *Uncivil Behavior: The Tactics Lawyers Resort To When They're Not Restrained,* California Lawyer, Jul. 1999, at 44.

[116] *See, e.g.,* Dianne Molvig, *1999 Bench-Bar Survey: Lack of Civility Still A Major Concern Among Respondents*, The Wisconsin Lawyer, Dec. 1999, at 10.

[117] *See, e.g.,* Ohio Supreme Court Commission On Professionalism, A Lawyer's Creed and Aspirational Ideals (1997).

[118] *See, e.g.,* ABA Commission On Professionalism, In The Spirit Of Public Service: A Blueprint For The Rekindling Of Professionalism – The Stanley Commission Report (1986).

[119] *See, e.g.,* Dianne Molvig, *1999 Bench-Bar Survey: Lack of Civility Still A Major Concern Among Respondents*, The Wisconsin Lawyer, Dec. 1999, at 10.

[120] *Id.*

[121] *See, e.g.,* Bruce J. Winnick, David B. Wexler, & Edward A. Dauer, *Preface: A New Model For The Practice Of Law,* 5(4) Psychology, Public Policy, and Law 795 (1999); Susan Daicoff, *Making Law Therapeutic for Lawyers: Therapeutic Jurisprudence, Preventive Law, and the Psychology of Lawyers,* 5(4) Psychology, Public Policy, and Law 811 (1999); Rand Jack & Dana Crowley Jack, Moral Vision And Professional Decisions: The

Changing Values Of Women And Men Lawyers (1989); Benjamin Sells, The Soul Of The Law (1994); Susan Swaim Daicoff, Lawyer, Know Thyself (2004); *See also,* websites of several organizations that promote alternative models of practicing law: www.iahl.org (International Alliance of Holistic Lawyers); collaborativelaw.org; www.mediate.com, collaborativelaw.com; www.transformingpractices.com..

[122] Alan Dershowitz, Letters To A Young Lawyer 50 (2001).

[123] *See, e.g., Id.* at 57; Richard A. Zitrin and Carol M. Langoford, The Moral Compass of the American Lawyer (1999); Richard A. Zitrin and Carol M. Langford, Legal Ethics in the Practice of Law (2002).

[124] See, e.g., Mathew M. Dammeyer & Narina Nunez, *Anxiety and Depression Among Law Students: Current Knowledge and Future Directions*, 23(1) Law and Human Behavior 55 (1999); Ann L. Iijima, *Lessons Learned: Legal Education and Law Student Dysfunction*, 48(4) Journal of Legal Education 524 (1998); Suzanne C. Segerstrom, *Perceptions of Stress and Control in the First Semester of Law School*, 32(3) Willamette Law Review 593 (1996); G.A.H. Benjamin, A. Kaszniak, B.D. Sales & S.B. Shanfield, *The Role Of Legal Education In Producing Psychological Distress Among Law Students And Lawyers*, American Bar Foundation Research Journal 225 (1986); Fernando J. Gutierrez, *Counseling Law Students*, 64 Journal of Counseling and Development 130 (1985); Lawrence Dubin, *The Role of Law School in Balancing a Lawyer's Personal and Professional Life*, 10(1) The Journal of Psychiatry and Law 57 (1982).

[125] *Id.*

[126] *See, e.g.,* Vernelia Randall, *The Myers-Briggs Type Indicator, First Year Law Students and Performance*, 26 Columbia Law Review 63 (1995); P. Miller, *Personality Differences and Student Survival in Law School*, 19 Journal of Legal Education 460 (1967); J.M. Satterfield, J. Monahan, and M.E.P. Seligman, *Law School Performance Predicted By Explanatory Style*, 15(1) Behavioral Sciences and the Law 95 (1997).

[127] P. Miller, *Personality Differences and Student Survival in Law School*, 19 Journal of Legal Education 460 (1967).

[128] *See, e.g.,* Fernando J. Gutierrez, *Counseling Law Students*, 64 Journal of Counseling and Development 130 (1985); Alan A. Stone, *Legal Education On The Couch*, 85 Harvard Law Review 392 (1971).

[129] *See, e.g.,* Alan A. Stone, *Legal Education On The Couch*, 85 Harvard Law Review 392 (1971); Pearl Goldman & Leslie Larkin Cooney, *Beyond Core Skills and Values: Integrating Therapeutic Jurisprudence and Preventive Law Into the Law School Curriculum*, 5(4) Psychology, Public Policy, and Law 1123 (1999); Marjorie A. Silver, *Emotional Intelligence and Legal Education*, 5(4) Psychology, Public Policy, and Law 1173 (1999);

Robert C. Bordone, *Teaching Interpersonal Skills for Negotiation and for Life,* 16(4) Negotiation Journal 377 (2000).

[130] Walter C. Willett, Eat, Drink, And Be Healthy: The Harvard Medical School Guide To Healthy Eating (2001); *See also,* Institute of Medicine of the National Academy of Science, Dietary Reference Intakes for Energy, Carbohydrate, Fiber, Fat, Fatty Acids, Cholesterol, Protein, and Amino Acids (2006); Mollie Katzen & Walter Willett, Eat, Drink & Weigh Less: A Flexible and Delicious Way to Shrink Your Waist Without Going Hungry (2006).

[131] Among the exceptions are athletes involved in strenuous exercise that requires them to ingest and burn quick energy sources.

[132] *See,* Institute of Medicine of the National Academy of Science, Dietary Reference Intakes for Energy, Carbohydrate, Fiber, Fat, Fatty Acids, Cholesterol, Protein, and Amino Acids (2006).

[133] *Id.*

[134] *See, e.g.,* Walter C. Willett, Eat, Drink, And Be Healthy: The Harvard Medical School Guide To Healthy Eating (2001); Institute of Medicine of the National Academy of Science, Dietary Reference Intakes for Energy, Carbohydrate, Fiber, Fat, Fatty Acids, Cholesterol, Protein, and Amino Acids (2006); Mollie Katzen & Walter Willett, Eat, Drink & Weigh Less: A Flexible and Delicious Way to Shrink Your Waist Without Going Hungry (2006).

[135] *See e.g.,* The Truth About Dieting, Consumer Reports, June 2002, at 27; Walter C. Willett, Eat, Drink, And Be Healthy: The Harvard Medical School Guide To Healthy Eating 37 (2001).

[136] *See e.g.,* The Truth About Dieting, Consumer Reports, June 2002, at 26; Institute of Medicine of the National Academy of Science, Dietary Reference Intakes for Energy, Carbohydrate, Fiber, Fat, Fatty Acids, Cholesterol, Protein, and Amino Acids (2006).

[137] *See, e.g.,* R.B. Cellia, Direct Metabolic Regulation in Skeletal Muscle and Fat Tissue by Leptin, 29(10) *International Journal of Obesity* 1175 (2005).

[138] *See, e.g.,* Leo Galland, The Fat Resistance Diet: Unlock the Secret of the Hormone Leptin (2005); Ron Rosedale & Carol Colman, The Rosedale Diet (2004).

[139] *See, e.g.,* Audrey F. Manley, Physical Activity and Mental Health: A Report of the Surgeon General (1996); Institute of Medicine of the National Academy of Science, Dietary Reference Intakes for Energy, Carbohydrate, Fiber, Fat, Fatty Acids, Cholesterol, Protein, and Amino Acids (2006); Janet Buckworth & Rod K. Dishman, Exercise Psychology (2002); Walter C. Willett, Eat, Drink, And Be Healthy: The Harvard Medical School Guide To Healthy Eating (2001).

[140] *See,* Institute of Medicine of the National Academy of Science, Dietary Reference Intakes for Energy, Carbohydrate, Fiber, Fat, Fatty Acids, Cholesterol, Protein, and Amino Acids (2006).

[141] *See e.g.,* The Truth About Dieting, Consumer Reports, June 2002, at 26.

[142] *See, e.g.,* Audrey F. Manley, Physical Activity and Mental Health: A Report of the Surgeon General 209 (1996); Janet Buckworth & Rod K. Dishman, Exercise Psychology 229 (2002).

[143] *See, e.g.,* www.dietpower.com for a desktop or notebook computer weight, nutrition and exercise manager; www.keyoe.com for a PDA-handheld weight, nutrition and exercise manager.

[144] *See, e.g.,* Handbook of Health Psychology (Andrew Baum et al. eds., 2001); Edward P. Sarafino, Health Psychology: Biopsychosocial Interactions (4th ed. 2001); Health Psychology (Derek W. Johnson et al. eds., 2000); Shelley E. Taylor, Health Psychology (5th ed. 2002); Bruce S. Rabin, Stress, Immune Function, and Health: The Connection (1999); Herbert Benson & Miriam Z. Klipper, The Relaxation Response (2000); Martha Davis, Mathew McKay & Elizabeth Robbins Eshelman, The Relaxation & Stress Reduction Workbook (2000).

[145] *See, e.g.,* Martha Davis, Mathew McKay & Elizabeth Robbins Eshelman, The Relaxation & Stress Reduction Workbook (2000); Herbert Benson & Miriam Z. Klipper, The Relaxation Response (2000); Andrew Goliszek, 60 Second Stress Management: The Quickest Way To Relax And Ease Anxiety (1992); Edward Charlesworth and Ronald Nathan, Stress Management 47-165 (1991).

[146] *See, e.g.,* Martha Davis, Mathew McKay & Elizabeth Robbins Eshelman, The Relaxation & Stress Reduction Workbook (2000); Herbert Benson & Miriam Z. Klipper, The Relaxation Response (2000).

[147] *See, e.g.,* Martha Davis, Mathew McKay & Elizabeth Robbins Eshelman, The Relaxation & Stress Reduction Workbook (2000); 30 Scripts For Relaxation Imagery And Inner Healing (Julie T. Lusk ed., Vol. 2, 1992); Stephen Levine, Guided Meditations, Explorations And Healings (1991); William Fezler, Creative Imagery: How To Visualize All Senses (1989).

[148] *See, e.g.,* Nischala Devi, Deep Relaxation (Nischala Devi Productions audiocassette, 1994); Nischala Devi, Dynamic Stillness-Meditation (Nischala Devi Productions audiocassette, 1994); Mathew McKay, Progressive Relaxation Breathing (New Harbinger Publications audiocassette 1988); Andrew Weil & Jon Kabat-Zinn, Meditation For Optimum Health: How To Use Mindfulness And Breathing To Heal Your Body And Refresh Your Mind (Sounds True audiocassette 2001); Jack Kornfeld, Sharon Salzberg and Shinzen Young, Beginner's Mind: 3 Classic

Meditation Practices Especially For Beginners (Sounds True audiocassette 1999).

[149] *See , e.g.*, Peter Hauri, Shirley Linde & Philip Westbrook, No More Sleepless Nights (2nd ed. 1996); Gregg D. Jacobs, Say Goodnight To Insomnia (1999).

[150] *E.g.,* Peter Hauri, Shirley Linde & Philip Westbrook, No More Sleepless Nights (2nd ed. 1996); Gregg D. Jacobs, Say Goodnight To Insomnia (1999).

[151] *See, e.g.,* Peter Hauri, Shirley Linde & Philip Westbrook, No More Sleepless Nights (2nd ed. 1996); Gregg D. Jacobs, Say Goodnight To Insomnia (1999).

[152] *See,* More information available through the American Sleep Apnea Association on their website at: http://www.sleepapnea.org

[153] Website listings of accredited sleep disorders centers are available at: http://www.aasmnet.org/listing.htm

[154] This model of stress is based on the ideas of a number of theorists and researchers. *See, e.g.,* Aaron T. Beck, Cognitive Therapy And Emotional Disorders (1976); Edward A. Charlesworth & Ronald G. Nathan, Stress Management (1991); Handbook Of Stress, Medicine, And Health (Cary L. Cooper ed., 1996); Cary L. Cooper, Philip J. Dewe, & Michael P. O'Driscoll, Organizational Stress: A Review And Critique Of Theory, Research, And Applications (2001); Albert Ellis, Reason and Emotion In Psychotherapy (1962); J.J. Hurrell, L.R. Murphy, S.L. Sauter, & C.L. Cooper, Occupational stress: Issues and Developments in Research (1988); R.L. Kahn, & P. Byosiere, Stress in Organizations, In Handbook of Industrial and Organizational Psychology 571 (Vol.3, 2nd ed. 1992); R.S. Lazarus, Emotion And Adaptation (1991); R.S. Lazarus & S. Folkman, Stress, Appraisal and Coping (1984); Richard S. Lazarus & Bernice N. Lazarus, Passion and Reason (1994); Hans Selye, History and Present Status of the Stress Concept, In Handbook of Stress 7 (1982); K.T. Strongman, The Psychology Of Emotion (4th ed. 1996); James C. Quick, Lawrence R. Murphy and Joseph J. Hurrell, Stress And Well-Being At Work: Assessments And Interventions For Occupational Mental Health (1992).

[155] *See, e.g.,* David G. Myers, The Pursuit of Happiness: Who Is Happy- and Why (1992).

[156] *See, e.g,* Daniel Goleman, Emotional Intelligence (1995); Daniel Goleman, Working With Emotional Intelligence (1998); The Handbook Of Emotional Intelligence (Reuven Bar-On & James D.A. Parker eds., 2000).

[157] *See,* John D. Mayer, Peter Salovey, & David R. Caruso, *Emotional Intelligence As Zeitgeist, As Personality, And As A Mental Ability, in* The Handbook of Emotional Intelligence (Reuven Bar-On & James D.A. Parker eds., 2000).

[158] Marjorie A. Silver, *Emotional Intelligence and Legal Education,* 5(4) Psychology, Public Policy, and Law 1173 (1999).

[159] Lawrence Richard, *The Lawyer Types,* 79(7) ABA Journal 74 (1993).

[160] K.J. Lively, *Reciprocal Emotion Management: Working Together to Maintain Stratification in Private Law Firms,* 27(1) Work & Occupations 32 (2000).

[161] *See,* Antonio R. Damasio, Descartes' Error: Emotion, Reason, And The Human Brain (1994); Antonio R. Damasio, Looking for Spinoza: Joy, Sorrow And The Feeling Brain (2003).

[162] James R. Averill, *Inner Feelings, Works Of The Flesh, The Beast Within, Diseases Of The Mind, Driving Force, And Putting On A Show: Six Metaphors Of Emotions And Their Theoretical Extensions, in* Metaphors In The History Of Psychology (David E. Leary ed., 1990).

[163] Antonio R. Damasio, Descartes' Error: Emotion, Reason, And The Human Brain (1994); Richard S. Lazarus & Bernice N. Lazarus, Passion and Reason (1994).

[164] *See e.g.,* Richard S. Lazarus, Emotion and Adaptation (1991); Richard S. Lazarus & Bernice N. Lazarus, Passion and Reason (1994).

[165] *See, e.g.,* Antonio R. Damasio, Descartes' Error: Emotion, Reason, And The Human Brain (1994); Richard S. Lazarus & Bernice N. Lazarus, Passion and Reason (1994); Daniel Goleman, Emotional Intelligence (1995); Joseph LeDoux, The Emotional Brain (1996).

[166] *See, e.g.,* Joseph LeDoux, *The Emotional Brain* (1996).

[167] Michael Gershon, *The Second Brain: The Scientific Basis of Gut Instinct and a Groundbreaking New Understanding of Nervous Disorders of the Stomach and Intestines* (1998).

[168] John T. Cacioppo & Wendi L. Gardner, *Emotion,* 50 Annual Review of Psychology 191 (1999).

[169] *See,* Antonio R. Damasio, Descartes' Error: Emotion, Reason, And The Human Brain (1994); Antonio R. Damasio, Looking for Spinoza: Joy, Sorrow And The Feeling Brain (2003).

[170] Lawrence Richard, *The Lawyer Types,* 79(7) ABA Journal 74 (1993).

[171] *E.g.,* Robert Plutchnik, Emotions and Life (2003); Richard S. Lazarus, Emotion & Adaptation (1994); T.D. Kemper, *How Many Emotions Are There? Wedding The Social And The Autonomic Components,* 93 American Journal of Sociology 263 (1987); P. Shaver, J. Schwartz, D. Kirson, & C. O'Connor, *Emotion Knowledge: Further Exploration of a Prototype Approach,* 52 Journal of Personality and Social Psychology 1061 (1987).

[172] *See, e.g.,* Handbook of Health Psychology (Andrew Baum et al. eds., 2001); Edward P. Sarafino, Health Psychology: Biopsychosocial Interactions (4th ed. 2001); Health Psychology (Derek W. Johnson et al. eds., 2000); Shelley E. Taylor, Health Psychology (5th ed. 2002); Bruce S. Rabin, Stress, Immune Function, and Health: The Connection (1999).

[173] Richard L. Bednar and Scott R. Peterson, Self-Esteem: Paradoxes And Innovations In Clinical Theory And Practice (1995).

[174] Nathaniel Branden, The Six Pillars Of Self-Esteem (1995).

[175] Martin E. Seligman, The Optimistic Child 27-36 (1995).

[176] *See,* M. H. Guindon, *Toward Accountability In The Use Of The Sef-Esteem Construct,* 80 (2) Journal Of Counseling & Development 204 (2002); M. Rosenberg, Conceiving The Self (1979).

[177] *See,* Carl R. Rogers, On Becoming A Person (1961); N.E. Betz, E. Wohlgemuth, D. Serling, J. Harshbarger & K. Klein, *Evaluation of a Measure of Self-Esteem Based on the Concept of Unconditional Self-regard,* 74 Journal of Counseling and Development 76 (1995).

[178] *See,* Saint Thomas Aquinas, Summa Theologiae: A Concise Translation (Timothy McDermott, ed., 1991); Terry D. Cooper, Sin, Pride and Self-Acceptance: The Problem of Identity in Theology and Psychology (2003); Michael Eric Dyson, Pride: The Seven Deadly Sins (2006).

[179] Marianne Williamson, A Return to Love: Reflections on the Principles of "A Course in Miracles" 190-191 (1996).

[180] G.A.H. Benjamin, A. Kaszniak, B.D. Sales & S.B. Shanfield, *The Role Of Legal Education In Producing Psychological Distress Among Law Students And Lawyers,* American Bar Foundation Research Journal 225 (1986); R. Frances, G. Alexopoulos, & V. Yandow, *Lawyers' Alcoholism,* 4(2) Advances In Alcohol And Substance Abuse 59 (1984); Forsyth & T.J. Danisiewicz, *Toward A Theory Of Professionalization,* 12(1) Work and Occupations 59 (1985);M.D. Gupta, *Machiavellianism Of Different Occupational Groups,* 18(2) Indian Journal of Psychometry and Education 61 (1987); J.P. Heinz & E.O. Laumann, Chicago Lawyers: The Social Structure of the Bar (1984); S. Reich, *California Psychological Inventory: Profile Of A Sample Of First Year Law Students,* 38 Psychological Reports 871 (1976); N. Solkoff & J. Markowitz, *Personality Characteristics Of First Year Medical And Law Students,* 42 Journal Of Medical Education 195 (1967); R. Tomasic, *Social Organization Amongst Australian Lawyers,* 19(3) Australian and New Zealand Journal of Sociology 447 (1983).

[181] J.M. Dabbs, Jr., E.C. Alford, & J.A. Fielden, *Trial Lawyers and Testosterone: Blue-collar Talent in a White-collar World,* 28(1) Journal of Applied Social Psychology 84 (1998).

[182] Connie J.A. Beck, Bruce D. Sales, & G. Andrew H. Benjamin, *Lawyer Distress: Alcohol-Related Problems And Other Psychological Concerns Among A Sample Of Practicing Lawyers,* 10(1) Journal of Law

and Health 1 (1995-96); Barbara S. McCann, Joan Russo, & G. Andrew H. Benjamin, *Hostility, social support, and perceptions of work,* 2(2) Journal of Occupational Health Psychology 175 (1997).

[183] Redford Williams, The Trusting Heart (1989); Redford Williams & Virginia Williams, Anger Kills (1998).

[184] J.C. Barefoot, K.A. Dodge, B.L. Peterson, W.G. Dahlstrom & R.B. Williams, *The Cook-Medley Hostility Scale: Item Content And Ability To Predict Survival,* 51 Psychosomatic Medicine 46 (1989).

[185] *See, eg.,* Carl Semmelroth & D.E.P. Smith, The Anger Habit: Proven Principles To Calm The Stormy Mind (2000); Carl Semmelroth, Then Anger Habit Workbook: Proven Principles To Calm The Stormy Mind (2002); Ron Potter-Efron & Pat Potter-Enron, Letting Go Of Anger: The 10 Most Common Anger Styles And What To Do About Them (1995); William Davies, Overcoming Anger And Irritability (2001).

[186] David G. Myers, The Pursuit of Happiness: Who Is Happy - and Why (1992).

[187] Dean Ornish, Love & Survival: The Scientific Basis For The Healing Power Of Intimacy (1998).

[188] Dean Ornish, Love & Survival: The Scientific Basis For The Healing Power Of Intimacy 2-3 (1998).

[189] *See, e.g.,* Steven Keeva, Transforming Practices: Finding Joy And Satisfaction In The Legal Life (1999); Bruce J. Winnick, David B. Wexler, & Edward A. Dauer, *Preface: A New Model For The Practice Of Law,* 5(4) Psychology, Public Policy, and Law 795 (1999); Susan Daicoff, *Making Law Therapeutic for Lawyers: Therapeutic Jurisprudence, Preventive Law, and the Psychology of Lawyers,* 5(4) Psychology, Public Policy, and Law 811 (1999); Rand Jack & Dana Crowley Jack, Moral Vision And Professional Decisions: The Changing Values Of Women And Men Lawyers (1989); Benjamin Sells, The Soul Of The Law (1994); Susan Swaim Daicoff, Lawyer, Know Thyself (2004); *See also,* websites of several organizations that promote alternative models of practicing law: www.iahl.org (International Alliance of Holistic Lawyers); collaborativelaw.org; collaborativelaw.com; www.transformingpractices.com; www.mediate.com.

[190] *See,* C.R. Snyder, Kevin L. Rand, & David R. Sigmon, *Hope Theory: A Member of the Positive Psychology Family, in* Handbook of Positive Psychology (C.R. Snyder & S.J. Lopez eds., 2002).

[191] S.C. Segerstrom, S.E. Taylor, M.E. Kemeny, & J.L. Faheym, *Optimism Is Associated With Mood, Coping and Immune Change in Response to Stress,* 74(6) Journal of Personality & Social Psychology 1646 (1998).

[192] J.M. Satterfield, J. Monahan, and M.E.P. Seligman, *Law School Performance Predicted By Explanatory Style,* 15(1) Behavioral Sciences and the Law 95 (1997).

[193] Susan Mineka & Arne Ohman, *Phobias and Preparedness: The Selective, Automatic, and Encapsulated Nature of Fear,* 52(10) Biological Psychiatry 927 (2002); Joseph LeDoux, The Emotional Brain: The Mysterious Underpinnings of Emotional Life (1998).

[194] Susan Mineka & Arne Ohman, *Phobias and Preparedness: The Selective, Automatic, and Encapsulated Nature of Fear,* 52(10) Biological Psychiatry 927 (2002); Joseph LeDoux, The Emotional Brain: The Mysterious Underpinnings of Emotional Life (1998).

[195] Susan Jefffers, Feel The Fear And Do It Anyway (1987).

[196] *Id.*

[197] Martin E. P. Seligman, Learned Optimism: How To Change Your Mind And Your Life (1998).

[198] See, e.g., Douglas Stone, Bruce Patton & Roger Fisher, Difficult Conversations: How To Discuss What Matters Most (2000); Rick Brinkman & Rick Kirschner, Dealing With People You Can't Stand (1994); Robert M. Bramson, Coping With Difficult People (1988).

[199] Stone et al., *supra* note 197.

[200] Milton Rokeach, The Nature of Values (1973).

[201] I have garnered this list from the works of many others. *See, e.g.,* Milton Rokeach, The Nature of Values (1973); Milton Rokeach, Rokeach Value Survey (1983); Don E. Beck & Christopher C. Cowan, Spiral Dynamics (1996); Dorothy D. Nevill & Donald E. Super, The Values Scale: Theory, Application and Research (1989).

[202] David G. Myers, The Pursuit of Happiness: Who Is Happy - and Why (1992).

[203] *See, e.g.,* Tim Kasser, The High Price Of Materialism (2002).

[204] *See, e.g.,* Sheelagh O'Donova-Polten, The Scales of Success: Constructions of Life-Career Success of Eminent Men and Women Lawyers (2001); Kenneth G. Dau-Schmidt, *The Fruits of Our Labor: An empirical Study of the Distribution of Income and Job Satisfaction Across the Legal Profession,* 49(3), Journal of Legal Education 342 (1999).

[205] Suzanne C. Kobasa, *Commitment and Coping in Stress Resistance Among Lawyers,* 42(4) Journal of Personality and Social Psychology 707 (1982); Mary E. Sweetman, David C. Munz & Robert J. Wheeler, *Optimism, Hardiness, and Explanatory Style as Predictors of General Well Being Among Attorneys,* 29 Social Indicators Research 153 (1993).

[206] *See, e.g.,*(listed alphabetically by author) Joseph Allegretti, The Lawyer's Calling: Christian Faith And Legal Practice (1996); Carl Horn III, LawyerLife: Finding A Life And A Higher Calling In The Practice Of Law (2003); George W. Kaufman, The Lawyer's Guide To Balancing Life And

Work (1999); Steven Keeva, Transforming Practices: Finding Joy And Satisfaction In The Legal Life (1999); Mike Papantonio, In Search Of Atticus Finch: A Motivational Book For Lawyers (1995); Benjamin Sells, The Soul Of The Law (1994).

[207] Steven Keeva, Transforming Practices: Finding Joy And Satisfaction In The Legal Life 11 (1999).

[208] Oliver Wendell Holmes, The Mind and Faith of Justice Holmes: His Speeches, Essays, Letters, and Judicial Opinions 29 (1943).

[209] D. Von Drehle, *The Crumbling Of A Pillar In Washington,* The Washington Post A20 (Aug. 15, 1993). Quote also appears in Sidney J. Blatt, *The Destructiveness of Perfectionism,* 50 American Psychologist 1003 (1995).

[210] Some have attributed this quote to Ralph Waldo Emerson, while others claim it to be the words of Bessie Anderson Stanley. After hours of research and the help of many librarians, I have discovered that no one seems to be certain about its origin. However, it is the thought that counts.

[211] Stephen R. Covey, The 7 Habits Of Highly Effective People (1989).

[212] American Bar Association, At The Breaking Point: The Report Of A National Conference On The Emerging Crisis In The Quality Of Lawyers' Health And Lives, And Its Impact On Law Firms And Client Services (1991); American Bar Association, The State Of The Legal Profession - 1990: Report Of The Young Lawyers Division (1991).

[213] Two of the best time management books in print are: Stephen R. Covey, A. Roger Merrill and Rebecca R. Merrill, First Things First (1994); Alec Mackenzie, The Time Trap (1990).

[214] Stephen R. Covey, A. Roger Merrill and Rebecca R. Merrill, First Things First (1994).

[215] Alec Mackenzie, The Time Trap 55 (1990).

[216] Two of the best time management books in print are: Stephen R. Covey, A. Roger Merrill and Rebecca R. Merrill, First Things First (1994); Alec Mackenzie, The Time Trap (1990). In particular, Mackenzie's book is filled with the types of specific behavioral tips discussed in this chapter.

[217] *E.g.,* Kenneth Blanchard and Spencer Johnson, The One Minute Manager (1982); Alec Mackenzie, The Time Trap 104 (1990).

[218] *See, e.g.,* Anthony Perez Cassino, *Associate Satisfaction Tied to Pro Bono,* New York Law Journal, October 13, 2000, at 24.

[219] National Association for Law Placement, Keeping the Keepers: Strategies for Associate Retention in Times of Attrition (1998); National Association for Law Placement, Beyond the Bidding Wars: A Survey of Associate Attrition, Departure Destinations, and Workplace Incentives (2000).

[220] James D. Cotterman, Compensation Plans for Law Firms 80 (4th ed. 2004).

[221] Catalyst, Beyond a Reasonable Doubt: Building the Business Case for Flexibility (2005)

[222] David H. Maister, Managing the Professional Service Firm (1993).

[223] David H. Maister, True Professionalism (1997).

[224] Clarence Hibbs, *Attorneys: High Performance And Family Relationships, in* High Performing Families: Causes, Consequences, And Clinical Solutions 71 (Bryan E. Robinson & Nancy D. Chase eds., 2000)

[225] North Carolina Bar Association, Quality of Life Survey of North Carolina Attorneys: Report of Quality of Life Task Force 42 (1991).

[226] American Bar Association, Young Lawyers Division, The State Of The Legal Profession – 1990 48 (1991).

[227] Bryan E. Robinson, *The Workaholic Family: A Clinical Perspective,* 26 American Journal Of Family Therapy 65-66 (1998).

[228] American Bar Association, Young Lawyers Division, The State Of The Legal Profession – 1990 17 (1991).

[229] American Bar Association, Young Lawyers Division Survey: Career Satisfaction 16 (1995).

[230] Sharon K. Houseknecht et al., *Marital Disruption Among Professional Women: The Timing Of Career And Family Events,* 31 Social Problems 273 (1984).

[231] Teresa M. Cooney & Peter Uhlenberg, *Family-Building Patterns of Professional Women: A Comparison of Lawyers, Physicians, and Postsecondary Teachers,* 51 Journal of Marriage and the Family, 749.(1989).

[232] American Bar Association, Young Lawyers Division, The State Of The Legal Profession – 1990 48 (1991).

[233] Lawrence R. Richard, *The Lawyer Types,* 79(7) ABA Journal 74 (1993); Lawrence R. Richard, Psychological Type And Job Satisfaction Among Practicing Lawyers In The United States (1994; Ph.D. dissertation, Temple Univ., Philadelphia, available through University Microfilms International Dissertation Services.)

[234] *Id.*

[235] Fiona H. Travis, Should You Marry A Lawyer: A Couple's Guide To Balancing Work, Love & Ambition (2004).

[236] Pub. L. 104-191, 110 Stat. 1936 (2006).

[237] *Jaffe v. Redmond,* 5/8 U.S. 1 (1996)..

[238] As amended by the ABA House of Delegates in February 2002.

[239] *See,* Carl Anderson, Thomas McCracken, & Betty Reddy, *Addictive Illness in the Legal Profession: Bar Examiners Dilemma,* Professional Lawyer 16 (May 1996); Hilary Duke, *The Narrowing of State*

Bar Examiner Inquiries into the Mental Health of Bar Applicants, 11 Georgetown Journal of Legal Ethics 101 (1997).

[240] *See, e.g.,* Medical Society of New Jersey v. Jacobs, Civ. A. No. 93-3670 (WGB), 1993 WL 413016, (D. N.J. Oct. 5, 1993); Ellen S. v. Florida Board of Bar Examiners, Case No. 94-0429, 1994 U.S. Dist. LEXIS 10842 (S.D. Fla. 1994); Clark v. Virginia Board of Bar Examiners, No. 94-211-A, 1994 WL 364443 (E.D. Va. 1994).

[241] P.L. 101-336, 42 U.S.C. §§12101 *et seq.* (1990).

[242] P.L. 101-336, 42 U.S.C. §§12101 *et seq.* (1990).

[243] 29 U.S.C. §794.

[244] *In Re Applications of Anne Underwood and Judith Ann Plano,* 1993 WL 649283 (Dec. 7, 1993).

[245] 42 U.S.C. §12119; *See, e.g.,* 14 Mental and Physical Disability Law Rptr 65 (Sept. 1996); *See also,* Wayne F. Cascio, *The Americans With Disabilities Act of 1990 and the 1991 Civil Rights Act: Requirements for Psychological Practice in the Work Place, in* Psychology in Litigation and Legislation (Julie Blackman, Wayne F. Casio, Stephen J. Ceci, Gary B. Melton, & Michael O. Miller, eds., 1994).

[246] 42 U.S.C. §12210; *See,* Nancy Jones, *The Alcohol and Drug Provisions of the ADA: Implications for Employers and Employees, in* Implications of the Americans with Disabilities Act for Psychology 151 (Susan M. Bruyere and Janet O'Keeffe eds., 1994).

[247] H. Conf. Rep. No. 596, 101st Cong., 2d Sess., at 64.

[248] U.S. Equal Employment Opportunity Commission, A Technical Assistance Manual on the Employment Provisions of the Americans with Disabilities Act §II-3 (1992).

[249] As amended by the ABA House of Delegates in February 2002.

[250] 42 C.F.R. §2.35(a).

[251] June 11, 2003.

[252] August 8, 2003.

[253] P.L. 101-336, 42 U.S.C. §§12101 *et seq.* (1990).

[254] 42 U.S.C. §12119; *See, e.g.,* 14 Mental and Physical Disability Law Rptr 65 (Sept. 1996); *See also,* Wayne F. Cascio, *The Americans With Disabilities Act of 1990 and the 1991 Civil Rights Act: Requirements for Psychological Practice in the Work Place, in* Psychology in Litigation and Legislation (Julie Blackman, Wayne F. Casio, Stephen J. Ceci, Gary B. Melton, & Michael O. Miller eds., 1994).

[255.] North Carolina Bar Association, Quality of Life Survey of North Carolina Attorneys: Report of Quality of Life Task Force (1991).

[256.] G.A.H. Benjamin, E.J. Darling & B.D. Sales, *The Prevalence of Depression, Alcohol Abuse, And Cocaine Abuse Among United States Lawyers,* 13 International Journal of Law and Psychiatry 233 (1990).

257. G. Andrew, H. Benjamin, Elaine J. Darling, & Bruce Sales, *The Prevalence of Depression, Alcohol Abuse, and Cocaine Abuse Among United States Lawyers*, 13 Int'l J. Law & Psychiatry 233, 241 (1990); Eric Drogan, *Alcoholism in the Legal Profession: Psychological and Legal Perspectives and Interventions*, 15 Law & Psychol. Rev. 117, 127 (1991); Stephanie B. Goldberg, *Drawing the Line: When is an Ex-Coke Addict Fit to Practice Law?*, A.B.A. J. 50 (Feb. 1990); see also Angie Fought, *Help for Addicted Lawyers*, 18 Pa. Lawyer 29 (March/April 1996); Jeffrey J. Fleury, Comment, *Kicking the Habit: Diversion in Michigan - The Sensible Approach*, 73 U. Det. Mercy L. Rev. 11, 14 (1995).

258. E.g., Michael A. Bloom & Carol Lynn Wallinger, *Lawyers and Alcoholism: Is it Time for a New Approach?*, 61 Temple L.Rev. 1409 (1988); Laurie B. Dowell, *Attorneys and Alcoholism: An Alternative Approach to a Serious Problem*, 16 N. Ky. L.Rev. 169 (1988); Patricia Sue Heil, Comment, *Tending the Bar in Texas: Alcoholism as a Mitigating Factor in Attorney Discipline*, 24 St. Mary's L.J. 1263, 1265 (1993).

259. E.g., Terence Williams, "I Won't Wait Up Tonight" (Hazelton Educational Materials, 1992).

260. American Psychiatric Association, Diagnostic and Statistical Manual of Mental Disorders, at 197-98, 213-214 (4th ed., text rev. 2000).

261 J. A. Ewing, *Detecting alcoholism: The CAGE questionnaire.* 252 Journal of the American Medical Association 1905 (1984).

262. William R. Miller & Stephen Rollnick, Motivational Interviewing: Preparing People to Change Addictive Behavior (1991)

263. See G. Alan Marlatt & Judith R. Gordon, Relapse Prevention: Maintenance Strategies in the Treatment of Addictive Behaviors (1985); Dennis L. Thombs, Introduction to Addictive Behaviors (1994).

264. E.g., Ralph E. Tarter, Howard B. Moss, & Michael M. Vanyukov, *Behavioral Genetics and the Etiology of Alcoholism, in* The Genetics of Alcoholism (Vol. 1) (1995); Richard Rende & Robert Plomin, *Diathesis-Stress Models of Psychopathology*, 1 Appl. & Prevent. Psychol. 177 (1992).

265. Robert M. Anthenelli & Marc A. Schuckit, *Genetics, in* Substance Abuse: A Comprehensive Textbook - 2d ed. (Joyce H. Lowinson, Pedro Ruiz, Robert B. Millman, & John G. Langrod, eds. 1992).

266. E.g., Patti Juliana & Carolyn Goodman, *Children of Substance Abusing Parents, in* Substance Abuse: A Comprehensive Textbook - 2d ed. (Joyce H. Lowinson, Pedro Ruiz, Robert B. Millman, & John G. Langrod, eds. 1992).

267. Edward J. Khantzian, Kurt S. Halliday, & William E. McAuliffe, Addiction and the Vulnerable Self (1990).

268. E.g., Boris Tabakoff & Paula L. Hoffman, *Alcohol: Neurobiology,* Substance Abuse: A Comprehensive Textbook - 2d ed. (Joyce H. Lowinson,

Pedro Ruiz, Robert B. Millman, & John G. Langrod, eds. 1992); Stephen A. Maisto, Mark Galizio, & Gerard J. Connors, Drug Use and Misuse (1991).

[269] P.I. Ordorica & E.P. Nace, *Alcohol,* in Clinical Textbook of Addictive Disorder 91 (R. J. Frances & S. I. Miller eds., 2nd ed. 1998).

[270.] Marc Galanter & Herbert D. Kleber, The American Psychiatric Press Textbook of Substance Abuse Treatment (1994).

[271] A.I. Alterman, A.T. McLellan, C.P. O'Brien, & J.R. McKay, *Differential Therapies And Options,* in Clinical Textbook Of Addictive Disorders 447 (R. J. Frances & S. I. Miller eds., 2nd ed. 1998).

[272] Greenlick "Bridging The Gap" Between Treatment And Research In Addiction (Institute of Medicine, National Academy of Sciences, 1998).

[273] C.P. O'Brien & A.T. McLellan, *Myths About The Treatment Of Addiction, 347* Lancet 237 (1996).

[274] D.D. Simpson & B.S. Brown, *Treatment Retention And Follow-Up Outcomes In The Drug Abuse Treatment Outcome Study (DATOS),* 11 Psychology of Addictive Behaviors 294 (1998).

[275] National Institute on Drug Abuse, NIH Pub. No. 99-4180, Principles Of Drug Addiction Treatment: A Research-Based Guide (1999).

[276.] See Dennis L. Thombs, Introduction to Addictive Behaviors (1994); Marc Alan Schuckit, Educating Yourself About Alcohol and Drug Problems: A People's Primer (1995).

[277.] American Psychiatric Association, *Practice Guideline for Treatment of Patients with Substance Use Disorders: Alcohol, Cocaine, Opioids* (1995); Rebecca Schilit & Edith S. Lisansky Gomberg, Drugs and Behavior: A Sourcebook for the Helping Professions (1991).

[278] A.T. McLellan & J.R. McKay, *The Treatment Of Addiction: What Can Research Offer Practice?*, in Bridging The Gap Between Research And Treatment In Community Based Addiction Treatment (Greenlick ed., Institute of Medicine, National Academy of Sciences, 1998).

[279.] See, e.g., Peter M. Monti, David B. Abrams, Ronald M. Kadden, & Ned L. Cooney, Treating Alcohol Dependence: A Coping Skills Training Guide (1989)..

[280.] American Psychiatric Association, *Practice Guideline for Treatment of Patients with Substance Use Disorders: Alcohol, Cocaine, Opioids* (1995).

[281] E.F. McCance-Katz & T.R. .Kosten, *New Treatments for Chemical Addiction* (1998).

[282] R.F. Anton, S.S. O'Malley, D.A. Ciraulo, et al., *Combined Pharmacotherapies and Behavioral Interventions for Alcohol Dependence: The COMBINE Study – A Randomized Controlled Trial*, 295 JAMA 2003 (2006).

[283] E.F. McCance-Katz & T.R. Kosten, *Psychopharmacological Treatments,* in Clinical Textbook Of Addictive Disorders 596 (R.J. Frances et al. eds., 2nd ed. 1998).

[284.] See, e.g., Stephen A. Maisto, Mark Galizio, & Gerard J. Connors, Drug Use and Misuse (1991). R. J. Frances & S. I. Miller (Eds),

[285.] Albert Ellis, John F. McInerney, Raymond DiGiuseppe, & Raymond J. Yeager, Rational-Emotive Therapy with Alcoholics and Substance Abusers (1988).

[286.] Timothy J. O'Farrell (ed.), Treating Alcohol Problems: Marital and Family Interventions (1993).

[287] D.A. Patterson, Recent Advances In Substance Abuse Treatment: The Development Of Effective Practice Methods (2000). Available at: http://swknox2.csw.utk.edu/ Substance %20Abuse/sld001.htm.

[288.] Compare, e.g., William R. Miller & Ricardo F. Munoz, How to Control Your Drinking (rev. ed., 1982).

[289.] See Barbara S. McCrady & William R. Miller (eds.), Research on Alcoholics Anonymous (1993).

[290.] Edgar P. Nace, *Alcoholics Anonymous,* in Substance Abuse: A Comprehensive Textbook (Joyce H. Lowinson, Pedro Ruiz, Robert B. Millman & John G. Langrod, eds. 1992).

[291] C. Timko, R.H. Moos, J.W. Finney, & B.S. Moos *Outcome Of Treatment For Alcohol Abuse And Involvement In Alcoholics Anonymous Among Previously Untreated Problem Drinkers.* 21 Journal of Mental Health Administration, 145 (1994).

[292] Project MATCH Research Group. *Matching Alcoholism Treatments To Client Heterogeneity: Project MATCH Post-Treatment Drinking Outcomes,* 58 Journal of Substance Abuse 7 (1997).

[293] North Carolina Bar Association, Quality of Life Survey of North Carolina Attorneys: Report of Quality of Life Task Force (1991).

[294] G.A.H. Benjamin, E.J. Darling & B.D. Sales, *The Prevalence of Depression, Alcohol Abuse, And Cocaine Abuse Among United States Lawyers,* 13 International Journal of Law and Psychiatry 233 (1990).

[295] W.W. Eaton, J.C. Anthony, W. Mandel & R. Garrison, *Occupations And The Prevalence Of Major Depressive Disorder,* 32 Journal Of Occupational Medicine 1079 (1990).

[296] Robert M. Carney, Kenneth E. Freedland, Michael W. Rich & Allan S. Jaffe, *Depression As A Risk Factor For Cardiac Events In Established Coronary Heart Disease: A Review Of Possible Mechanisms,* 17(2) Annals Of Behavioral Medicine 142 (1995); Andrew B. Littman, *Review of Psychosomatic Aspects of Cardiovascular Disease,* 60 Psychotherapy And Psychosomatics 148 (1993).

[297] Arthur Shwartz and Ruth M. Schwartz, Depression: Theories and Treatments - Psychological, Biological and Social Perspectives (1993).

[298] *See, e.g.*, PDR Drug Guide for Mental Health Professionals (2nd ed., 2004).

[299] David O. Antonuccio, William G. Danton & Garland YY. DeNelsky, *Psychotherapy Versus Medication For Depression: Challenging The Conventional Wisdom With Data,* 26(6) Professional Psychology: Research and Practice 574 (1995).

[300] Sidney J. Blatt, *The Destructiveness of Perfectionism,* 50 American Psychologist 1003 (1995).